WOMEN SPEAK
The Eloquence of Women's Lives

Karen A. Foss
Sonja K. Foss

WAVELAND
PRESS, INC.
Prospect Heights, Illinois

For information about this book, write or call:

Waveland Press, Inc.
P.O. Box 400
Prospect Heights, Illinois 60070
(847) 634-0081

CONTENTS

The Eloquence of Women's Lives

Contents

ACKNOWLEDGMENTS

Many voices contributed to this project; it truly was a collaborative effort. Among the most significant collaborators were our publishers, Carol Rowe and Neil Rowe; we thank you for trusting our vision of *Women Speak*.

Our special thanks to the women whose eloquence created this book. You could not have been more generous, courageous, or insightful in sharing the processes and products of your lives. In choosing you because of your "ordinariness," we came to realize how truly extraordinary you all are.

Our photographers — Diana Schoenfeld, Thomas Lanham, and Mary Rose Williams — were integral to the process of capturing women's voices. Your forays into women's lives required a great deal of time, adaptability, patience, and photographic artistry in order to produce the documentation we wanted.

Assistance with typing and transcribing was provided by Carole Sharp of St. Louis University and Terry McElrath of Humboldt State University; Tamara Burk transcribed her own family stories. Sharon Bracci Blinn provided assistance with proofreading. You helped give birth to women's voices by performing tedious and difficult jobs with good humor and exceptional skill.

We are grateful to those upon whom we intruded as we collected our examples of women's expressions: Melanie Johnson and Ron Johnson, Michelle McKeegan and Edward Olsgard, and Mary Hosley and Jim Hosley, whose homes were photographed; Linda Edwards and Joe Edwards, owners of Blueberry Hill, who allowed us to photograph the women's restroom there; and all of the family members, friends, and acquaintances who appear in the women's talk throughout the book in various ways as the women share their lives.

There are also special women in our lives who encouraged us to speak, particularly our mother, Hazel M. Foss. You have been a role model for us — a woman who has not been afraid to speak the truth of her experience — and who always encouraged us to do the same.

Other special women who contributed to *Women Speak* because of their influence on us are the women with whom we served as camp counselors at Camp Wilani in Veneta, Oregon, especially Kitty Danziero (Danny), Jane Kraus (Sticker), Sheryl Langhofer (Murf), Elly Perrine (Tad), Linda Phelps (Cece), Vickie Rooks (Stormy), and Jeanne Seward (Laurel). From your creation of a supportive women's culture, we developed self-confidence and an appreciation for women's friendships. Belle Edson is another woman whose presence in our lives is a constant reminder of women's culture in action; you are a valued friend and colleague.

From Sonja, additional thanks are due Linda Hale, a "strong-minded woman" and supportive role model. I still miss her generosity of spirit, individual style, and capacity to laugh at her critics as well as herself. The wonderful women— abigails—at the University of Oregon are very much contributors to this book, especially Judy Bowker, Jane DeGroot, Pamela Dunkin, Cindy Griffin, Donna Hammer, Marla Kanengieter, Cheris Kramarae, Diana Brown Sheridan, Jean Ward, Mary Rose Williams and Lu Xing "Lucy." You claim you are indebted to me in various ways, but the debt is mine. Your friendship and support have been invaluable and have demonstrated for me the wonder of women's culture. Four men are among those who contributed to my thinking about the communication that is significant in my life by providing examples of it. Robert Trapp, Kurt Nordstrom, and Daniel Wildeson, you are truly "honorary women" in your gentle spirits and patience with and appreciation for women's ways. I also am grateful for the love of my husband, Anthony J. Radich. Since your gift of *The Feminine Mystique* many years ago, you have encouraged the expression of my own voice with your care, support, laughter, and inspiration.

From Karen, special acknowledgment goes to two groups of women—one on each coast. To my women friends from Massachusetts, especially Marlene Fine, Sally Freeman, Fern Johnson, Susan Parrish Sprowl, and Cindy White— you provide me with ongoing reminders of the power and richness of women's friendships. In the West, thanks and appreciation to Elizabeth Hans, Lesley Meriwether, and Christine Myers. You were once my students, but I always have learned as much from you and with you as you ever did from me. I am also grateful to the women's studies faculty at Humboldt State University; you demonstrate over and over to me the transformative possibilities of women's culture. Among this group, Kathryn Corbett, Deborah Fort, Kathleen Preston, and Ann Skinner-Jones have been especially important sources of inspiration for me. Thanks, too, to all of the women who have worked with me at the Women's Center while this book was in progress—especially Tracy Brown, Beth Canerdy, Shannon Capaul, Kim Halliday, Lynda Madrone, Callie Rabe, Chaz Varney, and Cynthia Wright; you continually have shown me that the women's movement remains tenacious, lively, and diverse. Finally, I cherish the gentleness, laughter, and love of my husband, Stephen W. Littlejohn, ever willing to be a co-adventurer in exploring women's ways.

Finally, we wish to share our indebtedness to one another. We were partners in many forms of women's eloquence before we labeled them that, valued them, or knew we would write about them some day. Our first experience with women's friendship was with one another; it still hasn't been matched.

A NEW CONTEXT FOR THE STUDY OF WOMEN AS COMMUNICATORS:

RE-VISIONING PUBLIC ADDRESS

The moment we . . . hesitate to tell the truth that is in us and from motives of policy are silent when we should speak, life flows no longer into our souls. Every truth we see is ours to give the world, not to keep for ourselves alone, for in so doing we cheat humanity . . . and check our own development.[1]

In this appeal, made in 1890, Elizabeth Cady Stanton called for women to speak the truth of their experiences and asserted the significance of such speech. Women face a number of obstacles, however, in their efforts to answer Stanton's call and may feel, as she suggested, hesitant to communicate their perspectives. They may discover, for example, that when they do communicate, men simply do not listen. They also may find that, if they are heard, their perspectives are interpreted within male frameworks or deliberately are distorted in order to preserve those frameworks and the power embedded in them. In these and other ways, women's communication has been muted and misinterpreted, producing inaccurate accounts both of women's communication and of women's lives.

[1] Elizabeth Cady Stanton, "Womanliness," cited in *Feminism: The Essential Historical Writings*, ed. Miriam Schneir (New York: Random, 1972), p. 156.

But the silencing and distorting of women's communication does not mean that women have not been authentic and effective communicators. Women have an eloquence of their own, manifest in a variety of contexts and forms, that creates worlds of immense richness for them and those around them. Our purpose in *Women Speak* is to help give voice to women's eloquence. To this end, we offer thirty examples of various forms of women's communication — ranging from architecture, baking, children's parties, and costume design to needlework, photography, talk at a reading group, rituals, and shopping — that reveal the substance and style of women's communication.

Women's forms of communication generally have not been viewed as significant forms of communication by scholars of public address — those interested in the nature, impact, and significance of discourse in the public arena. In this chapter, we provide an explanation for the lack of significance accorded women's communication by describing eight assumptions that have guided the study of public address. For each assumption, we suggest how it has discouraged the study of women's communication and explain how we have responded to it in *Women Speak* in order to take women more fully into account. While it clearly is at odds with some traditional notions of public address, we see our approach in *Women Speak* as building on and extending the assumptions and insights of this area of study in order to arrive at an increasingly accurate picture of communication.

Assumptions Challenged

We believe that eight primary assumptions have served as the foundation for the study of communicators and texts by scholars in the area of public address: (1) Significant communication is produced by noteworthy individuals; (2) Significant communication is produced by historical individuals; (3) Significant communicators are male; (4) Significant communication is produced by individuals; (5) Significant communication occurs in the public realm; (6) Speechmaking is the most significant form of communication; (7) Significant communicative texts are finished products; and (8) Suitable frameworks for assessing communication are derived from male perspectives.

Some of these assumptions clearly are acknowledged as cornerstones of the study of public address; others have not been fully articulated or explicitly acknowledged as guiding its study of communication. Each of these assumptions is, of course, evolving, and in several cases, scholars are beginning to address some of the same issues we raise. Nevertheless, we see these assumptions as representing some basic foundations of how public address has been studied in the communication field. Thus, they offer a useful entry point for our efforts to explore how women's communication has been treated in this area of the communication field and to understand how we have diverged from that treatment in *Women Speak*.

Significant communication is produced by noteworthy individuals.

A basic assumption that has guided the selection of communicators for study in public address is their noteworthiness. Those whose discourse is examined and analyzed typically are known for remarkable or extraordinary achievements. Communicators' successes, reputations, and positions in society, in other words, have been privileged over other possible criteria—such as a text's functions, quality, content, or style—in the selection of discourse to be studied. A perusal of essays published in communication journals reveals this bias in favor of noteworthy individuals, with many of the same "worthies" serving as the subject of repeated inquiry. John Adams, Spiro Agnew, William Jennings Bryan, Jimmy Carter, Abraham Lincoln, Norman Vincent Peale, and Nelson Rockefeller, for example, all have been the subject of more than one essay in communication journals. Even when the speaker's performance is deemed less eloquent in comparison with other orators, as is the case with Robert Hall's study of Lyndon Johnson, Johnson's position as President of the United States made his discourse inherently worthy of investigation.[2]

The criterion of noteworthiness is self-perpetuating. The choice to focus on the discourse of those who have attained positions of merit or whose achievements are exceptional means that their discourse is viewed as important; those whose discourse is taken as important are seen as important. Left out of this cycle entirely is the discourse of ordinary people; no matter how exceptional in terms of content or impact, such discourse is not granted significance because the communicators themselves are not noteworthy.

Exceptions exist to the assumption that significant talk is conducted by noteworthy individuals. In *Rhetoric of the People*, a volume of essays edited by Harold Barrett, the purpose is to "offer a study of the ordinary citizen's rhetorical involvement in public life."[3] In the first essay in this volume, Bower Aly asserts, "We have heard too little about oratory as it has been spoken, not by the so-called giants but by the fellows at the forks of the creek; not by Abraham Lincoln alone but by the other boys at Clary's Grove."[4] Aly suggests that public discourse, not literature, music, painting, or sculpture, has been the "characteristic American art." He asks, "Should not the characteristic American art receive a consideration better designed to reveal

---

[2] Robert N. Hall, "Lyndon Johnson's Speech Preparation," *Quarterly Journal of Speech*, 51 (April 1965), 168-76.

[3] Harold Barrett, ed., *Rhetoric of the People* (Amsterdam: Rodopi, 1974), p. 9.

[4] Bower Aly, "The Contemporary Rhetoric of Politics and Statecraft," in Harold Barrett, ed., *Rhetoric of the People* (Amsterdam: Rodopi, 1974), p. 22.

its courses than we are likely to find in a discussion limited to great orators?" [5]
The essays that follow Aly's introduction include, among other ordinary
speaking situations, the tactics of students working in Eugene McCarthy's
Presidential campaign; frontier speaking; and the communication used by
African Americans to protest the showing of the film, *The Birth of a Nation*,
on a college campus. This volume, however, remains an anomaly and not a
forerunner of a shift in approach to the study of public address.

Anthologies of speeches compiled for use in public address classes generally
privilege noteworthy individuals whose speaking becomes such by virtue of
the position that person achieves. James Andrews and David Zarefsky's
American Voices: Significant Speeches in American History, for example,
includes speeches "from the point of view of those who tried, with varying
degrees of success," to shape the course of American history.[6] With the exception
of two individuals—Oliver Wendell Holmes, Jr., and Anita Taylor, a speech
communication scholar—Halford Ryan includes only politicians in his
collection of American rhetoric.[7] The speeches chosen for inclusion in
Contemporary American Speeches, edited by Richard Johannesen, R. R. Allen,
and Wil Linkugel, are broader in scope.[8] In addition to speeches by well-known
political figures such as Martin Luther King, Jr.; Jesse Jackson; and Ronald
Reagan, they have included speeches by Edward Cornish, president of the World
Future Society; Glenna Crooks, director of the policy division of the American
Pharmaceutical Association; and several students. With the exception of the
students, however, all of the individuals have credibility because they hold
formal positions of power in organizational or political contexts—even though
their names may not be household words.

The noteworthiness criterion, when applied to women communicators, has
taken two directions. The earliest consideration of women's speaking was the
study of noteworthy women involved in various reform movements—usually
temperance, anti-slavery, and women's rights—since women did not have access
to political positions in which they could excel as orators in the same ways
as could men. Robert Oliver summarizes the rationale for singling out women's
collective reform efforts rather than individual women orators for study:

> With the few exceptions that have been noted, the contribution of women,
> at least in the nineteenth century, to the public speaking platform, has
> largely been in numbers of passionate advocates and agitators, rather than

[5] Aly, p. 22.
[6] James Andrews and David Zarefsky, *American Voices: Significant Speeches in American History, 1640-1945* (New York: Longman, 1989), p. xv.
[7] Halford Ross Ryan, *American Rhetoric from Roosevelt to Reagan: A Collection of Speeches and Critical Essays*, 2nd ed. (Prospect Heights, IL: Waveland, 1987).
[8] Richard L. Johannesen, R. R. Allen, and Wil A. Linkugel, *Contemporary American Speeches: A Sourcebook of Speech Forms and Principles*, 6th ed. (Dubuque: Kendall/Hunt, 1988).

in outstanding individual achievement. After centuries of training in submission, and from the midst of a social situation that took their subordination wholly for granted, it was too much to expect that they could quickly produce eloquent orators equal to the best of the men.[9]

The entrance of increasing numbers of women into public life in the twentieth century led to the development of a second approach to the study of noteworthy women as communicators. Women whose communication had some impact on the political realm—most often those with some connection to the office of the American Presidency—began to be included in anthologies of speeches. In this approach, women are considered noteworthy if, for example, they run for or are somehow connected with the highest political office. Thus, speeches by Shirley Chisholm, Presidential candidate, and Geraldine Ferraro, candidate for the office of vice president, are included in public address texts.[10] Eleanor Roosevelt's communication also has been the subject of study.[11] While she gained a reputation for her speechmaking largely after her husband's death, Roosevelt's initial renown came from the credibility granted her by her role as First Lady. A woman whose discourse is included in speech anthologies and also is the subject of scholarly investigations is Barbara Jordan; the speech that appears most often in anthologies and is studied most frequently is her keynote address to the 1976 Democratic national convention, where a Presidential candidate was nominated.[12] A Presidential dimension, then, seems to be useful in gaining scholarly attention as a woman communicator in the political realm.

In *Women Speak*, we consciously sought to expand the scope of significant women communicators beyond those active in movements or involved in political activities by privileging ordinariness over noteworthiness. We believe the communication of all individuals is significant in its impact on their own lives and the lives of their families, friends, co-workers, and communities and that we can understand much about how communication works in the world by studying the communicative acts of ordinary people. We believe this is

[9] Robert T. Oliver, *History of Public Speaking in America* (Boston: Allyn and Bacon, 1965), p. 447.
[10] Shirley Chisholm's speech, "For the Equal Rights Amendment," appears in Ryan, pp. 220-24; Ferraro's "Acceptance Speech to the 1984 National Democratic Convention" is reprinted in Ronald F. Reid, ed., *Three Centuries of American Rhetorical Discourse: An Anthology and a Review* (Prospect Heights, IL: Waveland, 1988), pp. 727-32.
[11] For essays about Roosevelt, see, for example, Helen Jane Wamboldt, "Speech Teacher to the First Lady of the World," *Communication Quarterly*, 12 (November 1964), 5-6; Maurine Beasley, "Lorena A. Hickok: Journalistic Influence on Eleanor Roosevelt," *Journalism Quarterly*, 57 (Summer 1980), 281-86; and Maurine Beasley, "Eleanor Roosevelt's Press Conferences: Symbolic Importance of a Pseudo-Event," *Journalism Quarterly*, 61 (Summer 1984), 274-79.
[12] See Wayne N. Thompson, "Barbara Jordan's Keynote Address: Fulfilling Dual and Conflicting Purposes," *Central States Speech Journal*, 30 (Fall 1979), 272-77; and Wayne N. Thompson, "Barbara Jordan's Keynote Address: The Juxtaposition of Contradictory Values," *Southern Speech Communication Journal*, 44 (Spring 1979), 223-32. Jordan's speech appears in Ryan, pp. 225-29.

particularly true of women, who often assume the responsibility for communication in a wide range of interpersonal contexts.

We selected for inclusion in *Women Speak* the texts of ordinary women —
women who are not known for special talents or achievements outside of the
circles of their families, friends, or communities — but who nevertheless express
themselves in significant and eloquent ways. Each woman's voice represented
here, then, is significant not on the basis of her contribution to public society
but for its expression of her personal, lived experience in ways that are
meaningful to her and those around her. A few of the women included are
"noteworthy" as that term typically is defined — Judy Chicago and Ursula Le
Guin, for example. We have treated these women no differently from any of
the others in an attempt to emphasize the value and eloquence of each woman's
expression, whether or not it has been marked by public acclaim.

In addition to ordinariness, another bias informed our selection of women:
we have included women who appear to engage in self-conscious reflection
about their lives as women. Interested in understanding how gender informs
women's communication, we chose to include women who have given some
thought to how their status as women affects their lives and their forms of
expression. Not all of the women in this book would use the term *feminist*
to describe themselves, but their awareness that their status as women has made
a difference in their lives suggests the adoption of a stance that we see as
feminist.

Significant communication is produced by historical individuals.

A second assumption that has dominated the study of public address is that
historical figures are the preferred subjects of investigation. While most public
address textbooks do not explicitly assert the need for a speaking event to have
occurred in the past in order for it to be seen as significant, this appears to
be a prevailing assumption. Anthony Hillbruner's early discussion of the
importance of historical description, for example, presumes that the speaker
and text under examination belong to the past rather than to the present:

> The critic's first job . . . is to discover what was happening at the juncture
> of history in which the speech event took place. The critic takes this
> segment of time, puts boundaries around it, isolates it, so to speak, by
> figuratively putting it under a microscope. After the examination, he notes
> the salient features of the period and describes its notable characteristics.[13]

Lester Thonssen and A. Craig Baird also presume that the speaking situation
under investigation occurred in the distant past when they state that "critical

---

[13] Anthony Hillbruner, *Critical Dimensions: The Art of Public Address Criticism* (New York: Random, 1966). p. 9

appraisal depends heavily upon the critic's ability to effect faithful recon-structions of social settings long since dissolved." [14]

Anthologies of speeches offer perhaps the best evidence that this assumption still pervades the study of public address. Speeches important in the founding of the American republic, the Civil War, reform movements of the late nineteenth and early twentieth centuries, and both World Wars — all historical events — dominate even contemporary texts. In fact, many such texts end at a historical point well before the books' dates of publication. Robert Oliver's text, for example, ends with the speaking of Woodrow Wilson, and the collections by Andrews and Zarefsky ends with speechmaking in 1945. Even in the anthologies that include speeches from contemporary times, such as the one by Reid, the contemporary period is given far less attention than the speaking of earlier periods.

The emphasis on historicity in determining significant discourse was a prominent feature of neo-Aristotelian criticism, the earliest method that evolved in the speech communication discipline to analyze and evaluate speeches. Neo-Aristotelian criticism, so named because advocates of this approach rely for their critical method on the principles of effective speaking described by Aristotle, involves three major dimensions: (1) the reconstruction of the historical context in which the speech occurred, including background information about the speaker, details of the times, and a description of the particular occasion; (2) the analysis of the speech itself according to the classical canons of invention, or the discovery of subject matter; organization or speech structure; style; delivery; and memory; and (3) assessment of the effectiveness of the speech for the audience and occasion.[15] The emphasis on the recreation of the historical context clearly dominated many early studies of discourse, and far more attention often was devoted to describing context than actually analyzing speeches.[16] Roderick Hart, in an editorial about scholarship in public address, summarizes this assumption when he states that in early public address studies, the emphasis "was on the *history* of public address rather than the history of public *address*." [17]

While predominantly historical studies appear with less frequency in current scholarship in the area of public address, the speechmaking of individuals in the past continues to be preferred to the study of ongoing events and speakers

[14] Lester Thonssen and A. Craig Baird, *Speech Criticism: The Development of Standards for Rhetorical Appraisal* (New York: Ronald, 1948), p. 312.

[15] For a summary of neo-Aristotelian criticism, see Sonja K. Foss, *Rhetorical Criticism: Exploration & Practice* (Prospect Heights, IL: Waveland, 1989), pp. 75-109.

[16] See, for example, Jerald L. Banninga, "John Quincy Adams' Address of July 4, 1821," *Quarterly Journal of Speech*, 53 (February 1967), 44-49; and Robert M. Post, "Charles Stewart Parnell Before Congress," *Quarterly Journal of Speech*, 51 (December 1965), 419-25.

[17] Roderick P. Hart, "Contemporary Scholarship in Public Address: A Research Editorial," *Western Journal of Speech Communication*, 50 (Summer 1986), 285.

whose discourse is in the process of development. The hindsight, reflection, and alleged objectivity available with a speaking event in the past are privileged over the study of contemporary texts whose significance on the course of public events has not yet been demonstrated or fully understood.

We do not believe that significant communication is produced only by individuals in the past. Thus, rather than include in *Women Speak* women communicators who are important historically, we deliberately have chosen to include the communication of contemporary women, most of whom we know personally. We see our choice to study women who are our contemporaries as offering several advantages. Primary among them is the accessibility of these women; we were able to talk with most of the women about their communication choices. In addition, we believe we were able to gather more accurate examples of their communication and more revealing insights into them because of our personal relationships with the women.

We acknowledge that our decision to feature women we know has some disadvantages, as defined by traditional research approaches. In many instances, however, we found ourselves rethinking concepts and assumptions that we might otherwise have taken for granted if we had limited ourselves to historical women. We are not able, for example, to assess the communication we have included in *Women Speak* in terms of its effects on later events. Because we cannot, however, we were encouraged to question the appropriateness of long-term effects as a goal and to explore other goals that may be as important in the study of communication. We also are not able to be objective about the women and their texts. We suggest, however, that no one ever is objective about anything, but more important, we believe that our involvement in these women's lives enabled us to learn more about these women and their communication than we could have if we had attempted to distance ourselves from them.

Another disadvantage that might be noted is that the women included tend to be European Americans, educated, of middle class and middle aged — reflections of the communities in which we live and of the women with whom we are most likely to have contact. Thus, we have not included equal representations of women from different geographical settings, ages, races, sexual preferences, or educational levels, although there is some variety across these dimensions. We believe, however, that efforts to offer a balanced representation of texts in terms of such variables suggest a false kind of generalizability. We do not want to imply that the experiences of one African-American woman represent those of all women of color or that one lesbian's voice offers an understanding of lesbian communication. We believe that each woman's discourse has some idiosyncratic dimensions as well as some features that may characterize women's communication generally. In *Women Speak*, we want neither to homogenize women by treating them as if the differences among them do not matter nor do we want to emphasize the differences by highlighting them.[18] We simply are asserting that a woman's voice need not be typical or representative before it offers something of value.

As a consequence of selecting women we know for inclusion in *Women Speak*, we had to decide whether to use first or last names in our references to them. Because we are on a first-name basis with most of the women, we felt comfortable calling them by their first names, and first names also are more in keeping with the personal voices these women share. First names also felt more appropriate to us because of the accommodation last names may represent to a male framework. A woman's family name often is a patriarchal name not of her own choosing, and many of the women themselves expressed a lack of identification with their surnames. At the same time, we realize that in professional contexts, women often are called by first names when men are not, a practice that trivializes and devalues women. Thus, the use of last names would have signaled our desire for these women to be accorded status in traditionally recognized ways in the public realm.

We resolved the dilemma by alternating our references to the women between the two options. We call them by both their given and last names when we first refer to them; in subsequent references, we alternate between the two. We came to appreciate the integrated sense of personal identity and professional status, intimacy and respect, that the practice of alternating first and last names suggests.

With our decision to include the communicative texts of friends and acquaintances in *Women Speak*, our intent is not to suggest an end to historical investigations of communicators not known personally to the scholar. Rather, we seek to broaden the scope of public address to include individuals whose communication is in process and who can work with the scholar to offer the fullest possible picture of their texts and themselves as communicators.

Significant communicators are male.

A third assumption that has governed the study of public address is that men count as communicators, while women do not. The valuing of men as communicators and the concomitant exclusion of women has assumed various forms throughout the history of the communication discipline, although the neglect of women's forms of eloquence in the public realm has been particularly well documented. Karlyn Kohrs Campbell explains:

---

[18] We have borrowed the notion of *homogenization* from Bettina Aptheker, who writes of her desire, in documenting women's experiences, "not to homogenize. It was not to invent one 'woman' as a kind of universal iconography. The purpose was to interpret, to form patterns, to make intelligible the multiple, highly complex and ever-changing ensemble of social relations in which women are lodged." See *Tapestries of Life: Women's Work, Women's Consciousness, and the Meaning of Daily Experience* (Amherst: University of Massachusetts Press, 1989), p. 12.

> For centuries, the ability to persuade others has been part of Western man's
> standard of excellence in many areas, even of citizenship itself. Moreover,
> speaking and writing eloquently has long been the goal of the humanistic
> tradition in education.
>
> Women have no parallel rhetorical history. Indeed, for much of their
> history women have been prohibited from speaking, ... Further, once
> they began to speak, their words often were not preserved, with the result
> that many rhetorical acts by women are gone forever; . . .[19]

Even when evidence of women's communication has existed, however, such
material often has not been incorporated into the study of public address.
Andrews and Zarefsky, for example, include texts only by Sojourner Truth,
Lucy Stone, Frances Willard, Susan B. Anthony, Elizabeth Cady Stanton, and
Margaret Sanger in their anthology of fifty-six speeches. Johannesen, Allen,
and Linkugel's volume includes speeches by only nine women, three of whom
are students, implicitly suggesting that, apart from the students, other women
were not available for inclusion. While the presence of even a few women
in such anthologies is helpful in suggesting women's contributions to public
life, it confirms that men continue to serve as the standard for communicative
performance and that women are peripheral in terms of significant discourse.

Anthologies of women's speeches have begun to appear in an effort to offer
a full complement of women's speeches for examination and to counter the
view of women as peripheral. In *Outspoken Women*, Judith Anderson has
compiled the speeches of American women reformers between 1635 and 1935;
she includes, among others, Jane Addams, Dorothea Dix, Angelina Grimké,
and Ida Wells-Barnett.[20] Patricia Scileppi Kennedy and Gloria Hartmann
O'Shields, in *We Shall Be Heard*, divide their treatment of women speakers
into three eras. In the Pre-Civil War period, speeches by women such as Lucretia
Mott and Ernestine Rose are included; in the Civil War phase, speeches by
Anna Dickinson and Belva Lockwood are representative; and in the period
from World War I to contemporary times, speeches by Eleanor Roosevelt and
Betty Friedan are presented.[21] Karlyn Kohrs Campbell offers a two-volume
set devoted to women's discourse. The first volume of *Man Cannot Speak For
Her* is a series of critical essays in which Kohrs Campbell analyzes the discourse
of leaders in the early women's movement; key texts of these speakers comprise
the second volume.[22]

[19] Karlyn Kohrs Campbell, *Man Cannot Speak For Her: A Critical Study of Early Feminist Rhetoric*, vol. 1 (Westport, CT: Greenwood, 1989), 1.

[20] Judith Anderson, *Outspoken Women: Speeches by American Women Reformers, 1635-1935* (Dubuque: Kendall/Hunt, 1984).

[21] Patricia Scileppi Kennedy and Gloria Hartmann O'Shields, *We Shall Be Heard: Women Speakers in America, 1828 - Present* (Dubuque: Kendall/Hunt, 1983).

[22] Kohrs Campbell, *Man Cannot Speak For Her*, vol. 1; and Karlyn Kohrs Campbell, comp., *Man Cannot Speak For Her: Key Texts of the Early Feminists*, vol. 2 (New York: Praeger, 1989).

The significance of the male as communicator has been demonstrated in the communication discipline not only in the exclusion of women's communicative texts as data for study. Basic definitions that undergird the communication discipline have been developed without the input of women and thus reflect male perspectives on communication. The definition of *rhetoric* provides an example of such omission. Most of the commonly accepted definitions of rhetoric have not strayed far from Aristotle's "the faculty [power] of discovering in the particular case what are the available means of persuasion."[23] Such definitions, in which the essence of rhetoric is persuasion, do not necessarily fit women's values or experiences of interaction. Sally Miller Gearhart suggests that such definitions contain a male bias because of their emphasis on conversion and conquest—on the effort to change people and things.[24] Such definitions, which exclude the experiences and values of many women, perpetuate the notion of the male as the significant communicator.

In *Women Speak*, we have chosen to see women as significant communicators, and we offer our thirty texts by women as a step toward balancing the distorted picture of communication that has emerged from the study of largely men's communication. We hope the women's texts will be used not only to discover the nature and function of women's communication but as a starting point to question and reconceptualize definitions, constructs, and theories of communication that were developed from the study of men's communication. Notions such as credibility, effectiveness, protest, power, and leadership may assume quite different forms when they are developed from texts by women.

Significant communication is produced by individuals.

A prevailing assumption in the communication discipline has been that individual speakers are solely responsible for the texts they create. The early models used to describe pictorially the process of communication involved a speaker, in a particular context, imparting a message to an audience, which provided feedback of some sort.[25] While not stated explicitly, the speaker is assumed to be one person rather than a couple or a group. The emphasis on the speaker's background in the initial efforts to analyze and evaluate communication using neo-Aristotelian criticism—family influences, education, and impact of political context on the individual—further reaffirmed the sense that the speaker is singly accountable for the text.

[23] Aristotle, *Rhetoric*, trans. Lane Cooper (New York: Appleton-Century-Crofts, 1932), 1.1, p. 7.
[24] Sally Miller Gearhart, "The Womanization of Rhetoric," *Women's Studies International Quarterly*, 2 (1979), 195-201.
[25] For samples of such communication models, see C. David Mortensen, *Communication: The Study of Human Interaction* (New York: McGraw-Hill, 1972), chpt. 2. The Shannon and Weaver model, p. 37, and the Schramm model, p. 41, are classic communication models that demonstrate the implicit responsibility accorded the speaker for the communication transaction.

Even when scholars working in the area of public address move to the study of collective processes such as social movements, they continue to emphasize the individuals in the movement—in particular, its leaders—thus suggesting individual responsibility for a communicative text and its impact. Leland Griffin's article on historical movements offers an example of this perspective; he asserts that the leaders of social movements are those responsible for moving the social movement from one stage of development to another through their skill at "arousing public opinion." [26] Herbert Simons' work on the communication of social movements also suggests that leaders are responsible for the outcome of the movement: "The primary rhetorical test of the leader—and, indirectly, of the strategies he employs—is his capacity to fulfill the requirements of his movement by resolving or reducing rhetorical problems." [27] More recently, Charles Stewart, Craig Smith, and Robert Denton suggest: "Leaders must persuade persons to join in the cause, to organize into effective groups, and to unify through coalitions to carry the message to target audiences and to confront institutions and resistance forces." [28] Thus, even when group effort is involved in a communication situation, the general model is of individual initiators of communication who, largely alone, are responsible for the messages produced and their ultimate effectiveness.

We believe that communicative texts often are the result of more than one person, collaborating in various ways. To focus on one individual as the creator of a text often is inaccurate in that it ignores the contributions of those around the communicator to its creation. More accurate, we believe, in women's lives, is a view of "author-ity" as a process of collaboration that emerges in interaction with others.[29]

We have highlighted such collaboration in *Women Speak* in various ways. First, we have included texts that are produced jointly by two or more persons, something usually not seen in traditional anthologies of discourse. Because we believe that designating primary and secondary contributors in such cases often is difficult because of the myriad connections between them, when two or more women jointly created a text, we have alphabetized their names in the headings. The woman whose name is listed first should not be thought of as the primary communicator.

---

[26] Leland M. Griffin, "The Rhetoric of Historical Movements," *Quarterly Journal of Speech*, 38 (April 1952), 185.

[27] Herbert W. Simons, "Requirements, Problems, and Strategies: A Theory of Persuasion for Social Movements," *Quarterly Journal of Speech*, 56 (February 1970), 11.

[28] Charles Stewart, Craig Smith, and Robert E. Denton, Jr., *Persuasion and Social Movements* (Prospect Heights, IL: Waveland, 1984), p. 80.

[29] This view of *author-ity* is described by Judy Nolte Lenskink in "Expanding the Boundaries of Criticism: The Diary as Female Autobiography," *Women's Studies: An Interdisciplinary Journal*, 14 (1987), 46.

Second, we have focused on the communicative texts themselves over the individual creators to discourage an over-emphasis on the individual communicators. Thus, we have organized the book by forms of expression—arranged alphabetically—rather than by the names of the women who created them. We hope, through this arrangement, to increase awareness of the many connections the women see between themselves and the families and friends with whom they share their expressions and their lives. These women also are tapping into a collective authorship of other women who have preceded them. Each of the texts represents a genre with a long tradition—shopping, baking, and gardening, for example—by which women express themselves. By featuring quilting, then, rather than a particular woman as a quilter, we are suggesting that the experience is shared by many women and that the woman who represents that form in *Women Speak* draws on the experiences of many others in her quilting.

Significant communication occurs in the public realm.

The focus in the study of public address, as its name suggests, has been on communication in the public arena. Communicators may address others in various formats and contexts, but those messages that occur in public, formal contexts are those that have received attention in studies of public address. Herbert Wichelns, in an essay that set the parameters of the speech communication field and distinguished it from literary criticism, suggested that the public arena would constitute the province of the new discipline:

> [I]ts atmosphere is that of the public life, . . . It includes the work of the speaker, of the pamphleteer, of the writer of editorials, and of the sermon maker. It is to be thought of as the art of popularization. Its practitioners are the Huxleys, not the Darwins, of science; the Jeffersons, not the Lockes and the Rousseaus, of politics.[30]

By definition, we recognize, scholarship in the area of *public* address is supposed to deal with public rather than private discourse. The realm of the private belongs to the scholar interested in interpersonal communication, the conversational analyst dealing with patterns in everyday talk, or the ethnographer studying various cultural expressions. We suggest, however, that the delineation of a realm of study confined to *public* discourse unnecessarily limits the kinds of knowledge that can be generated about communication.

One limitation of the designation of an area of study called public address is the assumption that the discourse that has the most impact and influence

---

[30] Herbert A. Wichelns, "The Literary Criticism of Oratory," in *Studies in Rhetoric and Public Speaking in Honor of James A. Winans*, ed. A. M. Drummond (New York: Century, 1925), pp. 181-216; rpt. in *Methods of Rhetorical Criticism: A Twentieth-Century Perspective*, ed. Bernard L. Brock and Robert L. Scott, 2nd ed. (Detroit: Wayne State University Press, 1980), p. 72.

on human beings is public discourse. People's lives are most affected, this assumption suggests, by a President's inaugural addresses, speeches outlining economic policies, or calls to the nation to engage in war; by the discourse of social movements that challenge the social or political status quo; and by the discourse of ministers preaching their sermons. Certainly, such discourse *does* have major effects on people's lives; discourse that catapults a nation into war, for example, disrupts life patterns in significant ways, just as a woman's decision to join the feminist movement can affect her life in profound ways. But much of the discourse produced in such contexts has been studied as if the primary effects are those that affect the course of *national* or *world* events.

The communication that affects human beings much more often than discourse at the national and international level is the communication experienced close up—how our employers, friends, partners, and children communicate with us; the stories we tell; the clothing we wear; the gardens we grow; and the places in which we live. These messages do matter in terms of how our lives are lived; they affect the nature of our families, the friendships we form, the organizations in which we work, and the nature of the communities in which we live. These, in turn, are the sites of the problems with which politicians, government officials, and reform advocates must deal. By limiting their investigations to the public realm, however, scholars of public address have not had the opportunity to study the impact of such messages on the course of individual lives, nor have they generally sought explanations for public events in such messages in the private realm.

The designation of an area of study concerned only with public address has consequences beyond our understanding of communication in general; it also has consequences for the perception and treatment of women's communication. Because women's discourse is largely in the private realm, a focus on the public generally omits consideration of such discourse. When it is considered, however, women's discourse is devalued because it is attached to the private sphere, which has assumed negative connotations because of its connection to women. Men's operation in the public sphere is seen as superior, as Cheris Kramarae explains: "masculine intellect is seen in contrast to and as transcending the feminine character, which is biologically driven and firmly bound to the body and home. Men make the move away from the body and the home to reason and public activities." [31]

Valerie Endress points out another consequence of the public-private dichotomy for the study of women's communication. It results, she explains, in a particular definition of politics that includes only men's activities and communication. In this view, politics takes place in the public sphere and deals

---

[31] Cheris Kramarae, "Feminist Theories of Communication," in *International Encyclopedia of Communications*, vol. 2, ed. Erik Barnouw (New York: Oxford University Press, 1989), 159.

with issues "such as the political economy, international relations, war and peace, and domestic political dissent . . . ." [32] The politics involved in women's lives — evident in issues such as power differences and their impacts on women, the feminization of poverty, birth control, abortion, motherhood, sexism, and racism — are not seen as legitimate political concerns. The realm of the interpersonal and the private — where women's communication achieves its significance — is simply not considered political.

In *Women Speak*, we have chosen to disrupt the dichotomy of the private and public realm by including many texts that would be difficult to categorize as belonging only to one realm or the other. A woman's work in interior design, for example, is private in that the results are seen in the home; at the same time, it is a public statement to those who visit the home and witness the work. Similarly, to classify shopping as either public or private is difficult. It takes place in a public setting, but the communicator generally is unknown in that setting. The critical communication during shopping takes place intrapersonally if the shopper is alone or interpersonally if she is with others.

We also have chosen to question the emphasis on public communication in the study of public address by including some very private forms of communication — forms of communication not intended for and often not made visible in the public realm. These include such forms as personal letters, talk between a mother and child, and talk among members of a women's reading group. We have included such texts to facilitate awareness that such communication is powerful and significant in its impact on its creators and those with whom they interact.

As a result of our refusal to privilege the public over the private, many of the texts included in *Women Speak* reveal a vulnerability rarely displayed in the study of public address. Our decision to include ourselves in the book — for our sewing in section 7 and as part of the women's reading group in section 28 — was made, in part, because of the personal tone being revealed in the texts we were collecting. We felt we best could understand the concerns expressed and the vulnerability experienced by the women who contributed to *Women Speak* by being among them ourselves. For the women whose texts are included, the act of sharing their talk was scary because it reveals dimensions of their private lives on which they may be judged to be inadequate or inappropriate as women, wives or partners, mothers, professionals, or communicators, to name but a few.

For other women, what they discuss is not especially private, but it involves risks of another kind — admitting to behaviors that are accorded little value in the male domain. The essay on shopping is one example, as is our own

[32] Valerie A. Endress, "Feminist Theory and the Concept of Power in Public Address," in *Women and Communicative Power: Theory, Research, and Practice*, ed. Carol Ann Valentine and Nancy Hoar (Annandale, VA: Speech Communication Association, 1988), pp. 103-04.

discussion of sewing. We felt vulnerable admitting—especially to our professional colleagues who may read this book—that we match fabrics to earrings and that we cut squares and triangles out of fabric for use in making quilts. Many of us, particularly those in the speech communication field, wondered what effect such disclosures might have on our professional lives.

Despite these concerns, all of the women chose to use their own names in *Women Speak*, although we gave them the option of choosing pseudonyms. We believe the courage they have shown in allowing previously invisible, concealed forms of communication to be revealed will contribute to a much richer and more accurate understanding of women's communication, and we hope we have been able to present their texts with the sensitivity and care they deserve.

Speechmaking is the most significant form of communication.

In the study of public address, the speech has been privileged as the object of study over other forms of communication. Speeches are assumed to be the most influential type of communication in their impact on the course of human events. This focus in the study of public address was noted by participants at a conference held to explore new directions for the study of communication:

> Much of our theory has presupposed formal platform speaking and has thereby ignored a multitude of presentational and transactional possibilities. This emphasis . . . discouraged expansion of theory to encompass a wide variety of presentational forms ranging from 1848 campaign songs to rock and roll light shows. The emphasis on platform public speaking also inhibited the critic's exploration in such obvious rhetorical transactions as small groups and confrontation interchanges.[33]

The focus on speechmaking not only has excluded from consideration various forms of discursive communication such as journals, letters, and conversations but also has excluded non-discursive forms, particularly those involving visual imagery. Images in the form of advertisements, television, film, signs, dress, architecture, and the interior design of buildings constitute a major part of the communicative environment. Yet, studies of visual imagery typically have not been considered part of the study of public address.

Although forms of communication that are not platform speeches are receiving more attention in the current study of communication, speechmaking

[33] Thomas O. Sloan, Richard B. Gregg, Thomas R. Nilsen, Irving J. Rein, Herbert W. Simons, Herman G. Stelzner, and Donald W. Zacharias, "Report of the Committee on the Advancement and Refinement of Rhetorical Criticism," in *The Prospect of Rhetoric: Report of the National Developmental Project*, ed. Lloyd F. Bitzer and Edwin Black (Englewood Cliffs, NJ: Prentice-Hall, 1971), p. 222.

remains the primary object of study in public address. This emphasis continues in classes in "American Public Address" and "British Public Address," which typically involve only the study of speeches. Anthologies of public speeches continue to be the most frequently published type of textbook for use in such courses.[34]

When speeches are privileged over other forms of communication, women's communication tends to be excluded from consideration. Most women do not give speeches on a regular basis; speechmaking simply is not a common form of expression for women. This is due, in part, to the reduced opportunities for women to hold decision-making positions in the public realm — positions in which they would be likely to give speeches. But even were this not the case, speeches are not the forms of communication women consider most important in their lives. Mabel Murphy, a quiltmaker, aptly summarized this notion when she was asked to say a few words upon receiving an award for her quiltmaking from the Missouri Arts Council. She began, "I'm not a speaker; I just talk." [35] Her statement suggests the discomfort many women feel with the traditional public speaking mode — it is not a "native" form of expression for them. To include speeches as primary forms of discourse in the study of public address, then, reveals women's communication in a very limited, male-defined context and excludes much of the communication that has a critical impact on women and those around them.

The emphasis on discursive over non-discursive communication also constitutes a means by which women's communication is omitted from study in public address. Much of the communication women produce is not only not in the form of speeches, but it often is not verbal. Perhaps because they have been excluded from traditional discursive forms, women often express themselves through non-discursive channels such as gardening, needlework, child care, housework, interior design, and baking. These forms of communication, where women may find the fullest and richest expressions of their lives, however, are not appropriate texts for study when speechmaking is the privileged form of communication.

In *Women Speak*, we have attempted to provide a sample of texts that more accurately characterizes women's communication than do formal speeches. While we have chosen to call these forms of expression *texts*, they are not necessarily texts in the traditional sense of written or spoken artifacts. Rather,

[34] One exception is *Rhetorical Dimensions in Media: A Critical Casebook*, ed. Martin J. Medhurst and Thomas W. Benson (Dubuque: Kendall/Hunt, 1984), which explores eight different media — including television, music, and popular magazines — to demonstrate how rhetoric functions. The book consists, however, of essays about these media and is not a compilation of the media texts themselves.

[35] Mabel Murphy, luncheon, Missouri Arts Council conference, Lake of the Ozarks, Missouri, March 30, 1990.

they are better described as *expressions* that assume a variety of forms. Some involve words, and others consist largely of non-discursive forms of communication.

The process of presenting this range of material in book form was not always easy, and we came to understand why so many public address scholars have chosen to collect speeches. Because of their varied formats, deciding how best to capture and represent the women's expressions was a demanding and time-consuming process. To present a garden, the process of raising a child, or a quilt in a form suitable to a book is difficult, and the photographs, essays, and interviews we used in our efforts to depict these communicative events do not always do justice to them. We have attempted, however, to capture these women's expressions from as many angles as possible. We have included background information about them, incorporating their own words as part of that material;[36] actual transcripts as texts, where appropriate; and photographs of the non-discursive forms. In some cases, we also have included texts with which a woman works or from which she creates—instructions from a pattern for sewing a garment or a list of flowers in a garden, for example—because these provide important materials and vocabularies that are part of the creative process. We hope the excitement of working with the varied, multi-dimensional texts will help offset the necessarily incomplete artifacts we had to use to present those texts.

Significant texts are finished products.

The special value accorded formal public speeches in the study of public address is accompanied by a closely related assumption—that the texts to be studied are pieces of discourse with clear and distinguishable boundaries. This does not mean that critics, on occasion, have not been concerned with the evolution of texts, their ongoing impact, and similar issues concerned with the process by which a text is created.[37] For the most part, however, speeches have been treated as finite events—as messages delivered in particular contexts for particular audiences, after which their effectiveness is assessed. While scholars in communication acknowledge that communication is a process and generally have moved to a transactional view of it—seeing communication as a process jointly constructed by the interactants that does not necessarily

---

[36] All quoted material in the text that is not footnoted was obtained from personal interviews with the women.

[37] For example, the development and evolution of Lincoln's inaugural speech is discussed by Marie Hochmuth Nichols, "Lincoln's First Inaugural," in *American Speeches*, by Wayland Maxfield Parrish and Marie Hochmuth Nichols (New York: David McKay, 1954); rpt. in *Methods of Rhetorical Criticism: A Twentieth-Century Perspective*, 2nd. ed., ed. Bernard L. Brock and Robert L. Scott (Detroit: Wayne State University Press, 1980), pp. 73-113.

have a clear beginning and ending — the typical text studied in public address is a finished speech.

In *Women Speak*, we have taken the notion of process seriously and have attempted to make visible the ongoing nature of communication. Almost all of the texts are depictions of portions of a larger process. The talk between a mother and her son, the essay on mothering, and the transcript of talk at a women's reading group are a few examples. We consider each of these texts unfinished in the sense that the process involved in their creation is a never-ending one. Even when definite closure seems to have been obtained — a house is built, a photograph is taken, a poem is published — there is continued interaction around that form of expression. Homeowners, for example, continue to share their perceptions of the architect of their house with those who visit; a photographer's work continues to prompt new interpretations — even for her; and poetry continues to affect its readers in various ways after it has achieved a finished state as a published text.

We became very aware of the ongoing nature of these texts in talking with these women. They admitted that they see their expressions quite differently from one day to the next, and how they describe them one day might vary greatly from what they say about them on another. For others, our interviews helped them articulate their feelings about their forms of communication and come to new understandings about them, and the exploration of their own insights undoubtedly will continue after this book is published. We were cognizant, then, of having to stop the clock on the process of these texts, and we encourage you, as you analyze them, to see them as tentative and fluid communicative forms.

The effort to capture process resulted in artifacts of various lengths. Some of the samples included here are long — because we sought to capture the essence of the process, which most accurately is revealed over a period of time. The interaction between a mother and her son, for instance, is one of the longest; we felt, however, that a shorter text would not capture adequately the repetition, interruption, and shifts in topic and attention that characterize the parenting of small children. Other texts are quite short — the photographs of the graffiti from a women's restroom, for instance — because they show virtually the complete discourse. While some of the texts undoubtedly will prove more difficult to analyze than the tangible and completed speeches typically studied, we hope that they inspire a range of rich analyses because of the manner in which they seek to present a multi-dimensional picture of women's communication.

Suitable frameworks for assessing communication
are derived from male perspectives.

Male standards have been used to assess women's communication performance and effectiveness, even when such standards are inappropriate for analyzing their communication. In studies of women speakers, issues of gender that have an impact on the rhetor, message, and audience often are not mentioned. In Wayne Thompson's study of Barbara Jordan's keynote address to the 1976 Democratic national convention, for example, he suggests her effectiveness was due to two clusters of value appeals; considerations of gender are not part of his analysis.[38] In other studies, the women communicators are judged by male criteria for effectiveness; more likely than not, women are found not to measure up. Such is the case with Kathleen Edgerton Kendall and Jeanne Fisher's study of Frances Wright's oratory. They examine her oratory according to Aristotle's criteria for *ethos* and find that, while meeting the criteria for eloquence, she ultimately failed to gain extrinsic *ethos*: "Eloquence without extrinsic ethos produces museum pieces of oratory, not catalytic compositions that influence the course of history." [39]

We believe that a feminist framework is a more appropriate one for assessing women's communication than frameworks grounded in men's communication, and we regard *Women Speak* as a feminist project. We have taken a feminist perspective on women's communication in an effort to avoid employing male frameworks as guides for our presentation of women's texts. While many definitions of feminism have been used as the starting point for feminist frameworks and approaches,[40] one we find useful because of its communication orientation is that feminism is the belief that women and men are entitled to equal opportunities for self-expression. From this definition emerge three basic assumptions on which a feminist perspective or framework is based — in communication or any other discipline.[41]

The first assumption is that gender is a critical component of human social life; it serves as a lens through which all experience is filtered. The distinction

---

[38] Thompson, "Barbara Jordan's Keynote Address: The Juxtaposition of Contradictory Values."
[39] Kathleen Edgerton Kendall and Jeanne Y. Fisher, "Frances Wright on Women's Rights: Eloquence Versus Ethos," *Quarterly Journal of Speech*, 60 (February 1974), 65.
[40] Various definitions of feminism are offered in Cheris Kramarae, Paula A. Treichler, and Ann Russo, *A Feminist Dictionary* (Boston: Pandora, 1985), pp. 158-60.
[41] Just as there are many definitions of feminism, so a variety of feminist perspectives are possible; we are not claiming to offer the "correct" version here. For discussions of feminist perspectives on research in communication, see: Kathryn Carter and Carole Spitzack, eds., *Doing Research on Women's Communication: Perspectives on Theory and Method* (Norwood, NJ: Ablex, 1989); Carole Spitzack and Kathryn Carter, "Women in Communication Studies: A Typology for Revision," *Quarterly Journal of Speech*, 73 (November 1987), 401-23; H. Leslie Steeves, "Feminist Theories and Media Studies," *Critical Studies in Mass Communication*, 4 (June 1987), 96-135; Brenda Dervin, "The Potential Contribution of Feminist Scholarship to the Field of Communication," *Journal of Communication*, 37 (Autumn 1987), 107-20; and "Forum on Feminist Scholarship," *Women's Studies in Communication*, 11 (Spring 1988), a compilation of essays by various authors about women's scholarship. Our perspective on feminist scholarship is elaborated in Karen A. Foss and Sonja K. Foss, "Incorporating the Feminist Perspective in Communication Scholarship: A Research Commentary," in Kathryn Carter and Carole Spitzack, eds., *Doing Research on Women's Communication: Perspectives on Theory and Method* (Norwood, NJ: Ablex, 1989), pp. 65-91.

between sex and gender is crucial to a feminist perspective: sex is considered a biological given, while gender is a social and psychological construction that involves cultural notions of appropriate behavior for women and men. Feminist scholars call into question assumptions about gender that have been taken for granted and explore how traditional constructions of gender have subordinated women's experiences. They examine the implications of this subordination for the communication practices of both sexes.

A second assumption central to a feminist perspective is that women's perceptions, meanings, and experiences—including their communicative experiences—are different from men's and deserve to be taken seriously. Explanations for the source of these differences vary—including women's experience of oppression, their unique biological characteristics and how these have been incorporated into gender constructions, and the socialization process that establishes particular expectations for women. Whatever they see as the source of these differences, feminist scholars seek to develop constructs and theories of communication that recognize the effectiveness, impact, and eloquence of women's communicative experiences as well as men's.

A third assumption of scholars who assume a feminist perspective is that feminist scholarship is done to improve women's lives—to accomplish fundamental changes in the social order and in the construction of gender that subordinates and devalues women. Feminist scholars, through their research, attempt to improve women's lives in two ways. First, they seek to include in their research and theorizing the voices of women; this is an effort at inclusion. Through this effort, feminist scholars expand awareness of the omission of women from our disciplines and make problematic definitions and constructs previously assumed to be accurate and comprehensive descriptions of human behavior. A second way in which they seek to improve women's lives as a result of their research is through a process of reconceptualization of theoretical constructs using the knowledge gained from the study of women's data. They re-examine traditional definitions and constructs of, in our case, communication phenomena, to discover if the concerns and experiences of women were considered in their formulation. If they were not, they reformulate or reconceptualize those definitions and constructs to fit women's experiences.

A feminist framework informs the vision and design of *Women Speak*. We have given the construct of gender a central place in our framework for analysis of the texts, believing that how our culture has constructed definitions of and expectations for women cannot be ignored when dealing with women's communication. We also have taken seriously the assumption that women's experiences should be examined on their own terms—from the perspectives of women themselves. To this end, we have chosen to compile not women's speeches but rather various discursive and non-discursive forms that women themselves say are valuable for them. Finally, we hope that the framework for analysis of the texts, which encourages a reconceptualization of basic communication concepts to include women's perspectives, will hasten a re-visioning of the study of public address to include women as communicators.

We hope, then, that what we have produced, in collaboration with the women in this book, is appropriately subversive. With Deborah Cameron, we assert that women's talk is not inherently subversive but becomes so when women privilege it over the talk of men. We see *Women Speak* as offering a subversive alternative to traditional approaches to public address that have privileged male communication precisely because it asserts the inherent value of women's expression and declares it eloquent on its own terms.

FRAMEWORK FOR ANALYSIS

In the first chapter, we introduced *Women Speak* by providing the context—the study of public address—from which the book emerged. We suggested that a more accurate view of women's communication is gained when assumptions and practices that define significance in communication are expanded to include women. In this chapter, we offer suggestions for analyzing the texts in *Women Speak* to facilitate your examination of women's communication from a feminist perspective.

The systematic analysis of texts is the function of a particular approach to the study of communication called *rhetorical criticism*. *Rhetorical criticism* is the process of analyzing and assessing communication to discover such elements as the context in which it was created; its purpose within that context; its central ideas, structure, and style; and its impact on the communicator and others who are reached by it. By *rhetoric*, we mean humans' use of symbols for the purpose of communicating with one another. While some scholars make distinctions between the terms, *rhetoric* and *communication*, we are using them as synonymous. We have chosen to use the term *communication* rather than *rhetoric* in this book because its meaning is more widely understood, and fewer negative connotations are attached to it.

A variety of approaches or methods have been developed in rhetorical criticism to answer a variety of questions about how communication works— fantasy-theme analysis, pentadic analysis, metaphoric analysis, and neo-Aristotelian criticism, to name a few.[1] While any of these could be used for analyzing the texts in *Women Speak*, the framework we provide here is not grounded in any particular critical method. Because our goal is to facilitate the emergence of an increasingly accurate and comprehensive view of women's communication, we chose not to present a single, established method for use here.

Rather, the framework for analysis provided here is designed to encourage the discovery of characteristics of women's communication and use of those characteristics to question traditional communication concepts that may not describe women's communication. The framework also is designed to be used, when necessary, to suggest reformulations of these concepts to take into account women's perspectives and communicative practices. To accomplish these purposes, the framework consists of a series of questions to use in examining a text, grouped to provide a three-step process of analysis: (1) Examination and analysis of a text; (2) Formulation of hypotheses about women's communication on the basis of your analysis; and (3) Questioning of a communication concept in order to incorporate women's experiences into that concept.

The practice of rhetorical criticism in which you will engage as you analyze the texts in *Women Speak* is demanding. It requires a close and careful study of a text, using the questions as starting points. Any conclusions you draw about the text should be supported by direct references to the text; in other words, you should be able to justify your conclusions by offering reasons grounded in the texts themselves.[2] Because of the unusual nature of the texts in *Women Speak*, however, your task is likely to be even more demanding than the usual practice of rhetorical criticism, and you must be particularly creative, flexible, and imaginative as you engage in the process of analysis. The materials that serve as texts in *Women Speak* often provide evidence of only some aspects of the process involved in a form of expression, so you will be working with texts that contain gaps and omissions. In other cases, you will be dealing not with actual artifacts of communication processes but with essays about processes—the essays on shopping and motherhood, for example. Use all of the information provided about a form of expression as your text—both the

---

[1] For summaries of various critical methods developed for the analysis of communication, see: Sonja K. Foss, *Rhetorical Criticism: Exploration & Practice* (Prospect Heights, IL: Waveland, 1989); Bernard L. Brock, Robert L. Scott, and James W. Chesebro, *Methods of Rhetorical Criticism*, 3rd ed. (Detroit: Wayne State University Press, 1989); and Roderick P. Hart, *Modern Rhetorical Criticism* (Glenview, IL: Scott, Foresman, 1990).

[2] For more on the process of doing rhetorical criticism and the appropriate stance of the critic, see Foss, *Rhetorical Criticism*, pp. 11-29.

introductory material and the accompanying artifacts, whatever form they assume. Consider both the discursive or verbal as well as the non-discursive or nonverbal elements of the texts in your analysis.

Because of the necessarily incomplete nature of many of the texts in *Women Speak*, we especially encourage you to use your own experiences and those of women around you to provide a more complete picture of the text you are analyzing. For example, if you garden, you may wish to bring those experiences to bear on your analysis of the text on gardening; if you sew, your knowledge of sewing will help you fill in pieces of that process that could not be presented in the textual artifacts. If you do not personally engage in these expressions, you may want to talk with women who do in order to bring a more complete and informed understanding to your analysis.

In fact, rather than analyzing the specific garden or sewing project described in *Women Speak*, you may want to analyze the gardening and sewing processes of women you know, where you will have a wealth of information available as well as the opportunity for personal examination of the garden or garment. As we noted in the first chapter, the texts presented in *Women Speak* are not to be privileged in any way over those of other women. We are less interested in your use of these *particular* texts to discover the nature of women's communication than in your exploration of women's communication in its various manifestations in your own life.

Your analysis of texts in *Women Speak* does not need to begin with the first text—architecture—and proceed systematically and chronologically through the book. The texts are arranged alphabetically to discourage the privileging of the specific communicator over the form of expression. Feel free, then, to begin with the text that interests you most or that you feel most comfortable analyzing. If you are less experienced in working with non-discursive forms of communication, you may want to begin with texts in traditional verbal formats—such as the speech by Ursula Le Guin or the transcript of the women's reading group—before moving on to the less traditional text formats—such as children's parties or baking.

Step 1: Analysis of the Text

Women Speak makes accessible a wide sample of women's communication for analysis. Your task in this step is to develop as clear a picture as possible, from the text you have chosen for analysis, of how a particular woman (or women, in the case of collaborating creators) communicates. To accomplish this goal, you may want to consider the following aspects of the text in your analysis.

Nature of the Exigence

Consider the exigence, the need, or the situation to which the text is addressed. To what exigence is the woman responding? Is the need she chooses to address one she seems to have defined as originating within herself or in an external condition? Does the woman view the exigence as negative, consisting of an imperfection or undesirable condition? Is it, instead, positive for her, consisting of an opportunity to affirm, support, and celebrate? What attitudes, beliefs, traditions, and relationships affect the woman's definition of the exigence?

Nature of the Audience

Who is the audience for the text? Is the woman herself her own audience, or is the audience another individual or group? In some texts, both the woman herself and others may comprise the audience. In what ways does the woman involve her audience in the creation and presentation of her communication? In what ways does the audience's interaction with the woman help shape the nature of the text?

Nature of the Communicator

The woman who produced the text has made certain choices that are manifest in her text. Given what you know about the woman's background and perspectives, how do these seem to have shaped the choices she has made in the development of the text? How is her identity shaped by the text? What can you infer about the woman's attitudes, perspectives, or approaches to the world from your examination of the text? How might she herself be changed as a result of her text?

A communicator's sex and gender affect her own communication and how it is perceived by others. How does the fact that the communicator is a woman affect the nature of the text? How does the communicator's status as a woman affect your expectations for and evaluation of the text? The women who are included in *Women Speak* were selected, in part, because they demonstrate an awareness about and self-reflection on their status and experiences as women—they are feminist in their orientation to the world. What impact might the feminist orientation of the creator of the text have on its development and on your perception of it?

Nature of the Text

Examine the features of the text used by the woman to develop and present her perspectives. What seems to be the organizing idea or generating principle of the text? Some feminist scholars assert that caring and connectedness often are underlying or organizing principles for women's approaches to the world. Does caring characterize the organizing idea of the text in any way?

An organizing principle must be elaborated on or supported in a text in some ways. What are the primary materials and symbol systems used by the woman to develop the text's organizing principle? Blueprints in architecture or the specific vocabulary of sewing, for example, might constitute means by which an organizing principle is elaborated. How are these materials structured or organized? The woman has chosen particular language, colors, or textures — particular stylistic elements — to develop her ideas. What stylistic features characterize the text? How does the particular genre in which the woman works — costume design or letter writing, for example — affect the nature of the text?

Functions of the Text

Communication occurs in order to achieve certain purposes, whether or not a communicator is consciously aware of the full range of reasons for her communication. How does the text function for the woman who created it? How does it function for those who interact with her? Traditionally, persuasion has been the function or outcome on which communication scholars have focused in their analysis of discourse. To what degree is persuasion a primary function of the text? Do other functions seem to characterize the text more accurately? Journal writing, for instance, may be designed to facilitate discovery of the self, while the newsletter produced by and for the lesbian community may be designed largely to support and affirm.

Nature of the World Created

Communication creates our world or our views of reality. Communication is not simply talk about a reality that we already know in some objective way; our very reality is created by our communication about it. How we communicate, then, reflects and encourages particular beliefs about, actions toward, and knowledge of something. Identify the important features of the reality that appear to be created as a result of the text. Is it a world that is primarily physical, psychological, or social in nature? How do the woman's communicative choices focus attention on certain people, events, or ideas? Does the text establish a world populated by particular kinds of settings, characters, and actions? How might the world created by the text affect the woman's life? How might it affect other individuals who interact with the text? How effective is the text in creating the kind of reality the woman may want to create?

Worlds created by women through their communication relate to the patriarchal system or culture in which we all live in three primary ways: they may be designed to affirm and support the patriarchal system, to develop women-centered realities or places separate from it, or to adapt women's perspectives to the patriarchal system in an effort to integrate women's ways into that system. Is the world the woman creates in the text one that adjusts to the patriarchal system in some way? Does it help to create a woman-centered reality apart from that system? Does it try to do both? Is the world the woman creates with her text the result of her own experiences and definitions? Is it formulated largely from definitions and perspectives external to her?

Step 2: Development of Hypotheses About Women's Communication

After you have examined and analyzed a text, you have some knowledge that can be used as a starting point for making some general observations or hypotheses about the nature of women's communication. *Hypothesis* literally means "to suppose or propose," so the hypotheses you formulate are proposals, propositions, or initial ideas about the characteristics of women's communication. The hypotheses you formulate are starting points, then, for discovering what women's communication is like.

Your analysis of the text of the interaction between a mother and her child, for example, might lead you to speculate that women's communication seems to be characterized by interruptibility because it takes place in often unconnected bits and pieces. At this point, you don't know whether your hypothesis is true of all or most women's discourse; you simply know it is true about the text you have studied and might be true of other texts.

We hope you will continue your study of women's communication beyond one text by examining other texts and your own experiences with women's communication. After analyzing several of these texts, you will be able to tell whether the features of women's communication you have discovered in the analysis of one text are characteristic of the communication of many women or are simply idiosyncratic features of the communication of a particular woman.

You then will be able to reach some tentative conclusions about what women's communication, in general, is like. Are there certain kinds of subject matters about which women seem to communicate? Do particular stylistic or structural features seem to characterize women's communication? Given the diversity of women's experiences, are there features of content or style that can be found to characterize all or most women's communication? How do these differ from what you know about general features of men's communication? If features can be identified that characterize all or most women's communication, a basic exigence or condition to which women's discourse is addressed would seem to exist. Is there such an exigence that characterizes the lives of all women? What might it be? Why might women have developed particular forms of expression not shared by men? Do you see any truth to the assertion that women need to be bilingual—speaking the languages of both women and men—to function effectively in contemporary society?

Even if you analyze only one text of women's communication, however, you can begin to speculate, in the development of hypotheses, about the features that seem to characterize women's communication. You have taken one woman's communication seriously and thus have a beginning point for understanding women's communication. The understanding you gain can be used as the basis for the questioning of communication concepts, the next step in your analysis.

Step 3: Questioning a Communication Concept

You now have analyzed at least one example of women's communication and have developed some ideas about what women's communication might be like on the basis of your analysis. You now are ready to use the information you have gained about women's communication as a lens through which to examine a communication concept or notion to discover if it reflects the communication process as it is engaged in by women—in particular, by the woman whose text you analyzed. If it does not, you will want to suggest a reformulation of that concept so it fits women's communicative experiences. We suspect that what you discover as you question communication concepts may surprise you. You may come to see the world of communication theory as much more gender specific than you previously had imagined. The first step in this process is to engage in a critique of a communication concept.

Critique of a Communication Concept

The communication concept you select for critique will depend on the text you have analyzed and the results of your analysis. Did your analysis of the text suggest a certain concept as central to the text? If you have analyzed a text dealing with women's rituals, for example, you might be reminded of epideictic or ceremonial discourse and may wish to undertake a critique of epideictic discourse as it traditionally has been viewed. The hypotheses you formulated about women's communication also may suggest a concept you want to investigate. If you analyzed quiltmaking, for example, you might have discovered that women's communication seems characterized by intricate and complex structures. This notion might lead you to re-examine the traditional notion of organization or structure as it has been viewed in studies of discourse. You may find that chronological and problem-solution structural patterns, for example, which are common in public speeches, do not seem to fit the quilt as a communicative form. Notions such as the enthymeme, *ethos*, emotional appeals, self-disclosure, power, and rationality also might emerge from your analyses as candidates for critique. The concept of *eloquence* might be particularly appropriate for questioning, given the subtitle of *Women Speak*. How might eloquence, as it applies to women's communication, be conceptualized?

Once you have identified a communication concept that you want to question, begin by reviewing how that concept traditionally has been conceptualized. Does the concept, as it traditionally is defined, adequately describe the concept as revealed in the text you have analyzed? Does the traditional view of the concept seem to reflect men's communicative experiences more so than women's? Does it omit women's particular forms of communication by its definition or conception? Does it include but distort women's forms of communication?

Your answers to these questions will determine whether the traditional concept can be expanded to include women's ways of expression in its scope or whether the entire concept needs to be recast in order to do justice to women's communication. If you discover that the concept you are questioning does not seem to allow for the inclusion of women's ways of communicating, you will want to move to the next step of the questioning process — reconceptualization.

Reconceptualization of a Communication Concept

In the reconceptualization step, your goal is to formulate a new conception of a traditional notion of communication that takes women's ways of communicating into account.[3] Begin by identifying the aspects of the concept that seem irrelevant or inappropriate to the description of an aspect of women's communication you have discovered in your analysis. What aspects of the concept omit or distort women's communicative processes? You may discover, for example, that the concept of protest, as it traditionally has been viewed, includes opposition to an established system, but your analysis of a woman's text suggests that she establishes, in her protest, common ground with those who represent the system.[4] How might the notion of protest — or whatever concept you have chosen as your focus — be changed to include and accurately present women's perspective? Does a new, separate concept, with a new label, need to be developed to reflect major differences between how women and men tend to engage in that communication process? What are the essential features of such a concept as it is manifest in women's communication? Does it have a particular content and/or form?

[3] For examples of the process of feminist reconceptualization in a number of disciplines, see: Paula A. Treichler, Cheris Kramarae, and Beth Stafford, eds., *For Alma Mater: Theory and Practice in Feminist Scholarship* (Urbana: University of Illinois Press, 1985); and Christie Farnham, ed., *The Impact of Feminist Research in the Academy* (Bloomington: Indiana University Press, 1987).
[4] These are some of the findings discovered by Mary Rose Williams in her dissertation, "A Re-Conceptualization of Protest Rhetoric: Characteristics of Quilts as a Protest Form," Diss. University of Oregon 1990.

Consider possible effects the new concept might have on other, related concepts as they traditionally have been viewed in the communication discipline. What impact, for example, would a new conception of protest have on social movement theory? Which concept—the traditional one or your reconceptualized one—fits more accurately with your own communicative experiences? Would you respond differently to the concept had it been described or presented to you as you now have reconceptualized it? Do you feel more connected to or distant from the communication field as a result of your reconceptualization of the concept? Does your reconceptualization encourage you to evaluate women's communication in any different ways?

You may feel inadequate to the task of the rethinking and reconceptualizing of communication concepts. You are not an Aristotle, you may protest, able to make observations about communication that have staying power over centuries. Neither have you done sophisticated research that would entitle you to develop communication concepts. Remember, though, that all concepts are really just labels for explanations about how communication works, developed by inquiring people seeking to understand communication by studying some particular samples of it. Although you usually don't label them *concepts*, you often come up with ideas about how things work in your everyday life. We are asking you to do here, then, what you often do: to come up with explanations (or concepts) about something—in this case, how communication works. Your data are texts by women, which you use to develop an idea or concept about how an aspect of communication operates that takes seriously women's ways of communication.

The process of reconceptualization of a communication concept does not end with a reformulation of that concept. Once it has been reconceptualized, it needs to be tested through applications to other women's texts, including those in your own life, to see if it provides an accurate description of women's communication processes. You also will want to see what use you are able to make of your new knowledge in your own life. How have you changed as a result of your analysis of the text and your questioning of a communication concept? Are you more appreciative, for example, of the women's communication around you or of your own communication activities? Have you developed some ideas for increasing the effectiveness of your communication in some area? Have you come to realize that different criteria should be used to define communicative effectiveness for women and men? Have you become more sensitive to communication processes that exclude women's approaches? Are there ways in which you can give voice to women and women's perspectives in your life?

We hope you will use the framework offered here to stimulate your reading and thinking about women's communication and the process of communication in general. Most important, we hope you will approach your encounters with women's communication with a greater awareness and appreciation than you did before. The examination of women's communication from their own perspectives has only begun, and your analyses of women's texts and application of the knowledge you gain to the communication field and to your own life are important pieces in the expanding picture that constitutes our knowledge of how women speak.

1

ARCHITECTURE

Joyce Plath

"I thoroughly enjoy my work. Unlike the lonely painter who works to a large extent from the unconscious, I work with people. I like the combination of objective and subjective challenges that present themselves." For Joyce Plath, an architectural designer, the comparison between painting and architecture comes naturally: she has a Master's of Fine Arts in painting and taught art and women's studies at Humboldt State University before earning a degree in architecture. The catalyst for her interest in architecture was building her own "small house in the 1970s; I enjoyed the process of planning and building." She decided to apply to the graduate program in architecture at the University of California, Berkeley, almost on a whim: "Almost everyone I knew thought I couldn't do it since I had no math background. I found out I had been accepted into the three-year program in May—within a week of learning that I was pregnant with my first child. Since I wanted both the architectural training and the baby, I went ahead with both."

Plath, who works out of her home in Arcata, California, designs homes, apartment complexes, and commercial buildings. She is a strong advocate of infill—"using lots that have been overlooked by others and using small spaces efficiently to provide high-quality living environments." In addition to using existing space in cities creatively, she wants her structures to blend in with the style of the neighborhood. If she is building in an area characterized by Victorian architecture, for example, her design incorporates some features of that architecture—even for a contemporary home—so the building doesn't appear out of place. Plath's current projects include a new building for a hardware store that burned in Arcata; a fifty-unit apartment complex, also in Arcata; and two houses. She is also "rehabing" two historic commercial buildings in Eureka and several in Willits, California.

When designing a building, Joyce first attends to the site, "noting views, neighborhood, sun angles, topography, flat areas for play or gardens, areas that should not be viewed (neighbors' houses, junk cars), and acoustics." She finds difficult sites particularly interesting. She then interviews her clients to determine "lifestyle, hobby and home-office needs, other people who may live there (parents, extended guests, future children), and, of course, budget." Making her houses fit the physical needs of the owner is a major priority for her. She also likes her houses to "capture sunlight and views and to have outside space protected from wind"; her structures also must be visually pleasing in proportion and style.

Joyce speculates that women may design homes differently from men because, as primary caretakers, they often have developed strong preferences about arrangements that facilitate parenting. Plath is especially sensitive to spaces that accommodate children and parents in creative and efficient ways and admits that "my favorite houses are often for families with young children." She designs houses for such families so that the primary play area can be seen from the kitchen, for example. One couple with a young daughter was impressed that Joyce designed the windows in her room low enough so that she could see out of them. For families with teenagers, she tends to separate their spaces in order to give both parents and children some privacy.

Plath's sensitivity to issues of children and their environment stems from her own experience as a new mother in graduate school. Her son was born in February of her first year; he "was sleeping on a drafting table thirteen days later." She wrote her thesis on a prototypical infant day-care facility: "It was wonderful to combine the observations I had been making on my son's relationship to his environment with the new skills I had been learning in architecture school." Plath has another son—born five years after the first—and a half a daughter. Because she always had wanted a girl, she has become the legal guardian of a single friend's daughter; the daughter comes to visit every weekend and for a month in the summer, giving her mother a break from the parenting role and providing Joyce with the experience of raising a daughter. Joyce, now a single parent herself, hopes to design cooperative housing situations for single parents and seniors in the not-too-distant future.

Plath's travels to Africa and Asia have sparked her interest in housing issues in such countries. As a junior in college, she spent a year in India, and in her late twenties, she taught for three years in the Philippines and Thailand. She hopes to spend a year in Namibia soon, working as an "enabler—helping this very new country provide appropriate housing for itself." She taught a course in vernacular architecture for the developing world—looking at traditional building techniques and materials as they relate to climate and culture—for the Environmental Engineering Department at Humboldt State University.

The photographs and floor plans shown below are from a house Joyce designed for Melanie Johnson and Ron Johnson in Westhaven, California: "Their house remains my all-time favorite." In designing the house, Plath was confronted with an extraordinary site, overlooking the ocean and a creek. There were constraints on her design, however; in order for the project to qualify as a "remodel"—and thus be buildable as a site under coastal commission regulations—it had to be designed to fit exactly on the old house's foundation. In addition, the Johnsons wanted a generous study, a place to display art (Ron Johnson is an art history professor), maximum views of the ocean, and for as much of the outside to come into the house as possible. To create this feeling, they wanted windows that capitalized on the outside environment; they have a large window that overlooks the huge rock that sits next to their house. Not only did Joyce accommodate this wish, but she spent considerable time helping them select the style and finish for the windows—they wanted no window coverings. They finally chose a red fir that looks like the wood of the redwood trees that surround the house; they could not use redwood itself because it is too soft.

Plath also suggested adding a row of horizontal windows between the door level and the ceiling, with which the Johnsons are very happy. In fact, these windows present Joyce with one of her favorite views from the house— "the creek when walking down the stairs." This view is reminiscent of a "Zen view," described by Christopher Alexander in *A Pattern Language*, a book Plath sometimes recommends to clients. A "Zen view" is a glimpse of or framed view seen only from limited positions or on a pathway, like a stair landing, "in order to provide excitement and surprise."

Melanie and Ron Johnson were not only pleased with Joyce's design, but they liked how she worked with them as clients. "She didn't beat around the bush; she told us what she thought," according to Melanie Johnson. When they wanted the view from the kitchen to take precedence over efficiency— their dishes are stored on the opposite side of the kitchen from the dishwasher— they appreciated how Plath handled the situation: "She told us what would be most efficient architecturally, but then she designed what we wanted. She didn't keep talking about resale value." In other words, she "told us what her training told her she should do, but she allowed us to be really involved. She was sensitive to our personalities and lifestyle."

The photographs below show two views of the house. In the frontal view, the living room is on the left-hand side; notice the rock with the overlooking window. The dining room faces straight out, and the study is on the second floor, where the chimney is visible. The round window at the top of the house looks out from the master bedroom.

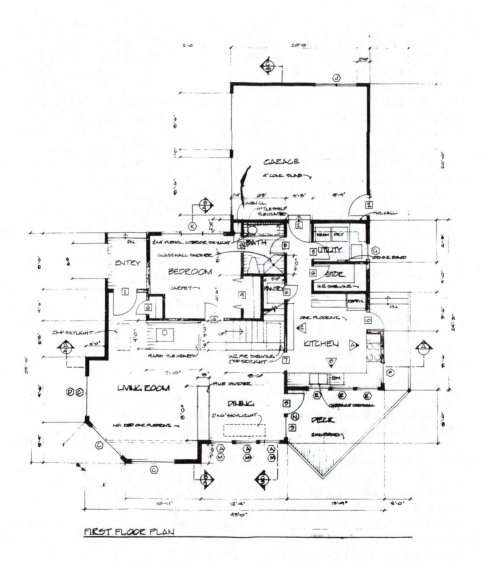

FIRST FLOOR PLAN

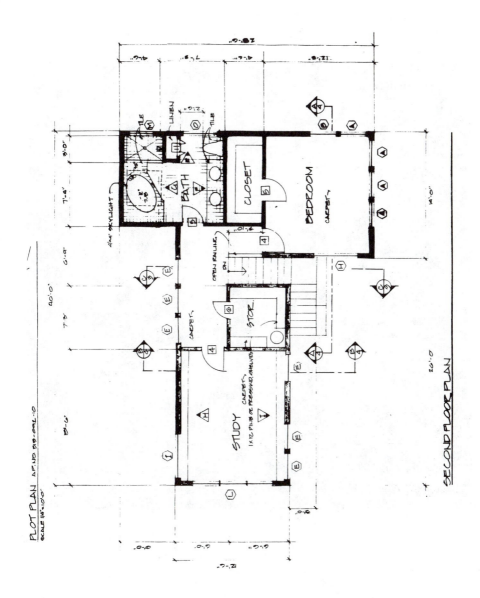

PLOT PLAN APT NO BLD-BLDG-10
SCALE 1/4"=1'-0"

SECOND FLOOR PLAN

Joyce Plath, home designed for Melanie Johnson and Ron Johnson
Photograph: Diana Schoenfeld

Joyce Plath, home designed for Melanie Johnson and Ron Johnson
Photograph: Diana Schoenfeld

2

BAKING

Mary Rose Williams

"My cheesecakes are a reflection of a desire I've always had to be very, very good at something," says Mary Rose Williams about the cheesecakes she creates. "I can't ski, I broke my foot in aerobics, I can't stand up on ice skates, and I'm not a great artist. I'm pretty average at everything except my cheesecakes." Williams has turned her expertise into a way to express her affection for her friends and their importance to her. Even when she was a student, living on a limited budget, Mary Rose's ability to make cheesecakes enabled her to give something special to others: "There wasn't a whole lot I could give because I just couldn't afford it, but I could make a cheesecake that was special for somebody."

Williams' mother introduced her to baking; as a child, she watched her mother, a housewife, develop a small business of making cakes for weddings, birthdays, and other special occasions. As a teenager, Mary Rose helped her mother with some of the cake decorating, and today, the two women's shared interest in baking is an important part of their relationship. Although Williams' mother rarely makes cheesecakes, she sends her daughter recipes for cheesecakes, and Mary Rose often talks through her ideas for new cheesecakes with her mother.

Williams married following her graduation from high school, and during the ten years of her marriage, her cooking and baking skills were practiced and refined. But not until she was divorced did Mary Rose begin to specialize in baking cheesecakes. She wanted to prove to herself that she could do something well and "wanted something that was a challenge. A lot of people like cheesecakes, but everybody talks about how hard they are to make, so I decided to conquer them." As Williams pursued associate's, bachelor's, master's, and doctorate degrees in Maryland, Virginia, Colorado, and Oregon, she continued to develop her expertise in the creation of cheesecakes.

Mary Rose's foray into the baking of cheesecakes consisted of following recipes developed by others and learning basic principles about how cheesecakes are made. She quickly discovered that the basic baking technique she had learned from her mother—"you get the basic recipe and then you throw in this and you throw in that according to how you *feel*"—had to be adapted carefully to cheesecakes. She learned that ingredients affect each other and the end product in very particular ways in cheesecakes, that the door of the oven never should be opened after a cheesecake is put in because it will fall flat, and that a cheesecake should cool completely before it is put in the refrigerator to prevent it from cracking. After making fifteen or twenty cheesecakes, Williams felt comfortable with the process and had settled on a basic recipe.

From then on, Mary Rose's cheesecakes assumed ever more dramatic forms. She now creates new recipes from her basic one, varying it according to the ingredients she is adding—perhaps raspberries, nuts, or unsweetened chocolate—and speculating on their impact on the recipe and modifying it to insure the desired sweetness, tartness, and level of moisture. She still has failures because untried ingredients may act in unexpected ways. Her addition of too many juicy strawberries to one cheesecake, for example, contributed too much liquid to the cheesecake, creating a moist, gooey pudding instead of a cake. She was dismayed by the failure because the cake was being made for a special birthday party. Then a friend suggested they transform it into a trifle; the "cake" was poured into a punch bowl and covered with mounds of whipped cream.

For Williams, the process of making a new cheesecake begins by thinking about the recipient. Does she like a graham-cracker crust, a pastry crust, or a chocolate-pecan crust? What is his taste in foods—does he like sweet or tart foods? What is her preference in style—simple and plain, ornamental, or abstract and modern? What is the occasion, and how can the cheesecake capture the essence of that event? Mary Rose's answers to such questions result in a cheesecake specially designed for the person and the occasion. One friend, for example, received a chocolate cheesecake swirled with raspberries, semi-sweet chocolate, and brandy for her birthday; it was topped with whipped cream, raspberries, chocolate, and almonds. Another friend was given a lemon and orange cheesecake, a tart and tangy cake with a pastry crust for his birthday. For a goodbye party for a faculty member leaving the university, Williams made chocolate cheesecakes and decorated the tops to match the table decorations.

Mary Rose's cheesecakes often are the central feature of celebrations among her circle of friends, who often ask her to create a cheesecake for an event or simply expect that one of her cheesecakes will be there. While Williams is proud of her cheesecakes and wants people to enjoy them, she feels "uncomfortable if they like them too much—if they really go overboard in their praise"—because she doesn't "make them for that." The fun, for Mary Rose, comes in the planning of the cheesecakes—designing exactly the right type of cheesecake for a person and an occasion. Although she can make a cheesecake quickly and easily, with short notice, she isn't comfortable doing so. There's enough time to mix the ingredients and bake the cheesecake but not enough to do the kind of creative planning that Williams enjoys and considers essential.

Below are four of the recipes (or *receipts*, as she grew up calling them) Mary Rose has developed for cheesecakes: her basic cheesecake, chocolate raspberry cheesecake, hazelnut cheesecake, and strawberry cheesecake.

The Basic Cheesecake

When I mention *cheesecake* to different people, they all have vastly different ideas of what a cheesecake looks or tastes like. One person may think of cheesecakes as being of one flavor—lemon. Another may conjure up thoughts of a tart, firm cake smothered with canned or fresh fruit. A third person may remember a cheesecake as something similar to a tart mousse—firm but creamy. I have discovered that the flavors of cheesecakes are as endless as the baker's imagination, toppings can be simple or elegant, and the cake's texture can range from firm and somewhat dry to soft and creamy. For all of these tastes and consistencies, there is one basic recipe with which I begin all of my cheesecakes.

The basic ingredients I use for the fillings for the cheesecake recipes that follow are:

    4 8-ounce packages cream cheese (the store's brand is not
        recommended—the consistency usually isn't as good as
        the more nationally known brands)

    3 eggs

    1 to 1 1/2 cups sugar (amount depends on other ingredients
        added)

    1/4 cup whipping cream

    1/2 cup sour cream

Also common to the cheesecake recipes that follow is the process of mixing and baking. Careful attention to the following details will save time, ingredients, and face.

1. Think about the flavor of cake you want to make, the topping you will put on it, whether or not the topping is logistically possible, and how you will transport the concoction once it is done.

2. Buy the ingredients for the cake at least three days in advance of baking.

3. On the morning of the day you will bake the cake, take the cream cheese out of the refrigerator to soften.

4. Bake the crust and let it cool completely before adding the filling.

5. Beat the cream cheese with the sugar until all lumps are gone. Then add the eggs and other basic ingredients. Finally, add the specialty ingredients.

6. When the filling is complete, pour it into a 9-inch spring-form pan.

7. Place a pan of water (I use a 12-inch cake pan) on the oven rack below the cheesecake.

8. Pre-heat the oven and place the cheesecake on the rack above the water.

9. Do not open the oven door again for at least 3 hours. Bake the cake at 350 degrees for 15 minutes, then turn the oven down to 300 and bake for 1 hour to 1 1/2 hours. **Do not open the oven door until the cake is baked and cooled.** You have to test the cake by eyeballing it. If the center looks sunken after 1 hour and 15 minutes, give the cake another 10 or 15 minutes, checking its looks every few minutes. (Remember, the cake will continue to bake after the oven is turned off, so don't overdo it.) After enough cakes, you'll get a pretty good sense of when the cake is just the right texture. When the time is up, turn off the oven and let the cake sit in the oven for at least 1 to 2 hours longer. When the oven is cool, remove the cake to a spot where there is no draft until it is completely cooled.

10. After the cake is completely cooled, refrigerate it for at least 8 hours. Do not remove the sides of the pan until after this refrigeration is complete.

11. To remove the sides of the spring-form pan, let the cake sit on the kitchen counter for about 5 minutes. Then, take a thin knife and loosen the sides of the cake from the pan. This may take a bit of coaxing, so be patient.

12. When the sides are removed, slip the knife under the cake to loosen the crust from the pan. Do this slowly and gently, all around the bottom. Slip a metal spatula under the crust and gently slide the cake from the bottom of the pan onto a cake plate.

Take a breather now. The worst is over! All that's left to do is top and eat.

The major ingredient necessary to make a superb cheesecake is patience. Ideally, you should bake the cake one day and decorate and eat it the next. Whatever your schedule, give yourself enough time to ruminate about the kind of cake you want to make and to bake and top it. After you get the hang of it, you'll soon be creating your own masterpieces.

Chocolate Raspberry Cheesecake

You will need these ingredients in addition to the basic ones:

Crust:
1 package plain chocolate cookies
2 tablespoons sugar
3 tablespoons butter (softened)

Cheese filling:
3 1-ounce squares unsweetened chocolate (melted)
2 1-ounce squares semi-sweet chocolate (chopped)

Raspberry filling:
1 1/2 cups frozen or fresh raspberries (Be sure to thaw frozen berries the night before you plan to bake the cake; do not drain them.)
2 tablespoons brandy
1 tablespoon sugar
1 teaspoon cornstarch

Topping:
1 square semi-sweet chocolate, shaved (to make curls)
1/4 cup raspberries, drained (save the juice)
1/2 cup slivered almonds
1 cup whipping cream
2 tablespoons sugar

On baking day, bring the butter and cream cheese to room temperature. Cook the raspberries, sugar, and brandy. Mix cornstarch with some cool raspberry juice or water (about 1 tablespoon of liquid). Add the cornstarch mixture to the raspberries. Cook and stir until mixture boils; remove from heat and cool.

While this mixture is cooling, make the crust. Crush chocolate cookies to make 1 1/4 cups of crumbs. Mix in 2 tablespoons of sugar, cut in soft butter, and press into bottom and up about 1/2 inch of the side of a spring-form pan. Bake in 375-degree oven for 8 to 10 minutes. Be careful not to bake it too long; the chocolate cookie crumbs seem to burn easily. You'll be able to smell if it's over-baking.

While the crust is cooling, make the cheese filling. Beat together the basic ingredients, and add 3 squares of melted unsweetened chocolate.

Pour 1/3 of the batter into the spring-form pan. Spoon on half of the raspberry mixture and sprinkle with 1 square of chopped semi-sweet chocolate. Layer 1/3 more of the cheese mixture, spoon on the rest of the raspberry filling, and sprinkle with 1 square of chopped semi-sweet chocolate. Cover with remaining cheese filling.

When you are ready to assemble the cake, whip the cream with 1 or 2 tablespoons of sugar. Be sure to whip the cream so that it is very stiff—almost to the stage of becoming butter. Using a pastry tube, pipe the whipping cream onto the top and sides of the cake. Be creative and have fun. Then sprinkle on drained berries, chocolate curls, and almonds. Dribble the raspberry juice down the sides of the cake and on the top. Feast!

Hazelnut Cheesecake

Before I moved to Oregon, I never tried to make a hazelnut cheesecake because I didn't have hazelnuts readily available. If you have the same problem, you can substitute the hazelnuts in the crust with ground walnuts, almonds, or pecans. The flavor will be slightly different; however, with the addition of some Frangelico liqueur, the crust will have a hint of hazelnut flavor.

Since this recipe MUST include some Frangelico, be sure to get to your liquor store before it closes for the weekend or holiday. If you are unfamiliar with Frangelico, here's a hint: It comes in a bottle in the shape of a monk. The liqueur is made from hazelnuts; if you forget the name when you go shopping, just ask for hazelnut liqueur.

You will need these ingredients in addition to the basic ones:

Crust:
1 1/2 cups finely ground hazelnuts
1 tablespoon sugar
2 tablespoons butter (melted)
1 or 2 tablespoons Frangelico liqueur

Filling:
3/4 cup ground hazelnuts
1/3 cup Frangelico liqueur (or to taste). Be careful not to add too much liquid to the batter, though. If you want to add more than 1/2 cup of Frangelico, also put in a couple of tablespoons of flour.

Topping:
1 cup sour cream
1 tablespoon sugar
1/3 cup ground hazelnuts
1/3 cup whole hazelnuts (chocolate-covered hazelnuts add a nice touch)
1 tablespoon Frangelico

Make the crust by mixing all of the crust ingredients together and pressing over the bottom and 1 inch up the sides of a spring-form pan. Bake in a

375-degree oven for about 10 minutes. Be careful not to over or under bake. The mixture will begin to smell "nutty" when it's time to come out of the oven.

While the crust is baking and cooling, mix the basic filling ingredients and beat in the ground hazelnuts and the Frangelico. Pour batter into pan and bake according to the usual directions.

After the cake has been cooled, refrigerated, and removed from the pan, prepare the topping. Mix the sour cream with the sugar. Spread on top and over the sides of the cake. (I like to let it fall over the sides for a nice decorative effect.) Sprinkle ground hazelnuts on the top. Then dribble the Frangelico over the cake and top with whole hazelnuts. You can arrange the hazelnuts in a particular pattern or just randomly distribute them. Be creative!

Strawberry Cheesecake

When I asked my friend's son, Jake, what kind of a cheesecake he wanted for his sixteenth birthday, he didn't hesitate a second in responding; he wanted strawberry. Since I had not made a cheesecake with strawberries in it (I only had put them on the top before), I was excited by the prospect of a new adventure. Surprisingly, my first effort was a great success; however, the second time I made the cake, it was a disaster. Therefore, I caution against adopting the theory that if 1 pint of strawberries is good, 1 quart will be better.

You will need these ingredients in addition to the basic ones:

Crust:
3/4 cup graham-cracker crumbs
3/4 cup ground nuts (walnuts, pecans, almonds, or hazelnuts)
3 tablespoons butter (melted)
1 1/2 tablespoons sugar
3/4 teaspoon cinnamon

Filling:
1 pint strawberries (cleaned, sliced, and drained; save juice
   for topping)
1 teaspoon vanilla

Topping:
8 to 12 whole, pretty strawberries
1/4 cup slivered almonds (more if you'd like)
1 cup sour cream
1 tablespoon sugar
Strawberry juice

Mix crust ingredients and press into bottom and up 1 inch on the sides of a spring-form pan. Bake at 375 degrees for approximately 10 minutes.

While the crust is baking and cooling, mix the basic ingredients together and add the vanilla. Add the pint of strawberries. If the strawberries are very juicy, check the batter to see if it is too thin. If it is, add a few tablespoons of flour. Don't overdo this, though, or you'll be able to taste the flour in the cake. If the strawberries aren't very juicy, you can add more of the juice you drained off of them, being careful to save a couple tablespoons of it for the top.

Pour the batter into the crust and bake according to the usual directions. After the cake has been cooled, refrigerated, and removed from the pan, prepare the topping.

Mix the sour cream and sugar. Spread on top and over the sides of the cake. Sprinkle on slivered almonds, arrange whole strawberries on top, and dribble strawberry juice on top and over sides. Be careful not to use too much juice, or the cake will look soggy.

Be ready to make another one soon. Strawberry season is short in most states, and people like to get a lot of strawberry eating in while they can.

3

CHILDREN'S PARTIES

Donna Hammer

"When planning Nick's party, I think about what would be fun for him—what he likes to share with his friends. But it also must be something of which I approve," explains Donna Hammer. Her son, Nicholas Hammer, celebrated his eighth birthday with a party on April 7, 1990, at Skinner's Butte Park in Eugene, Oregon, which his mother planned and orchestrated. Hammer brought to the planning of the party not only her concerns as a mother but also an awareness of how activities like a party can communicate values to Nicholas and other children—an awareness heightened by her graduate study in speech communication. She spent two weeks before the date planning the various aspects of the party—guest list, invitations, cake, and games.

The planning began with Donna and Nick talking over who he would invite to his party. Hammer wanted her son's close friends to come but also wanted the number to be manageable. The final guest list included five boys and one girl. Acknowledging that the invitation of one girl to a boy's birthday party is unusual, Donna explains that she is a family friend who rides with Nick to school each day. She had invited him to her birthday party, where he was the only boy; he, in turn, reciprocated.

Planning the games required the greatest amount of effort for Donna. She designed two games—"The Adventures of Nick's Maze" and "Everybody Wins"—which are described in greater detail below. The theme of "Adventures" was based on themes common to Nintendo video games, which feature mazes, magic potions, strange creatures, and weapons. Because Hammer objects to the sexism and violence in these games, however, she chose to create an alternative in which the children act as if they are in a video game—but without weapons, violence, or princesses to save. This game began with the children constructing masks to wear while negotiating the maze, and Donna describes the process of mask making below. The children enjoyed "being able to act out what they had seen on T. V.," and the game was active in contrast to the passivity of T.V. and videos.

"Everybody Wins" was inspired by the game, "Hot Potato," in which children pass an object around the circle and try not to be caught holding it when the music stops. For Hammer's version, the children passed a ball made out of paper, layered to hold prizes, while singing songs to provide the music. When Donna stopped singing, the children also stopped; the child holding the ball unwrapped it until she or he found a prize. The children's reaction to this game was puzzlement, according to Hammer; used to being rough and competitive in getting rid of the ball, they had to handle the ball gently as they tried to hang onto it.

The birthday cake Donna designed was a circus train, which she and her husband made the night before the party, after Nick had gone to bed. Birthday cakes are a chance "to do something creative," according to Hammer, and she always makes unusual cakes for Nick's parties. One year, for example, she made a castle out of a huge strawberry shortcake. Nick received a train last Christmas and "has really been enjoying it," so Donna used a train theme for the cake.

The birthday party began with the children constructing their masks and playing "The Adventures of Nick's Maze." At that point, Nick opened his presents and the children ate birthday cake. The party ended with the game, "Everybody Wins." In the section below, instructions are provided for the two games and for the baking and assembly of the cake. The photographs that follow show Hammer serving the cake, the mask-making process, and the party participants with their finished masks.

Come Help Us Celebrate!

For _Nicholas Hammer_
Date _April 7, 1990_
Time _1:30 pm - 3:30 pm_
Place _Skinner Butte Park_

Given by _Donna and Bo_
Phone _345-5443 (R.S.V.P.)_

See you there!

Games

Adventures of Nick's Maze

My plan was to use the maze format from the Nintendo game and allow the children to act as if they were in a video game. I set up a mask-making table so that the children could make a mask to wear while going through the maze. The masks weren't designed to represent any special characters; the children just used their imagination in constructing a mask they would enjoy wearing through the maze. The following items were used in making the masks: colored paper, glue, string, scissors, glitter, felt pens, and a hole punch. After the masks were made, the children lined up at the beginning of the maze.

I set up the maze before the children arrived at the park and used crepe paper and stakes to mark its path. The goal of the game was for the children to get to the end of the maze as fast as they could and find the magic key. There were six stopping points in the maze; each of these offered a different activity for the children. The six activities were:

(1) Plant seeds: I placed a large box full of dirt and a cup of pea seeds at the first point. The children had to plant three seeds carefully in the dirt and water them.

(2) Carnival game: This game is similar to those found at a fair or carnival. I wrapped five tin cans in newspaper comics and placed them on a box. The children were given three tennis balls to throw at the cans. Once they had knocked the cans off, they could move on.

(3) Magic potion: The children received a glass of magic potion, which was really sparkling apple juice. Because of the bubbles, they couldn't drink

it too quickly. Once they finished drinking the potion, they received a marshmallow.

(4) Magic belt: At this point, the children gave me the marshmallow they had received at the previous stop, and in return, I put a "magic belt" around the waist of each child, and he or she ran to the end of the maze. The magic belt was part of the knight's costume Nick wore at Halloween; it was studded with ornaments in various colors.

(5) Magic key: At the end of the maze was a box filled with dirt. Buried in the dirt were seven plastic eggs. Six of the eggs contained pennies, and one of the eggs contained the magic key. All of the children won because they found a penny or a key. The child who was the fastest to unearth and open an egg with a penny in it won a special prize as did the child who found the egg with the key in it.

Everybody Wins

Similar to "Hot Potato," this game involves passing an object around in a circle and stopping the action when the music stops. Unlike "Hot Potato," however, in which there is only one winner, in this game, everybody wins and competitiveness is deemphasized.

I designed a ball out of old wrapping paper and newsprint (mostly comics). I layered the paper so that I could hide prizes in the folds — stickers, colorful shoe laces, bubble gum, a pair of dice, and small globes. I used tape to hold the edges together loosely. To play the game, the children sat in a circle and passed the ball around. They had to be gentle with it so that it would not break. When the music stopped, the child holding the ball unwrapped it little by little until he or she found a prize. After sharing the treasure with the other children, the child left the circle, and the game continued. Instead of using recorded music, the children sang. I sang alone at first, and as children left the circle, they joined in. We mostly sang "Happy Birthday To You" and Christmas carols. By the end of the game, all of the children had a prize and could share or trade with one another.

Cake Recipe

The cake was in the design of a circus train. The ingredients consisted of:

    1 chocolate cake mix
    1 chocolate frosting mix
    12 sticks black licorice (the kind that are twisted)
    30 round hard peppermint candies
    8 Hershey's kisses
    2 lollipops
    15 gumdrops (assorted colors)

1/4 lb. candy-coated licorice drops
12 animal crackers (elephants, camels, and lions)
1 strawberry pie (for the train station)
1 pie crust
12 strawberries (sliced)
1 tablespoon brown sugar
dash of cream
dash of vanilla
3 Pepperidge Farm wafer cookies (these look like logs)

I baked the cake in five rectangular mini-loaf pans for the train cars. While the cake was baking, I cut the sticks of licorice in half and placed them on a large cutting board to make the train tracks. The open side of the licorice faced up so that the candy wheels could fit into them. After the cakes cooled, I arranged them on the tracks and frosted them. I placed six peppermint candies on each car for the wheels (three on each side). I also lined the top edges of each car in a different color with candy-coated licorice drops. I then decorated each car as follows:

Engine: I used two lollipops for the engineers. I cut most of the stick off, leaving just enough to stick into the top of the cake. I used different colored gumdrops for the smoke stacks and headlights.

Hershey's Kisses Car: I lined up two rows of kisses, side by side, on the top of the car.

Zoo Car: I lined up three rows of animal crackers side by side on the top of the car.

Candy Car: I covered the top of the car with gumdrops.

Logging Car: I stacked three Pepperidge Farm wafer cookies on the top of the car.

I made a fresh strawberry pie (Nick's favorite treat) for the train station. I laid the crust in a mini-loaf pan and filled it with the strawberries, sugar, cream, and vanilla. After the pie cooled, I carefully removed it from the pan and placed it on the cutting board. I decorated it with windows and doors made out of licorice and used frosting as glue. I also placed a few of Nick's Lego figures around the station, along with green paper frayed at the ends for grass.

Donna Hammer, serving birthday cake
Photograph: Mary Rose Williams

Donna Hammer, helping with masks
Photograph: Mary Rose Williams

Donna Hammer, Nicholas Hammer, and friends with masks
Photograph: Mary Rose Williams

4

COMEDY

OVER OUR HEADS

*Teresa Chandler, Marion Damon,
Annie Larson, and Karen Ripley*

"Improv is a lot of fun, and it looks like fun on stage. If it's done well, it looks very easy, but there are a lot of structures in improv, there are a lot of rules to follow to make something work."[1] This summary of improvisational comedy is provided by Teresa Chandler who, with Karen Ripley, co-manages an improvisational comedy group called Over Our Heads. The group has performed at the Michigan and West Coast women's music festivals; schools and universities around San Francisco and up and down the West Coast; at clubs and community centers in the San Francisco bay area; and at conferences.

Founded in Oakland/Berkeley in January, 1984, the group consists of Ripley and Chandler as well as Annie Larson and Marion Damon. Pamela Stoneham serves as an alternate for the group. Each member of Over Our Heads had worked in the performance arts in various ways before the formation of the group. Karen, who also performs on her own as a stand-up comic, wanted to be a comedian since she was a child, although the focus on improvisational comedy came later: "I found improv six or seven years ago and fell in love with it."[2] Teresa says she "was born a ham. I always wanted to do comedy, music and theater, the combination of them, which is what Over Our Heads is to me. I wanted to be Carol Burnett when I grew up—I thought Carol Burnett was a position, like president, and you could grow up and get the job."[3]

---

[1] Mary Richards, "'Over Our Heads': Unpredictable and Spontaneous," *Bay Area Reporter*, 28 May 1988, p. 26.
[2] Richards.
[3] Richards.

Chandler performs as a musician on her own as well as doing improvisation with Over Our Heads. Ripley and Chandler had worked together as clowns and comics and owned a restaurant together before starting Over Our Heads; they also share a publishing company called Ruby Network.

Annie Larson made the croissants for Karen and Teresa's restaurant. She studied acting and worked with various improvisational groups but had not performed for several years until she met Ripley and Chandler and realized she wanted to be on stage again: "Performing is one of the things that brings me the most joy in my life." [4] In the fall of 1985, Marion Damon joined the group; she had performed with several improvisational groups around San Francisco before becoming part of Over Our Heads. Pamela Stoneham, who fills in for group members, has been active as a teacher and participant in theatre sports in the San Francisco bay area, in which teams of actors create difficult scenarios for the other team to perform—a musical Western in Shakespearean language, for instance.

A performance of Over Our Heads includes improvisational skits based on audience suggestions, routines in which the audience fills in blanks in a conversation, stand-up comedy routines, and lesbian/feminist songs. For the skits, the group might ask the audience for suggestions for an interesting location, a character, and a prop. Using the first suggestions they hear, the group creates a routine—set in a treehouse, with a lesbian mom as a character, and a futon for a prop, for example. Another standard routine is for one of the members to begin a conversation with the audience and have the audience fill in the blanks. For example, a conversation might begin with the line, "I was out driving my car, and I almost hit a (someone in the audience calls out *church*). Just then, a bus came by, and there were twenty (someone says *donkeys*) on this bus. The story becomes increasingly bizarre as the tale unfolds.

Over Our Heads intersperses its routines with humorous songs, most of which are co-written by Ripley and Chandler. A common pattern is for Karen to write the music and lyrics for a song, with Teresa making suggestions and additions as well as doing the vocal arrangements for the group.

The group's approach to improvisation is based on the techniques of Viola Spolin, the "grandmother of improv." To those not trained in improvisational techniques, what the group does seems almost impossible—constructing on-the-spot skits based on words and characters suggested by the audience. Ripley captures the essence of improvisation when she says: "You're going to see something you have never seen before and will never see again." [5] But some basic principles guide how the group functions on stage—principles not unrelated to managing life. Chandler describes improvisation as essentially "life skills—things people should use all the time." The basic elements involved

[4] Richards.
[5] Richards.

in improvisation and life come down to three: trust, commitment, and support. For an improvisation to be successful, each character must engage in behaviors that convey these three capacities, and the basic rules of improvisation are derived from them.

The first rule of improvisation is never to deny anything. According to Teresa, "if you deny an action or a person [that someone is depicting in an improvisation], everything stops." Instead, the group approaches a scene with a "yes, and . . ." attitude. Each member tries to take what's there and affirm it in order to move the scene along, trusting in a humorous and successful outcome. Another rule of improvisation is that each member of the group approaches a scene with the desire to make the other performers look good. "If you worry about how you'll look or what you'll do, the performance will be less successful," according to Chandler. A third rule is to listen: "If you miss something because you're not paying attention, you may end up denying it later on—which means you're not being supportive."

As an all-female group, the members of Over Our Heads believe they do make different use of humor than male comics. Males tend to create humor by taking a "one-up" stance; something is funny because something or someone is being put down. Women do not tend to do this; instead, explains Teresa, they "play people from the inside out" and depict much deeper character portrayals. Over Our Heads offers reflections on the female experience that are funny to women precisely because it is able to suggest context and characters with which its audiences identify.

The lyrics to *I Survived a Fem*, written by Karen Ripley and Teresa Chandler, and a photograph of Over Our Heads in performance follow.

I Survived a Fem

Karen Ripley and Teresa Chandler

Readin' *Vogue* magazine and painting up her nails
Everything I hoped for sure went straight to hell.
My mind wanders—I can always go back to men
Goddess help me, I survived a Fem.

Chorus: I could always get a butch
        It wouldn't take much;
        She could take out the garbage
        And always fix my clutch.

I survived a fem with her long blonde hair
Tight black stockings, silky underwear
I'm just a poor girl who can't understand
Goddess help me, I survived a Fem.

Chorus

Waxing off her body hairs and dying all the rest
Even at 4:00 a.m. she always looks her best.
Eating only rabbit food just to stay slim.
Goddess help me, I survived a Fem.

Chorus

I'm tired of being lonely; don't want it anymore
Someone just caught my eye walking through the door
Ringlets made of auburn hair; those eyes—get a load of them
Goddess help me, here I go again.

Chorus

Annie Larson, Marion Damon, Teresa Chandler, Karen Ripley, Over Our Heads
Photograph: Irene Young

5

COSTUME DESIGN

Robin Ver Hage

A number of different interests came together for Robin Ver Hage when she chose to work in the area of costume design for theatre. She always has been drawn to fabrics and the variety of textures available in fabrics and started to sew at the age of 10. The idea that she could create and control her own world also was a source of theatre's appeal. Growing up, as she did, in a strict religious environment, she found herself in "a world I didn't have much affinity for or control over." Her emphasis in her undergraduate studies in art history, studio art, and dramatic literature contributed, as well, to Ver Hage's interest in theatre design, which draws on aspects of all of these disciplines.

Robin did not choose theatre as a profession until she found herself managing a restaurant following her graduation and decided she had to start thinking about how to earn a living in a more creative way. She returned to school, earning a Master's of Fine Arts degree in theatre design from the University of Michigan. She has taught costume design at Michigan State University, the University of Akron, and Wayne State University. Her free-lance work has included costume design for the Black Sheep Repertory in Manchester, Michigan; Opera Theatre of St. Louis; and The Muppets, Henson Associates, in New York City.

For Ver Hage, the process of theatre costume design is a complex one that requires her to seek inspiration from a number of different sources. In her approach to design, she seeks to discover, "within the play script, a means of visually serving the play." Robin believes that, in designing for the theatre, a designer needs to go back to the literature—to the play, in contrast to "some designers, who tend to start with the visual and push it onto the verbal." In her initial thinking about a play, she asks herself why the playwright chose to express ideas in a certain way.

In addition, Ver Hage's design process involves trying to feel the mood of the play, which then begins "dictating colors and shapes and textures." She thinks in broad, abstract terms at this point rather than trying to visualize specific costumes for specific characters. One play "may seem gray and brown to me, or another one orange and pink. Or it has to be soft fabrics." The costumes for the film, *Dangerous Liaisons*, illustrate this point. Those costumes, Robin suggests, clearly reflect the mood of the film: "A lot of the fabrics were slicker than they would have been in that period; you wouldn't see everybody in that whole world dressed in fabric surfaces that were quite that hard and reflective." But this "lying with fabric" helped to establish and reflect the mood of the setting, characters, and plot.

Ver Hage's process of design also involves the effort "to really get inside the characters," and this approach, she believes, distinguishes her from some other designers: "That's why I was drawn to theatre—because of character. Plot seems secondary to me; it's character that I'm real wrapped up in." As she reads a script, she thinks about how a character might express her or himself in dress; she then tries to design a costume that serves that character and can be used by the actor as a vehicle to bring the character to life on stage. Again, *Dangerous Liaisons* is an example of how costumes become such vehicles for the actors: "Those costumes were really vehicles for the actors to give you that world. The color choices, silhouettes, and the surface treatment really helped delineate the characters."

Yet another consideration for Robin in her costume design is the actor who will wear the costume. She tries to talk with the actors, find out how they are envisioning their characters, and incorporate at least some of those ideas into her designs. This isn't always possible, though: "In some productions, it's just lucky their bodies have clothes on them, and in other productions, you can have a private conference with the actors and talk about how they see the character and why." The actors' ideas about their costumes must be balanced by the costume designer's need to coordinate all of the costumes for presentation together on stage: "The problem is that an actor may have a wonderful idea about how the costume should be, but you have 50 bodies on stage that should present an aesthetically pleasing picture to the audience. It's not like getting dressed and going to lunch, where it doesn't really matter if you have red on and I have pink on and they don't go together. If you have to sit in an audience and pay money and look at that for an hour, you don't want red and pink together; it may disrupt the flow of the production. So you have to make those adjustments. And the actor doesn't usually see that." Consequently, Ver Hage often must deal with actors' hostility, which can make costume design "rather thankless" at times.

Robin loves many things about costume design and the theatre environment. She enjoys "being close to a play," discovering new things about it as a result of hearing it over and over again during rehearsals. She enjoys the deep friendships and strong emotional bonds that develop among those who work in the costume shop, the result of large amounts of time spent together. She also enjoys the magical deception of theatre: "Now, in the industrial world, there's so much emphasis on things literally being fine, very literally being what they are. But theatre is one place where you just take trash like polyester garbage and other bottom-line materials, broken mirrors, or whatever, and you're pulling it altogether to make something that on stage is so magnificent. That deception, where there's a question of 'what is it really?' has a lot of appeal; it's exciting."

But work as a costumer designer has its unappealing aspects. There are many places in a production where the process of costume design can break down — processes that the designer often cannot control. The director may change her or his mind about the direction for a production and doesn't communicate that change, the play script may be bad, the theatre may not have the resources to produce the kinds of costumes Ver Hage designs, or the designs created may be too difficult for the workers to complete within the scheduled work period, for example.

The very long hours required for garment production also are a problem with the profession. A costume shop is a place, Robin explains, "where people often produce garments at below minimum wage, burning the midnight oil, sewing their fingers off, just to get these costumes up on stage." A continuous schedule of 14-hour days is not unusual. Burn-out tends to happen after about 10 years in the profession of costume design as a result of this schedule; in fact, most of the people who studied costume design with Ver Hage are no longer in the business.

Robin herself is not currently working as a costume designer. When she moved to St. Louis with her husband, she accepted a position with the Missouri Arts Council, where she is a program administrator for the areas of theatre, literature, and arts education. She may return to costume design someday, perhaps in free-lance work, but for now, she is content to advise theatre groups seeking assistance from the Arts Council, watch theatre productions, care for her newborn daughter, and sew for herself.

The four sketches that follow are ones Ver Hage designed for the play, *Roshomon*, by Fayand Michael Kanin, based on stories by Ryunosuke Akuragawa; the play was presented at the University of Akron Kolbe Theatre in Akron, Ohio. The play is a story of a number of different persons who are witnesses to a crime. How the various people perceive the event and choose to recount it reveal much about their characters as well as the elusive nature of reality. The sketches here are for the costumes for the four main characters — the bandit, the guard, the sorceress, and the wigmaker — and they include the samples of fabrics Ver Hage attached to suggest the textures and colors she envisioned for the costumes.

Robin Ver Hage, design for costume for sorceress, **Roshomon**
Photograph: Thomas Lanham

Robin Ver Hage, design for costume for bandit, **Roshomon**
Photograph: Thomas Lanham

Robin Ver Hage, design for costume for wigmaker, **Roshomon**
Photograph: Thomas Lanham

Robin Ver Hage, design for costume for guard, **Roshomon**
Photograph: Thomas Lanham

6

DANCE

DeBorah D. Ahmed

"The foundation that inspires me to say what I have to say through my choreography and artistry will probably always come from the experiences of African people," asserts dancer DeBorah Ahmed. "I know a lot of choreographers who say they don't deal with the Black experience because they find it limiting, but I don't see the African world experience as limiting. Our experiences are vast; they have incorporated everything everybody else has experienced—war, famine, wealth, opulence—we've had it all." A dancer, teacher, choreographer, and arts administrator in St. Louis, Missouri, Ahmed is committed to building from and highlighting the African experience.

DeBorah began her study of dance with ballet lessons at the age of five in her hometown of St. Louis. Her interest in dance waned as she reached adolescence, and she quit ballet lessons at the age of 12. While she could not name the reasons for her discontent at the time, she now realizes that the European ballet tradition fit neither her cultural heritage nor her body structure. Despite her teacher's constant reminders, she found she simply could not "tuck in her behind," as her Caucasian classmates seemed to be able to do. Nor was she given the opportunity to perform in the ballet school's performances and recitals, "probably because I was a little Black girl."

In high school, Ahmed returned to dance when she discovered modern dance and jazz and found that they dealt with "music I wanted to move to, was inspired to move to." She served as president of Taberna, her high school dance club, where she learned she was a natural teacher and was able to try her hand at choreography for the first time. Following a performance of the dance club in her senior year, a stranger approached DeBorah and asked if she would be interested in a scholarship to Southern Illinois University to study dance with Katherine Dunham. Ahmed was not then familiar with Dunham, an internationally known dancer, choreographer, and teacher whose company was headquartered in East St. Louis and who blended dance forms from Africa and the Caribbean (particularly Haiti), ballet, burgeoning American modern dance forms, and traditional African-American jazz. DeBorah turned down the offer; she wanted to be an archaeologist. "I now realize what I blew!" she says.

At Grinnell College in Grinnell, Iowa, Ahmed studied anthropology, with the intention of being an Egyptologist. But she continued to study dance, participated in the dance club, and refined her skills in choreography. Although she graduated with an anthropology degree, her experience in London her junior year at Grinnell led to her decision to pursue a career not in her major but in dance.

DeBorah traveled to Europe with the "Grinnell in London" program, where she discovered a large community of Blacks from all over the world, including the Caribbean, Africa, and South America, living in London. She found that "the flavor and spirit of the whole area were totally different." She took African dance classes at a community center in the area and was introduced to traditional African arts, foods, and clothing. Her parents had not emphasized their African heritage while Ahmed was growing up, and her first exposure to Afrocentric cultural aesthetics was exciting and inspiring: "I was really falling in love with this side of myself."

DeBorah's awakening to her own cultural heritage led to her desire to specialize in African dance in her study, teaching, and performance. Her first job following her graduation was as director of the dance program of the Kuumba Theatre Workshop, a community theatre in Chicago, where she lived in a community of African Americans who "were very much into traditional African cultural ways." I was really ignorant of myself as an African American," Ahmed recalls, "and I knew I needed to steep myself in a group where I could get this information, energy, and support."

In Chicago, DeBorah auditioned for and joined the Muntu Dance Theatre, a traditional African dance company: "That was it! I just loved it!" The transition from classical ballet to traditional African dance, however, was difficult. She explains: "I had to basically throw away everything I knew about dance and start all over again." She kept her understanding of the body, how it functions, and how to take care of it, but she had to unlearn her previous training in "how to express movement." This meant learning not to put her arms and hands in the second position of ballet when they were to be at her sides and learning to stop pointing her toes when she jumped. "I'd go across the floor like a little ballerina trying to do African dance," she remembers. "It was rough, it was rough, it was rough." Eventually, though, she "started to get it. I still wasn't that good, but I began to understand what it was I was supposed to be doing and how it was supposed to look."

Ahmed continued her education in traditional African dance when she moved to New York City in 1979 to study dance with Chuck Davis and the International Afrikan American Ballet. While in New York, she had the opportunity to participate, in 1980, in Dance Africa, a showcase of the best in African dance in the country.

DeBorah's specialty is dance that originates in the area of West Africa that once comprised the ancient empire of Mali—the Ivory Coast, Gambia, Mauritania, Burkina Faso, Senegal, Guinea, and Sierra Leone. In contrast to the European dance tradition, the dance forms from this region are relaxed and spontaneous. They are characterized by dancing *with* the music rather than *to* the music, with interaction between musicians and dancers so that each inspires the other. This interaction is reflected, during the dance, when "the musicians talk to you. They can call your name out on the drum, and you can hear it among everything else that's going on because they'll watch you, they'll know your rhythm." Ahmed is still amused at how different this type of dance is from her earlier ballet training, where "everything is straight, pulled up, the music hits, and then you start."

Following her marriage, DeBorah and her husband moved back to St. Louis, where she accepted a position at Washington University, teaching African dance. In addition to teaching, Ahmed is the program administrator for Touring and Multi Discipline Arts at the Missouri Arts Council, where she coordinates the Council's Missouri Touring Program and works with arts organizations that utilize many art forms. She and her husband also work with an organization called Better Family Life, which provides and promotes activities for African Americans and the community at large, and they are the parents of a one-year-old son.

In 1984, DeBorah started her own dance company, Rhythms in Anoa Dance Theatre, named for Anoa, a character in the book, *Two Thousand Seasons*, by Ghanaan author Ayi Kwei Armah. Anoa is a guiding force that provides assistance to the main characters in the book and symbolizes coming into the knowledge of self. Anoa always is able to point the characters in the right direction, reminding them that in order to get where they want to go, they must remain in contact with their ancestral soul.

Ahmed's company focuses on various movement styles, especially those rooted in Afrocentric aesthetics, and its members are committed to seeing art as a liberating force for their community. They don't believe in art for art's sake: "art should have some connection to the community that birthed you as an artist and should be an inspiring force that allows those who view it to see the world a little differently." All members of the group work full time apart from the dance company, and their work with the company is generally unpaid; thus, the company suffers from the usual problems that plague arts organizations with few resources. But it performs regularly in churches, community centers, schools, and libraries.

DeBorah does most of the choreography for the company's performances, although she is encouraging other members of the company to contribute in this area. She develops her choreography around a theme or story line—always one that has an impact on her people and her community. In a piece called *Death Wish*, for example, she dealt with drug addiction; another, *Echoes of the Mother Land*, shows the relation between African-American and traditional African dance forms.

Ahmed's choreography is characterized by a blending of traditional African forms and modern jazz and the incorporation of many different aesthetic elements into her performances, including music, singing, and theatre. She also seeks to find time or meter in the music that isn't obvious and choreographs to those secondary rhythms in an effort to create a more interesting piece. Because her pieces usually are performed for audiences who know little or nothing about the context of African dance or her story line, DeBorah provides her audiences with program notes so that "people won't have to guess what I'm doing." "What are you saying here? Give me a hint," is her response to dance she doesn't understand. "Deliberately trying to keep people confused is not my style," says Ahmed.

The materials that follow provide an introduction to DeBorah's work in dance. Included are her notes for a piece she created, *The Judgement*, in which she outlines the story line and her initial thoughts on how it will be developed in movement, costumes, and scenery. The program notes also are included for a performance of Act I and Scene 1 of Act II of *The Judgement* in September, 1989, in Nashville, Tennessee. The occasion was a celebration commemorating the tenth anniversary of the involvement in arts education of Rossi "Bambataa" Turner and his Sankofa Dance Theatre. These are followed by photographs of Ahmed dancing a combination of different traditional West African movements.

Notes for *The Judgement*

May, 1989

Theme: How we must accept the responsibility and consequences of our thoughts, desires and actions

Players: 1 male dancer

    3 female
    1 musician
Setting: The present

Characters: A woman searching for (perceived) happiness
                The husband, who desperately tries to understand her and
                    make her happy
                The judge
                Her protective spirit/guiding angel
                The saxophonist—the voice of her soul and communication
                    link between her and her angel

Basis of story: The Egyptian drama of the weighing of the souls, where one's soul eventually rests is based upon one's life's deeds. Elegba, the Yoruban orisha who is the trickster, guardian of the roads, is the spirit that drives us to keep people and ourselves off balance.

Story line: The scale is ever present. It is balanced when before the judge but imbalanced when the woman travels each of her roads. Her angel holds the scale.

Act I

Scene I: The saxophonist (the Voice) is center stage and begins to play his music. The angel appears from behind him. They have a conversation with each other.

Scene II: The angel goes stage right or left and awaits the appearance of the woman. She moves to the saxophone Voice, expressing herself, awaiting the input/guidance of her angel. They dance together. She is going through an internal battle to experiment with different desires that she has.

Scene III: The angel moves stage right or left and the woman awaits the arrival of her husband. He and his wife dance together in conversation over her desire to explore her fantasies. She tells him that she is unhappy with her life and wants to explore different experiences. He doesn't understand why. He perceives that she is happy. The angel observes this and attempts to intervene to get her to see the ridiculousness of her desires, but to no avail. The angel then changes to Elegba and leads the woman to the various roads that she desires to take. The angel puts on the Elegba mask.

Scene IV: Elegba takes the woman to the judge to hear how her soul will be weighed upon her decision to take one of these roads as her life's path. She shall be granted permission to walk each of these roads and then make her decision.

Intermission

Act II

Scene I: Her angel accompanies her down her first road: The Party. She tries to lead, then follow, and finally is confused, overcome, frightened by the possibility of getting caught. One of the party people, however, gives the angel a part of the party desire for later on.

The second road is one of Opulence and Financial Success. Everything is green, purple, and gold. This time the players grab for her, but she fights to get away. She grabs a piece of one of the players but her angel makes her give it back, only to have the same player give the same piece back to the angel. The woman doesn't know that this has happened.

The third road is Sensuality. (I need 2 men and 1 woman.) She is seduced so greatly that her angel must pull her to safety. She is overcome with sensual pleasures. (I'll need to use different items to display sensuality, not just sexual behavior and innuendoes.) Her angel is given a token.

Her fourth road is Mental Powers. Everything is white, a feeling of coldness and starkness. She desperately tries some of the things learned on her earlier roads, but to no avail. Her angel has to pull her out in a frustrated state. Her angel is given a token.

Scene II: She revisits each road several times, trying to decide which one she wants to walk but cannot make up her mind. Her angel stands by and observes, surrounded by the token from each road. The woman collapses on the floor and drags herself to her angel to plead for help. The angel only gives her the tokens and leaves her there to decide.

Scene III: The judge reappears, the scales are balanced, and she is asked to pass her own judgement—decide her own fate. She is told that this power is within her and that no one decides our destiny but us. We are the masters of our fate—the captains of our soul (refer to "In Search of the Miraculous"). I need a 5-minute hourglass which will be her time keeper.

She begins to ask for help from the judge, her husband, her Voice, her angel, but none gives answers. They only point to her and the tokens. She takes turns putting each token on the scale, only to find them too heavy to keep the scale balanced. Her time is passing to make up her mind. She eventually realizes that she must have a piece of each token to make her life balanced and places 2 on each side of the scale.

While she is deciding and weighing the tokens, the others leave the stage to change into the Lamban clothes. The drums start at the point the hourglass ends and Lamban is done. The woman joins them and this is the end.

RHYTHMS IN ANOA DANCE THEATRE
St. Louis, MO

Rhythms in Anoa Dance Theatre uses afrocentricity as the basis of their creative force. Grounded in the concept of "Edutainment," the company seeks to provoke thought, as well as entertain. Rhythms in Anoa is multi-faceted, utilizing traditional African and African American movement and music, contemporary funk, theatre, and other genres to impart their message.

THE JUDGEMENT

In the Yoruba religion, which originated in Africa, Elegba is the trickster - the keeper of the roads. The spirit or force in life that keeps us off balance, uncertain of what decision to make. Maat, the ancient African/Egyptian goddess of balance and justice, held the balance scales on which our souls were weighed.

In life, we each chose the path that we must walk on. Sometimes one path presents itself as though the correct one, but we are fooled, then confused by what decision to take. But whatever road we take, our lives are judged when we reach the end. Our final resting place is determined by the outcome of The Judgement.

This is a story, yet to be completed , about a young woman who is unsure of what she wants out of life. She experiences confusion within herself and about the marriage while in this state. She has the fortune however, of having her Guardian Angel take her to each of the roads she fantasizes about travelling, the first of which her Angel travels with her.

*Dance program, **Rossi Turner's Dance Spectacular***

In Time:

- The Angel introduces herself and prepares the way for her child's/the Woman's rite of passage.

- The woman joins her Angel, frightened at first and then succumbing to her guiding force. Her Angel lets her know that though she shall travel many uncertain roads, she will always be close.

- The woman speaks about herself as she also resigns herself to what she must do.

- Her husband joins her. Their love is expressed, but she believes she must leave her marriage to understand herself. "Is marriage the best thing for me?" Her husband, weary of the emotional battles, resigns himself to letting her experience life the way she wants to.

- Her judge introduces herself. She reads the Woman's sentence to her so she will clearly understand that the road she ultimately chooses in life will be the one which her soul will be weighed. She accepts this reading and journeys to her first road - the Fast Lane/The Party.

Sankofa Dance Theatre
Rossi Bambaata Turner, Artistic Director

Linda Barrington - Whitaker
Tommy "Musa Amen" Smith
Karen DeBerry
Ronald "Doc" Hayes
Joan Wallace
Kevin "Magic" Blair
Clauressia Na'imah Dawson
Balawa
Cassandra Hambrick
Yolanda Love
Tyshena Hayes
Stephanie Hardy

Rhythms of Anoa Dance Theatre
St. Louis, MO
DeBorah Ahmed, Artistic Director

Medina Johnson
Adrean Stewart
Joey Henderson

This production is dedicated to
Ms. Mammie White
G. Rashid Abdul Bambaata Turner
Saaneah Tene Jamison
Chanda Tomineka Beach
Ms. Louise Shute
and to the memory of the South African Black
Consciousness leader Stephen Biko who was
killed on September 10, 1977 by South African
police.

Program

mistress of ceremonies
Ms. Yolanda Love

African fashions on parade

Ms. Elaine Fisher
Ms. Black U.S.A. 1989

Rossi Bambaata Turner

Rhythms of Anoa Dance Theatre
DeBorah D. Ahmed, Artistic Director

Intermission

Children of Sankofa

Mr. Patdro Harris

Sankofa & Rhythms of Anoa Dance Theatre's

Brother Bambaata

Finale
Mr. Patdro Harris, Rhythms of Anoa & Sankofa
Dance Theatre

DeBorah D. Ahmed, dancing
Photograph: Thomas Lanham

DeBorah D. Ahmed, dancing
Photograph: Thomas Lanham

DeBorah D. Ahmed, dancing
Photograph: Thomas Lanham

DeBorah D. Ahmed, dancing
Photograph: Thomas Lanham

7

DRESS

Karen A. Foss and Sonja K. Foss

"I understand that I have something of a reputation among my students and colleagues for interesting outfits," says Sonja Foss. Her sister, Karen Foss, agrees: "My students frequently comment on my outfits; they're amazed to learn that I sew them." By making their clothes and paying particular attention to the accompanying accessories, Foss and Foss are able to create their unusual attire.

Karen and Sonja learned to sew when their mother gave them patterns for Barbie doll clothes when they were in the fourth grade. Their mother thought she would be the one to sew the doll clothes, but that wasn't the case; Foss and Foss soon had produced a box full of doll clothes. When they began making clothes for themselves in the seventh grade, their mother was even more delighted and stopped sewing for them altogether.

The actual sewing of a blouse, dress, or suit is only part of the process Sonja and Karen go through to create an outfit. A pair of earrings often starts the whole thing off—a gift from a friend who knows of the sisters' preferences for large, unusual earrings or a purchase of their own, often made when traveling. Because the earrings Foss and Foss prefer tend to be of unusual design or color combinations, they often don't have anything in their wardrobes to match them; this prompts a search for fabric to make something that goes with them. "We both get comments from people about how well our earrings match our outfits," explains Karen. "What they don't realize is that we usually start with the earrings." According to Sonja, "this means that we're both usually carrying earrings around with us at all times, so that we're ready in case a fabric store crosses our paths!" The search for just the right fabric to match a pair of earrings may take months or even years. Earrings are not the only impetus for the two women's fabric purchases. Both like to buy fabric when they travel; the outfit they make then becomes a way to remember the trip.

Once they discover fabric that matches a pair of earrings or simply an interesting piece of fabric, Foss and Foss let it suggest the kind of outfit to make. If the fabric is casual, a shirt is a frequent choice or perhaps a skirt or casual dress. If the fabric is dressy, they'll make a dress or a suit. Selecting a pattern can take time, too; not all fabric stores carry all pattern books, so they often go to two or three stores before choosing a pattern. They have been known to spend an entire day going back and forth among fabric stores, "something our husbands just can't understand," says Karen.

The next step in the process is actually sewing the outfit, which they usually can do in a day or so, depending on the number of pieces and its complexity. People often wonder how Foss and Foss have time to make their own clothes; both are university professors, and virtually the only things they don't sew are jeans, coats, and sweaters. "I use sewing as a reward," Sonja explains. "When I finish writing an essay or preparing for a course, I reward myself: I get to sew something. So I usually spend a couple of days every few months or so sewing." Karen leaves her machine set up and tries to sew fifteen minutes every day.

When the outfit is finished, Foss and Foss cut the leftover fabric into patches for quilts; usually they have at least two quilts in process, "which means that we'll have the designs all figured out and templates made. Every time I finish something, I cut out pieces for my quilts and for Sonja's, too," says Karen. When they have collected enough pieces for the quilt tops, they sew them together. They don't do handstitching to attach the top to the batting and backing; they either tie their quilts or pay someone else to quilt them by hand or machine.

Foss and Foss' commitment to discovering interesting fabrics is evidenced in their willingness to endure adverse conditions to pursue their pastime. They have gone to special fabric sales at 6:00 a.m., have stood in long lines at sales to purchase fabrics at good prices, and once went to a fabric store in weather of 16 degrees below zero: "The owner of the store was shocked to see anyone there," Sonja recalls. Karen remembers one occasion, though, when her efforts to look at fabric were thwarted: "On the way to a papyrus-making factory in Cairo, our bus passed an open-air market, where I saw stall after stall of fabric stacked up. So after listening to a brief explanation of how papyrus was made, I decided to run back the few blocks and check out the fabric. As I approached the door, however, two men with long sticks, standing on either side, firmly lowered them in front of me and blocked my exit. It's the only time anyone's ever kept me from a fabric store!"

Foss and Foss typically choose outfits to sew that incorporate certain principles. First, they must be different from the clothing others are wearing: "We want our clothes to stand out," explains Karen. "It's hard for me to imagine buying something from a rack in a store, knowing other people are wearing exactly the same thing you are." Clothing was not, however, always a means of deliberate differentiation for the two women. Sonja explains: "In junior high and high school, we desperately wanted to fit in but never did. One reason was that our clothes were never quite right — never quite what the other kids were wearing. Our hemlines were never where theirs were, we never had Nehru blouses or owned circle pins when they were popular. And, of course, we thought, 'If we could just have that one item or if our hems were right, every-thing would be OK.'" "Our concern with differentiation was compounded," adds Karen, "by our being twins. It was bad enough that one of us had to have hemlines out of place; it was a hundred times worse that your sister did, too." The years of living with difference somehow encouraged Foss and Foss ultimately to choose difference, rather than conformity, in terms of their dress.

A second criterion Foss and Foss use in putting outfits together is that they must be bold and colorful. They tend to choose wild, abstract, geometric prints for their clothing. "Tiny flowers and plain colors usually aren't our style," says Sonja. Karen recalls finding some fabric with huge pink-and-orange tropical fish and flowers against a black background — a perfect match for some fish earrings she had just purchased. "I was delighted with my find," says Foss, "but the clerk commented as she was measuring the fabric out for me, 'This is the ugliest fabric I've ever seen!' Obviously, not everyone appreciates the same boldness in fabrics that we do!"

Foss and Foss are, for the most part, more interested in the print in a fabric than in its color. They admit, however, that they avoid beige or pale yellow fabrics, for example — "because they don't look good on us. We're not the type to wear only 'spring' or 'summer' colors, though," Sonja explains, "even though they might look the best on us. Karen came back from Japan with red-and-beige earrings for each of us. We ended up making outfits out of a beige striped fabric — which by itself looks fairly bad on us. But we added red scarves and red shoes and don't look too washed out."

Foss and Foss also pay attention to type of fabric in selecting what to buy. They never buy anything with polyester in it simply because after a year or so, it begins to "ball up," especially in areas of constant wear. They prefer all cotton, wool, silk, or rayon fabrics. The exception is when they are sewing for a lengthy trip when they will not have easy access to laundry facilities and irons. Then they buy fabrics with polyester in them so they will wash well and not wrinkle.

Sonja describes a fourth criterion Foss and Foss use in putting together an outfit: "it must be rhetorically effective." By that she means that it must communicate effectively whatever aspect of herself she wants to present on a particular occasion: "I'm a rhetorician; I study how symbols function and how people respond to them. To incorporate that knowledge into my dress seems natural to me. When I teach, I want to communicate that I'm a professional, a woman, an individual, interesting, confident about who I am, and contemporary, so I try to dress in ways that communicate these qualities. At other times, I deliberately dress in a 'funky' or casual way to communicate something quite different." Karen agrees and adds, "I'm currently director of women's studies and am quite conscious of the role my appearance plays in my position. I think I can encourage a new image for feminists by dressing in interesting ways and by not conforming to the stereotypical feminist in jeans and combat boots. It's 'perspective by incongruity' — here's a woman who pays attention to her dress, but she's a feminist. Sometimes, people have to rearrange their thinking to make that juxtaposition work in their heads."

In the following pages, various dimensions of the process Foss and Foss use to develop an outfit are illustrated, using one of Sonja's outfits. The outfit began, as so many do, with a pair of earrings. Sonja explains: "Two of my best friends married each other and, in fact, they got married in my house. They gave me a pair of earrings in the shape of overstuffed chairs for helping with the wedding." The earrings are purple; the pillows on the chairs are in black-and-white stripes. Foss found some purple-and-white-striped cotton fabric in the same purple as the earrings, but she also wanted to pick up the black and white in the earrings, which she did with fabric of a narrower stripe, but in black and white. A Vogue pattern for a three-piece outfit of below-the-knee pants, a sleeveless top, and a long coat allowed her to combine the two fabrics. The coat is in the purple stripe; the pants and top are in the black and white. The back of the pattern envelope, excerpts from the pattern instructions, and photographs of the earrings and the completed outfit suggest the process involved in the creation of a Foss original.

U.S. **$10.50**
CAN. $12.90
AUST. *$11.50
N.Z. *$12.65**
**Incl. G.S.T
*recommended price
*prix suggéré

SIZE / TAILLE
10

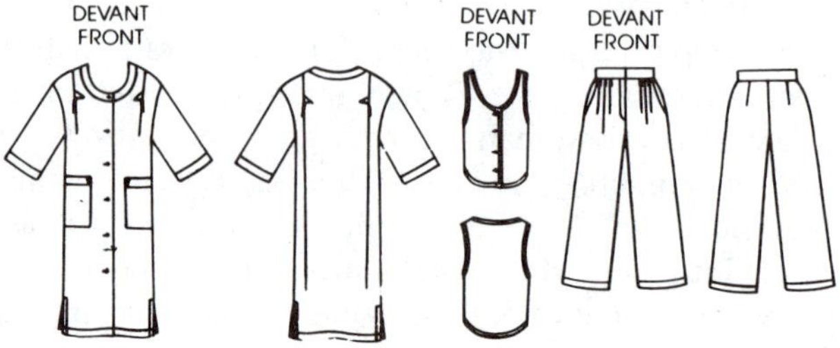

MISSES' COATDRESS, PANTS AND TOP. Very loose-fitting, straight coatdress, mid-calf, has neckband, dropped shoulders, front and back tucks, pockets, side hemline slits and ¾ sleeves with mock bands. Straight legged pants, above ankle, have waistband, front pleats, slanted pockets and mock fly zipper. Both have stitched hems. Close-fitting top has low, cutaway armholes, shaped hemline and narrow hem.
NOTIONS: Coatdress: Six ⅝"(15mm) Buttons. **Pants:** 7"(18cm) Zipper, One Hook and Eye Closure, Seam Binding and Pkg. 1¼ (3.2cm) Waistband Interfacing. **Top:** Four ⅝"(15mm) Buttons.
FABRICS: Med.wt. Linen, Silk-like Linen, Lt.wt. Wool Crepe, Silk-like Broadcloth and Chambray. Unsuitable for obvious diagonals. Allow extra fabric to match plaids or stripes. Use nap yardages/layouts for pile, shaded or one-way design fabrics. * with nap ** w/o nap

ROBE-MANTEAU, PANTALON ET HAUT. Robe-manteau, très ample, à mi-mollet, avec bande d'encolure, carrure élargie et manches ¾ à bandes simulées; plis devant et dos, poches plaquées et fentes de côté. Pantalon au-dessus de la cheville, à jambes droites, avec ceinture, plis devant, poches en découpe et braguette simulée à glissière. Ourlets piqués. Haut ajusté, avec entournures dégagées. Ourlet étroit arrondi.
MERCERIE - Robe-manteau: 6 boutons (15mm). **Pantalon:** Fermeture à glissière (18cm) - 1 agrafe plate - Ruban bordure - 1 paquet d'entoilage-ceinture (3.2cm). **Haut:** 4 boutons (15mm).
TISSUS - Lin moyen ou simili soie - Crêpe de laine léger - Toile légère (simili soie) - Chambray. Les grandes diagonales ne conviennent pas. Compte non tenu des raccords de rayures/carreaux. * avec sens (tissus pelucheux, à reflets ou certains imprimés) ** sans sens.

6	8	10	12	14	16	SIZE	TAILLE	6	8	10	12	14	16
COATDRESS						**INS**	**CM**	**ROBE MANTEAU**					
4⅛	4⅜	4⅝	5	5	5	**35*/****	**90**	3.80	4.00	4.30	4.60	4.60	4.60
3⅛	3¼	3⅜	3⅝	3⅝	3⅝	**45*/****	**115**	2.90	3.00	3.10	3.40	3.40	3.40
2⅜	2⅜	2⅝	2⅝	2¾	2¾	**60 ***	**150**	2.20	2.20	2.40	2.40	2.60	2.60
2	2	2¼	2⅜	2¾	2¾	**60 ****	**150**	1.90	1.90	2.10	2.20	2.60	2.60
INTERFACING						18,25	46,64	**ENTOILAGE**					
⅜	⅜	⅜	⅜	⅜	⅜	**36,45**	**90,115**	0.40	0.40	0.40	0.40	0.40	0.40
PANTS								**PANTALON**					
2¼	2⅜	2½	2⅝	2¾	2¾	**35*/****	**90**	2.10	2.20	2.30	2.40	2.60	2.60
2	2	2⅛	2⅛	2⅛	2⅛	**45*/****	**115**	1.90	1.90	2.00	2.00	2.00	2.00
1½	1¾	1¾	1¾	1¾	1¾	**60*/****	**150**	1.40	1.60	1.60	1.60	1.60	1.60
LINING (Pockets)								**DOUBLURE** (poches)					
½	½	½	½	½	½	**45**	**115**	0.50	0.50	0.50	0.50	0.50	0.50
TOP								**HAUT**					
1½	1½	1½	1½	1½	1½	**35*/****	**90**	1.40	1.40	1.40	1.40	1.40	1.40
1¼	1¼	1¼	1¼	1¼	1⅜	**45*/****	**115**	1.20	1.20	1.20	1.20	1.20	1.30
⅞	⅞	⅞	⅞	1⅛	1⅛	**60*/****	**150**	0.80	0.80	0.80	0.80	1.10	1.10

						WIDTHS	LARGEURS						
Lower edge						Coatdress	robe-manteau						à l'ourlet
42½	43½	44½	46	48	50			108	110	113	117	122	127
18½	19	19½	20	20½	21	Pants	pantalon	47	48	49.5	51	52	53.5
34	35	36	37½	39½	41½	Top	haut	86.5	89	91.5	95	100	105
						LENGTHS	LONGUEURS						
Finished back from base of neck						Coatdress	robe-manteau						nuque à ourlet
43¼	43½	43¾	44	44¼	44½			110	110	111	112	112	113
19¼	19½	19¾	20	20¼	20½	Top	haut	49	49.5	50	51	51.5	52
Finished side from waist													côté, taille à ourlet
33	33	33	33	33	33	Pants	pantalon	84	84	84	84	84	84

Back of pattern enevelope, Vogue 1546
Copyright © 1985 Butterick Company, Inc.

Vogue 1546
Page 1 (4 pages)

PANTS

5 Waistband

4 Back

2 Pocket

3 Side Front

1 Front

TOP

7 Back

8 Continuous Bias

6 Front

COAT DRESS

13 Back Neck Band

12 Front Neck Band

11 Back

14 Sleeve

10 Pocket

9 Front

PANTS USE PIECES: 1,3,4 and 5

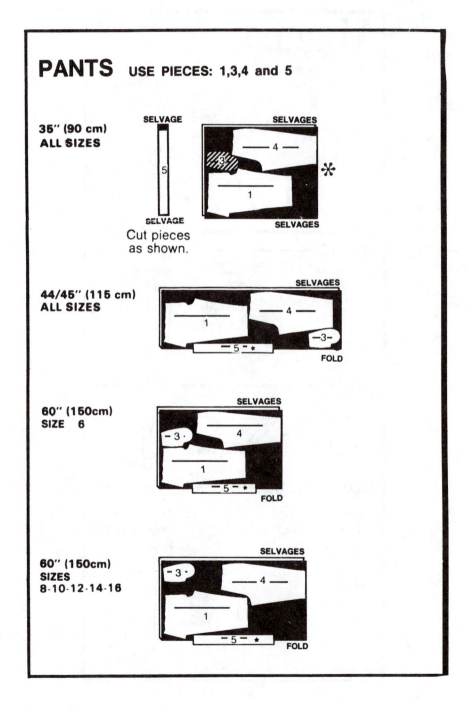

**35" (90 cm)
ALL SIZES**

Cut pieces
as shown.

**44/45" (115 cm)
ALL SIZES**

**60" (150cm)
SIZE   6**

**60" (150cm)
SIZES
8-10-12-14-16**

TOP

STEP 1 - FRONTS AND BACK

Turn opening edge of FRONT 6 to inside along outer foldline; press. Sew invisibly along inner edge, as shown. Baste across upper and lower edges.

Stitch BACK 7 and front sections together at shoulders.

Stitch back and front sections together at sides.

STEP 2 - CONTINUOUS BIAS

With right sides together, bring ends of CONTINUOUS BIAS 8 together, matching symbols. Stitch.

Starting at one uneven end, cut along cutting lines, forming one continuous bias strip.

To make binding for neck and armholes, with wrong sides together, fold bias strip lengthwise, having raw edges even. Press.

Turn front self facings to outside along remaining foldlines. Baste across upper edge.

Pin bias strip to neck edge, having raw edges even, and extending ends ½"(13mm) over inner edge of self facings, as shown. Stitch entire neck edge in a ⅝"(15mm) seam. Trim.

Turn self facings to inside, turning in bias strip along seam; press. Baste close to inner edge of bias, continuing across self facings to small ●'s, as shown.

Pin bias strip to armhole edge, having raw edges even, and turning in ends to meet at underarm seam, as shown. Stitch in a ⅝"(15mm) seam. Trim.

Turn bias to inside along seam; press. Baste close to inner edge of bias, as shown. **SLIPSTITCH** ends together.

TOPSTITCH armhole edge, as shown.

STEP 3 - FINISHING

Turn lower edge of self facing(s) to outside along foldline(s). Stitch ⅝"(15mm) from lower edge. Trim, as shown.

Turn self facing(s) to inside.

Turn ⅝"(15mm) on remainder of lower edge of garment, turning in ¼"(6mm) on raw edge; press. Baste close to inner pressed edge.

TOPSTITCH lower, front opening and neck edges, pivoting at small ●'s, as shown.

Make machine or hand buttonhole(s) in right front at marking(s).

Sew button(s) to left front at marking(s).

Earrings, starting point for outfit by Sonja K. Foss
Photograph: Diana Schoenfeld

Sonja K. Foss, completed outfit
Photograph: Diana Schoenfeld

8

FAMILY STORIES

Tamara Louise Burk, Jillian Louise Nickless,
and Cicely Louise Sutherland

As a means to retain her history and the history of women in her family, Tamara Burk began to record the stories told by her grandmother, her mother, and Burk herself. Her collection of the stories told by the women in her family was sparked by a course she took dealing with narrative and communication at the University of Maine, but her desire to do so was heightened by her recognition that her grandmother was aging: "I treasure my grandmother very much; I was panicked about her getting older without preserving her experiences and her perspectives."

Burk's collection of her family stories is part of her ongoing research about women's stories, which began as she completed her bachelor's and master's degrees in speech communication. She has studied the functions, strategies, and performance aspects of women's storytelling and plans to continue to investigate other dimensions of women's stories. Tamara sees several characteristic qualities of women's stories that make them unique communication events. Women's stories tend not to meet the male-defined criteria for a "good story." They may not have a point, and they may not be told in a chronological order. Rather, they often begin with a complicating action and go in various time orders to explain it. In addition, they may not be about "remarkable" events but rather about commonplace events in women's lives. Burk also is fascinated by the collaborative nature of women's stories and by how they unfold through the joint participation of the women.

Tamara's research on women's storytelling is part of her commitment to giving voice to women in various ways. A feminist activist, she has been involved in rape awareness and prevention efforts, has worked with women in a shelter for abused women, has helped develop a crisis hotline, and has worked to empower disadvantaged high school students dealing with such issues as gender, sexuality, and communication. "My mother's and my grandmother's lives and stories of oppression *very* much shaped who I've come to be today," says Burk. "Unfortunately, I wasn't spared many of the same oppressive experiences they had, but talking with them helps me to make sense of patriarchy (as if it will ever make sense), at least in a family and historical sense."

The transcript that follows is an excerpt of a session recorded while Tamara was together with her mother and her grandmother for her mother's wedding. Burk sequestered the three women in a room and prohibited the men from entering, explaining to them, "When men are here, the talk is different. Stay out!" She taped over six hours of talk among the women, recording the family stories. Some she had heard often, and others she never had heard before. Many of these are stories that only the women in her family tell—the "tellability rights" belong to the women, and the men simply do not tell them.

The three stories that follow deal with childbirth, a girl's discovery of her clitoris, and death; other topics covered by the three women in the storytelling session included religion, pregnancy, family members, racism, feminism, politics, homosexuality, childhood memories, child care, motherhood, menstruation, birth control, drugs, abortion, pets, marriage, abuse, divorce, surrogate motherhood, sex, rape, child raising, women and guilt, and housework. The storytellers are: Tamara's grandmother, Cicely Louise Sutherland, of San Lorenzo, California, the mother of one daughter and two sons; Tamara's mother, Jillian Louise Nickless, of Wakefield, New Hampshire, the mother of one daughter and one son; and Tamara Louise Burk, of Williamsburg, Virginia, with no children, although she and her partner often consider their dog, Bogart, to be part of their family. At the time of the telling of the stories, the women were 72, 45, and 23 years old, respectively. In the transcript, "G" refers to Sutherland, Tamara's grandmother; "M" refers to Nickless, Tamara's mother; and "D" is for "daughter," Burk herself.

Childbirth: Taxi Cabs and *Playboy* Magazine

G: I couldn't get comfortable when I had those twins, Oh God! I couldn't lie down, I couldn't stand up, I couldn't sit up. I weighed 157 pounds! [She gained approximately 50 pounds.]

M: 157?

G: Yeah.

M: That was rough, wasn't it?

G: Yeah, it was rough.

M: It was really rough. [thoughtful silence for several seconds]

G: I nearly didn't get to the hospital in time.

M: Hmmm. [sad look on face]

G: We were playing bridge, remember Marge and uh, and uh, Dick? They used to live over there, they had two little girls. They were over to play bridge that night.

M: Yeah, yeah. [remembering]

G: And Bob [husband] was, of course, full of booze.

M: Sure.

G: And he was drunk, and I started having pains and I thought, "Oh God." So uh, then,

M: We kids must have been in bed.

G: Yeah, you were.

M: Yeah.

G: We were playing bridge. And so uh, I went to the bathroom and there was some blood there and I thought, "Oh boy, I gotta get out of here." So I came out, I said, "Bob, I've got to go to the hospital." He said, "No, you don't, you're not due until September." Well, when, no, let's see, no, that was, uh, so anyway, Dick said, "Bob, if you don't take her, I'll take her, right now." So, we all got in the car [a taxi], and I laid right across the back seat and Marge was sitting on my, across my legs [pointing to where she was sitting] and was sitting on me to keep the children in, ya know, before we got there.

D: Ohhh. [painful look on face] She was sitting on your legs to keep the children in?!

G: Yeah, yeah. 'Cause I could of bore them right there, in the, in the car.

D: Sitting on your legs would keep them in?

G: Yes, well it closes up this part of you [pointing to crotch area] where you, you, the baby couldn't get out.

D: Wouldn't they fight to get out, though?

M: Oh, yeah, eventually, but she was probably on the brink.

G: Well, they tried to but not, they, they don't come out with boxing gloves on! (all laugh) Fight their way out. But uh, when I got, got there, they pulled up uh, uh a,

M: Gurney.

G: A wheelchair and to, get me out of the car.

M: Mmmm.

G: Went straight up to the, to the operating room, and they, they put a doctor's gown on me and that was that. They were born right there and then. God,

I was happy to get rid of that. It was so uncomfortable, it was no pleasure at all.

M: Hmmm.

G: Bob would take me for a drive and, I'd be sitting up like this [straight], and all of a sudden I'd be, reclined putting my feet a way out that way. Oh! My God! It was awful!

D: (Hesitantly) Were, they born dead?

M: No.

G: No, they, they were alive. One lived uh, an hour, and the other lived uh, four hours, and that was it.

D: Was it because they were so premature?

G: Yeah, it was.

D: You went a couple months early?

M: The Rh factor had something to do with it, too, didn't it?

G: Well, it was, I, yes, I had negative blood and I didn't know it, and Bob was positive see, so after having three children, you're bound to have trouble with negative blood.

D: Why? What's the Rh factor?

M: The Rh factor, if someone has an Rh negative factor and someone has an Rh positive factor, they don't mix. It's like putting oil and water together; they just don't mix.

G: They repel one another, see.

M: Now they have medication that can handle that.

G: Yeah, today they can do anything.

M: And it can change, ya know, the whole outlook on it, but back then,

D: Did you know that Uncle Teddy [grandmother's brother] was left in a shoebox?

M: Yes.

D: Wrapped in cotton?

M: Yeah, cause he was so tiny.

G: Well, they didn't throw him under the bed, you know!

D: (Laughing) Well, I know! I know.

G: (Laughing) Hey, Ted! [pretending to throw the shoebox]

D: Nanny, I can't imagine taking a seven-month old, or, a baby that's born in seven, two months early, and sticking him wrapped in cotton in a shoebox to keep him warm.

M: Why not? It's closed!

G: Well, a shoebox is keeping the heat in, you see. [later on in the conversation]

D: (To M) Did fathers ever go in [to the delivery room] then? Ever? Did Dad ever go in with you? What did Dad do while you were giving birth?

M: Your father, (laughing) um, first time around with Tim [son], no, he couldn't go in there. Second time with you,

D: Why?

M: Uh, they, they just didn't do it, it wasn't a common practice.

D: But he was there at the hospital?

M: Oh yeah, he was right there at the hospital.

G: They [fathers] could never do that [go into the delivery room] with mine.

M: I mean he [daughter's father] sat there reading *Playboy* magazine!

D: **Oh, Christ**! [mouth drops open]

M: And eating uh, uh lifesavers.

D: In the waiting room?

M: No! Right next to my bed! He had *Playboy* magazine! (laughing) With all these boobs hanging out and all these gorgeous bodies, and here I am plopping all over the place, ya know?

G: Ugh! (loud and deep tone of voice) (daughter laughs)

M: And then what really ticked me off was the doctor came in and borrowed the *Playboy* magazine, he says, "Are you through reading it?" He said, "I'd like to read it while I'm waiting." (laughs loudly)

D: Oh, God! Oh, God! Pornography lovers giving birth to kids!

M: This is uh, eighteen hours of,

D: Labor?

M: Of labor, yeah. I was pretty shot.

D: Wow. What do you do in labor, just sit around and wait?

M: Yeah, that's about it.

D: Does it hurt? When you're in labor?

M: Uh, there is pain.

G: There is pain, there's not an awful lot you can do, really, when uh, the baby's coming down.

M: The baby is just coming down the birth canal, you just wait it out.

G: There's a lot of men that (laughing), I think a lot of men couldn't handle it.

M: (To D) Well, it depends, it depends on the woman. The second time around, uh, you uh, let's see, Dennis [daughter's father] was right with me. Tammy [daughter] was more reasonable, she came out oh, in about four hours, but you were induced, too. My doctor was going out of the, the States, he was going to South America, and I wanted him to deliver you, so I asked him to induce you.

D: How do you induce labor?

M: You give medication and it'll, starts the baby reacting.

D: Was it time for me to come out?

G: Yeah.

M: No, not really. Well, it was, within two weeks, OK, so you came two weeks ahead of time. But anyway uh, it was induced and uh, everything went very well. Four hours later you were about to be born, Dennis says, "I have got to go to the bathroom. I'll be right back." He went out, I went into the delivery room, and you were born. He was in the bathroom, so he missed out on it. He was really upset, ya know, he wanted to be there.

G: Sorry, Dennis.

D: I came out this quick, Dennis just peed?

M: Oh yeah, oh sure.

G: Well, uh, they [babies], they do that [arrive quickly].

D: You should have crossed your legs and said, "Go get my husband!"

M: I wouldn't do that.

G: You don't want to cross your legs, you don't want to choke the, well (laughing) maybe you should of!

M: Yeah! (laughs.) Geez! (all laugh)

G: (In squeaky voice) C'mon let me out! [imitating daughter trying to get out of mother's body] (all laugh)

D: It [giving birth] hurts too much.

M: Oh, balony.

D: (To G) But you crossed your legs, you had someone sit on your legs in the taxi cab [during a miscarriage].

G: I had to, I had two, two twins in my lap.

D: Oh, God.

G: That was uh, that was uh, [becomes silent]

D: Kirt [daughter's partner] doesn't want to ever come in [to the delivery room]. He thinks he'll get sick and throw up.

M: Well, he might. Some, some people would, some people would, and other people wouldn't.

D: He really thinks he couldn't handle it.

M: I watched, uh I watched, Tim [mother's son] being born.

D: I want to videotape it!

M: And I watched, I watched you being born, too.

G: Videotape it? (yelling) Double wide! (all laugh) Double wide!

M: Ride the stirrups! You gotta ride the stirrups!

G: C'mon Tammy, **push**! (laughs.) Push! Push!

D: This is as bad as gynecology stories.

G: Oh, God, this is awful talk, ya know, what's all this?!

D: It's not awful talk, it's talk about women's experiences!

M: Yeah, but it [childbirth] was neat, though, Tammy.

D: (To G) What is more woman centered than childbirth?

G: What is, what, what, what, what, what, what?

D: I said, what is more woman centered than childbirth?

G: What is woman more what? (daughter laughs)

D: I, I said, this isn't gross, we're talking about women's experience, and I said, what could be more woman centered than childbirth?

G: Woman centered, oh, that's right.

D: There aren't many men who have babies.

M: (Singing loudly) Having my baby!

G: (To D) Uh, she's having a baby, that's what (laughing) she's doing. (all laugh)

M: (Laughs) Paul Anka.

D: Figures a man would sing it.

G: Paul Anka, he's got five [kids] I think, five or six.

M: I don't know I, I always thought birth was pretty neat. I think, it's a miracle, and it's, pretty neat the way Mother Nature takes over.

G: It's natural. (daughter laughs) That's right, it, it's natural.

M: Well, I think it's a lot of miracle.

G: We aren't, we aren't, women aren't,

M: When you figure that it starts from something that you can't even see, ya know, a sperm, you can't even see that, and here a human body can form that is so complicated.

G: Well, uh, the woman is, is uh, made to achieve that in nature, and uh, that's, that's what we're for!

M: No, no, well that's,

D: What the hell were men made for?!

G: They're for poking. (all laugh loudly)

D: Nanny, what did you used to make your tampons out of?

G: (Laughs) Old cigarette butts. (all start screaming and laughing)

And From Then On I Called You "Clit"

G: (To M) Tell us the story about clit.

D: (To G) Oh, you tell me that story! Go ahead, tell me!

G: (To D) (laughs) You tell me!

D: (To G) Tell me the story.

G: (To M) You tell it, you know it, I know it, too.

M: I can't remember it. What was this?

G: Oh, well, she [Tammy, age three] she was, uh, in the bathtub with Tim, [Tammy's brother, age five] and she wanted to know **why** she didn't have one of those.

M: Oh, God, yes! (screams loudly) Oh, oooooo.

G: Those things, ya know?

M: (Continuous laughter.) What things, Mum? Can you say the word? It's called a penis!

D: Well, wait, tell me the story!

M: Oh, God.

G: So, ah, she [daughter] started to howl, of course.

M: Oh, you were howling!

G: She wanted one [imitating daughter], "Rah, Rah I want one of those!" (in high-pitched voice) (all laugh)

M: And, ah, I ran in,

G: And your mother said, "You have one." [loudly imitating daughter] "Rah! Rah! Rah! Rah!" [jumps up and down clutching crotch] (all laugh loudly)

D: (To G) Nanny, that's not true!

G: (Laughs) That, that is!

M: That's true!

D: I went like this? [jumps up and down clutching crotch]

M: You were,

D: Rah! Rah! Rah! Rah! [in same high-pitched voice grandmother used] (all laugh loudly for several seconds)

G: And so, your mother said, "Well, you can't see it, it's just up inside." You said, "OK." So, you calmed down, you got out of the bath, and you got dried and you went to bed. Well, I don't know, it was several days later, you were out playing, and you came **screaming** inside [imitating daughter], (high-pitched voice). "Mother! Mother!" You were hurt, so you said, "Timmy hit me in the clit, clitoris!"

M: (Laughs) Timmy hit me.

G: Yeah, your mother had said, "It's not called a penis, it's a clitoris." And see, so you, somebody hit you right, right in the, in the, uh, vital spot, and you came in [imitating daughter], "Somebody hit me in the clitoris, Mommy!" (in high-pitched voice) (mother laughs.)

D: What did you do?

G: We laughed at you.

M: We laughed. I checked you out and made sure you were OK.

G: I told that to everybody I know, and from then on I called you "Clit."

D: Oh, God! (all laugh)

M: What happened, you were in the bathtub with your brother, you and your brother used to take baths together.

D: I remember, remember the time I took a shit in the tub?

M: I remember!

D: And we played with it?

M: You and Tim!

D: It was a submarine, "Dee Dee Dee Dee." [imitates playing with it] We were poking it, and it would go down and it would come back up and bubble.

M: (Laughs) Oh, God! I had to go in and clean up the mess!

D: I remember that, took a dump, we were playing with it, we were poking it and making it go around.

M: Oh, geez! God!

D: And Mom came in, "Rah! Rah! Rah!" [same imitating voice from previous story] We said, "We have a log, Mommy, look!" (all laugh)

G: Nobody's on it, though. (all laugh)

M: Yeah!

D: I remember that.

M: Oh, that was disgusting.

D: And you had to clean it up, didn't you?

M: I, of, well, who else? Who else?!

D: Oh, I'm never, never mind, listen to these stories, I'm never going to be a mother. I'm not gonna look at anyone's clit, I'm not gonna clean up crap. I'm not gonna have my kids,

M: Are you kidding? You were having a fit. I think all of a sudden, you, you found out the reason that Tim was a boy and you were a girl that night in the bathtub when you discovered that, but honest to God, you were hysterical. You thought you were missing a vital part of your body.

G: (Laughs) Oh, gosh!

M: And I, I came up there and you're standing in the tub and you're clutching yourself, ya know, and I thought, "What happened here?!" Ya know? Cause I had just gone out of the room. I usually stayed in the bathroom while you kids were taking a bath so that,

D: So we wouldn't take dumps, and,

M: Well, no, so that, you know, I didn't want you to hurt yourself.

G: (To D) That sounds like one of your tricks! (laughs) A dirty trick!

M: Oh, God! (all laugh)

G: Want to do a dirty trick?

M: You were having a fit over that [clit]. Boy, was that funny. I mean, it was one of those things that was a very serious thing, for you, at the time, and it had to be explained, but inside I was, you know, I was cracking up. Here was this kid and, if I'd only had a camera and a (laughing), a recorder to record it, it was really something. It was really something.

G: It was funny.

You Go When You're Supposed To

D: What did G. G. die of? [daughter's great grandmother]

G: G. G. died of old age.

D: G. G. died of old age.

G: She, she died of uh, of uh, what do they call it? Not staph, a flaff, a,

M: No, staph infection [staphylococcus]

G: Staph infection.

M: She had a staph infection.

G: She was in the hospital. I took her in to have a, have a uh, a biopsy taken of her shoulder. We didn't know what was in her shoulder; it was a lump, and it was sort of jelly like. So I took her to the doctor, and he told me to see another doctor, and they took x-rays, and uh, then they, uh, took a biopsy. She had the biopsy, and uh, in the hospital, and uh, and I went up to see her. They had her in a room with about, there, there were six of them in a room, and they were so jammed up you could hardly move through it, all these people. And she had no bandage on! And I thought, "Gosh, that [her shoulder] looks funny to me." And the second day, I went up there, uh, I was going to bring her home, and, the following day, and I thought, uh, "Gee, she's, she." She had stitches like that [pointing to where the stitches were] and I brought her home, and, and,

D: Is that when she became infected?

G: Oh, I know. I brought her home again, and uh, she uh, I was to take her in, I brought her home, it was a Tuesday, I think, a Wednesday, or a, a Thursday I was supposed to take her in. And she and I were playing cards that night, and uh, the Tuesday night I brought her home, and uh, she uh, when she wasn't borrowing from the deck she kept her shoulder against the jam of the door.

M: Door.

G: The door jam. And she had a bandage like this on [points to where bandage was on G. G.'s shoulder], and I said, "Oh, Mum, does that, does that hurt?" and she said, "Oh, no, it doesn't hurt." Well, the next morning, I was going to get, get her and she was sleeping for a long time and I thought, "Well, I better get, get her up 'cause she'd be hungry."

D: Right.

G: So I bring her breakfast to her and so forth, I made some porridge and uh, a cup of tea, some toast and so on, what she always had, so then uh, at lunch time I had to go take her back to, to uh, the doctor's, the following, uh that was uh, the following day, and she, the following day I was to take her back, see. And so, to see the doctor, and they were going to do what they were going to do, and so anyway, she uh, she got uh, she got uh, so I went in at noontime to ah, give her some lunch, I made some sandwiches. And so, I uh, I said to her, "Mum, we gotta be at the hospital at two o'clock this afternoon to see the doctor and so on." Well, I had to carry her to the car, she was so weak! Well, I got her there, to the, to the hospital, and I got a wheelchair to take her in. And they wheeled her in to the operating area, put her on a, she was sitting on a, a table, and they had to undo all this. [points to where the bandage was] The minute they undid it, the blood shot from here to the ceiling! [demonstrates the distance that the blood shot] It was just bleeding all over. So, they put on some kind of, uh, a rubber bandage and so they took her right to the hospital and sewed it up. They sewed it up, like, just like this [pointing to where the stitches were] ya know, with a million stitches. And, uh, I went to the hospital to see her, and I thought, "I don't like the look of this, there's uh, they were yelling, all these people laying around, flowers everywhere."

D: Isn't that the way you found her before, the first time when they sewed it up?

G: Yeah, this, this, was the second time they had sewed it up, yeah. And that was that. And then I was to bring her home, uh, the following day, and uh, I went up to get her. I called, I called before I went to get her, and I asked, "Is Mrs. White ready?" and uh, "She's not here," the nurse said. I said, "Well, she's due to come home today, I'm coming up there, uh, to get her." So, she said, "Just a minute" and she came back to the phone, she said, "She's in, uh, uh, isolation." I said, "What for?!" She said, "Well, she's got staph infection, and they're draining it in isolation." I went up there, they had a million tubes running up her nose and one into her, into her arm, and uh, an irrigation thing going up on her, on her, uh, shoulder in order to clean her out. And uh,

D: Was she conscious?

G: Yeah! She was conscious, and uh, I went in to see her. I had to get all dressed up in a suit, and a mask and gloves. My sister came down [to California from Canada]. I, I told her, I said, "Ya know, Mum, Mum's not very well here." So, she came down and uh, Oliver [great grandmother's brother] came down. And uh, about a week, a week after she'd been in the hospital, seven days or so, I'd go up and see her every day, and uh, see how she was doing that day. Well, after about so many days, uh, I went up one day,

D: And so, she was in isolation for a couple days?

G: Oh, for about a week.

D: A week?

G: So, I went up one day and I, I was outside her door and I heard, "Owwwooo! Owwwooo!" (high-pitched howling noise) And I thought (laughing), "Coming, what is, from her door!?" And I thought, "What on earth is going on?" I rushed off to put the suit on, and I went running into her room, "Mum, what's the trouble, what's the trouble?" "Well," she said, "I have to do this because they're not paying any attention to me." (all laugh loudly) Oh, God!

M: "Owwwooo!" [imitating grandmother] (all laugh)

G: Well, she wanted something, and they wouldn't answer her bell, you see, "Owwwooo!" (all laugh loudly)

D: How come they wouldn't answer her bell?

G: I don't know, I guess there weren't any nurses around. So (laughing) anyway, I said, "Well, we'll find somebody to help you." (laughs) It just scared the darn liver out of me, ya know?

M: Yeah, yeah.

G: And so, that went on for a while. And uh, she got so she was very, very, weak. So uh, we had uh, my sister had come down, and I took her to the hospital to see Mum and so on and so forth. And uh, I,

D: (To M) She says that constantly, just like you!

G: What?

M: So on and so forth.

D: So on and so forth. (mother laughs)

G: So what?

D: She [mother] says it constantly, and you keep saying it constantly, too.

G: Well, that's all right, isn't it?

D: Oh, I guess I'll allow it. (laughs)

G: Do you want to (laughing), do you want to dissect it? [referring to daughter's discipline, speech communication] (mother laughs)

D: Listen, have I ever made fun of your life's vocation? No, I haven't!

G: Well, uh, (laughing) I made,

D: You should just be happy that I'm a,

M: Finish the story!

G: Ya know, I made you famous [referring to storytelling research]. (mother laughs) So you'd better tuck your tail under your feet. (all laugh) So anyway, uh the, the uh, lab people kept, uh, coming in, these young fellows that uh, doing all the lab work, took blood about every half hour. And about after three days I said to, I said, "Look, my mother is 88 and, and she does not need all this attention with the blood work." I said, "I don't want you to do this." She, she didn't like it, either.

M: Yeah, yeah.

G: And uh, and so, they said, well, they were only following orders, and I said, "Leave this poor woman alone!"

M: Yeah.

G: And uh, with that I went, I, I took off! I took my sister, and we went to see the doctor.

M: I love this part. (mother and grandmother laugh) I love it!

G: So, I tore in there, and I said [speaking forcefully], "Doctor Rosenfeld," or whatever his name was, I said, "What do you, uh, why are you doing this to my mother, taking her blood all the time?!" I said, "She doesn't need that, you know that." She [G. G.] had even told the doctor, "I'm ready to die just as long as it's my time."

M: Yeah.

G: Mum, ya know, felt you go when you're supposed to. Try, try and be happy.

M: Yeah.

G: (Slight laugh) Be happy!

M: Yeah. (laughs) Be happy!

G: So, ah, I, I said [to the doctor], "This is my sister, I have three brothers, we all want to honor our mother's wishes, which is, she's willing to die, which is, it's her time to die. She's seen the, telephones come in, and the horse and buggy, and the cars, and the planes, and even to the man on the moon, what more do you want?" And that's what she said, "I'm ready to go."

D: Yeah.

G: I told him, "Leave her alone. I don't want any more heroics, and so on."

D: What did the doctor do?

G: He said, "Well, uh." He said, "Well, I thought she was getting better." I said, "For what?! For less than half a life? Do you want that woman to, to lie in bed for the rest of her life, maybe years?" And I said, "No. My sister and my three brothers did not want that." So uh, he said uh, he didn't say anything, he knew what I meant. So anyway, I had never talked to anybody like that in my life, ya know? I had never, I had always been on the shy side, ya know, I never liked to argue with people and so on and so forth. I always sort of would think to myself, "Well, you, you think what you want, I'll think what I want" sort of thing. And so uh, when I, (laughing)

M: So, you were in the doctor's office and you were very, very, angry,

D: Did you yell, did you yell at the doctor? Did you really give him hell? Was it a he?

G: I did! I told him, "I, just keep your hands off her!" I said, "I don't want her to live!"

D: (Laughs) Oh, God!

M: That was that.

G: Well, why is it, why, why would I want my mother brought back when it was her wish that, that she go? If she wants her wish, I think she should have it. And uh, she was eighty eight, and she had a wonderful life, she said so herself, and uh, so I think it's only fair to honor her wish. Heck uh, who wants to be lying in bed for years, and uh, doing nothing? I think that's uh, that's like worse than being in jail!

M: Yeah.

G: You know? So anyway uh, the doctor said uh, "Ya know, I think she's getting better." I said, "For what?"

D: So, is a staph infection contagious?

G: Oh yes! Very contagious!

M: Yes, highly, highly contagious.

G: It's in the air.

D: What, what kind of infection is it?

G: It's poisonous (laughing) is what it is!

D: No, I mean it just gets in like,

M: It gets into your system and just attacks everything in your body.

G: Yeah.

D: Do they still have it today?

G: Oh yeah!

M: Yes.

D: How do they treat it?

G: The best way they can.

M: Isolation and antibiotics.

G: Well, they, they irrigated her [G. G.], her wound here [pointing to shoulder] to get it out, you see, and it's a little too late because it's inside. By that time, it was through the bloodstream. So anyway,

D: So, did you take her home?

G: Uh no, I didn't take her home, I left her there in the hospital, but I didn't want them to keep on trying, trying to get her better, when she didn't want it. When (laughing) we came out of there [doctor's office], my sister and I, she said, "My God! I, how did you do that? You never do things like that!" I said, "Well, I was so damn mad I, it was about time I did!"

M: Yeah.

G: And uh, she said, "Gosh, I could never do that!" I said, "You would if you felt like I did."

M: Yeah.

G: Ya know, and uh, so uh, that's the way it was.

D: So, did she die in the hospital?

G: So she, she died shortly after. We, I was up there one day and, with my sister, and uh, we uh, she sort of was in a coma, she was sleeping, and, the last thing she did, was (voice falters), she had her hand on the bed and I had my hand right here [demonstrating how her hand was resting next to G. G.'s] and she said, she didn't say anything (voice shaking), she just sort of shifted her hand over. [demonstrating how G. G. placed her hand on top of grandmother's hand]

M: (Speaks softly) Yeah.

G: And uh, then I thought, "I guess this is it, this is the last of it, let's go!"

M: (Laughs) You got out of there, you didn't stay?!

G: [Cries, shaking her head no]

M: No.

G: [Very softly] No.

D: You left?

G: Uh huh. (daughter and mother start crying)

D: Why didn't you stay with her while she died?

G: (Sobbing noise) I couldn't do it. (takes a deep breath)

M: (Simultaneously laughs and cries) She couldn't do it.

G: (Laughs and cries) You got me crying now.

M: (Cries) It's OK, Momma. [Phone rings, mother answers it, daughter approaches grandmother to comfort her]

D: [Hugs grandmother.] I didn't mean to make you cry.

G: (Small laugh) It's all right. [visibly shaken]

D: And so, when you went back was she dead?

G: No. [daughter and grandmother sit silently for awhile]

D: That was a sign. Right?

G: [Distracted] Hmmm?

D: That was a sign.

G: Oh yes, she was,

D: It was the last time she got to hit ya! [trying to cheer grandmother up]

G: [Blows nose] [responding seriously] She didn't quite hit me, she, she grabbed my hand. [daughter and grandmother sit together silently for a minute, mother returns]

M: Now, was, was, Gran taken up to Canada?

G: No.

M: She was cremated down here?

G: Uh huh.

M: In the States?

G: Yeah. Well, what happened was uh (laughing), on with this story business, was that uh, my sister, she cannot stand the sight of anything like that!

M: Stand the sight of what?

G: To see, to see everybody sick in bed and so forth.

M: Oh, yeah.

G: On the, on the, on the edge of death, etcetera.

M: Yeah.

G: So uh, she said, Mum, Mum was not uh, was not uh, [pauses] she was out of it is what it is.

M: Yeah. [daughter hands grandmother a new tissue]

G: Thank you. She was out of it. Anyway, what happened was my sister and I left my Mum, in the hospital, and (laughing) my sister says uh, "Let's go to the mall." (all laugh loudly for several seconds)

D: Oh, God! Are you serious?! This is Jean?

G: Yeah!

M: This is Auntie Jean, yeah. (all laugh)

G: So we went to the mall, and (laughing) we bought clothes (mother laughs) and she says, (laughing) she says uh, "Ya know, when you got something like this, you, you gotta go out and buy something." (all laugh)

M: Yeah! (laughs very loudly) Spend!

G: Oh, gosh! So I went, we, she bought some clothes, and I bought a leather jacket! (all laugh)

M: Oh, good for you!

G: To go fishing with, ya know. Then we went on home.

M: Yeah.

G: That was about uh, four o'clock, yeah, about four o'clock, and by this time, Ted [brother] had come up, ya know, from (laughing), and my cousin Clara came down.

M: Yeah, yeah.

G: I wouldn't let Clara go up there and see her [G. G.]. [blowing nose] She came to me at the, to the hospital one day, and I said, "No, I don't think you should go and see Mum. She's in uh, uh, intensive care, etcetera, etcetera." So, we moved along, we weren't there very long. (laughs) So anyway uh, the day that Jean and I uh, went shopping we were by ourselves, and so Clara was home with Ted. (laughs)

M: Yeah. (laughs) You left them. Shopping! (all laugh)

G: We got our shopping done! (laughs very hard) I'm not gonna tell you this! (all laugh loudly for several seconds)

M: (Laughs) What did you do?!

D: (Laughs) I wish I had my camera! [because everyone was laughing so hard]

G: We went home and, uh, uh (laughing) I said, "Where is Ted?" Ted was outside somewhere so I (laughing), I went out to, to see him and here he was (laughing), Clara, Clara wore a wig (laughing so hard difficult to understand)

D: Clara what?

G: (Laughs) Wore a wig!

M: (Laughs) Wore a wig! (all laugh)

G: Ted was out in the backyard with her wig on! (all howl with laughter for several seconds)

D: Our family grieves in very interesting ways, you go shopping (mother screaming with laughter), and Ted dresses up like a woman!

G: Oh, God, I laughed so much, I got a picture of it! (all laugh) You can't, you can't believe it, ya know!

M: (Laughs) He had Clara's wig on, and Mum takes a picture!

G: Oh, God, he looked, (laughing) I said, "Don't do that. You'd better give her her wig back." "Oh, she doesn't want it!" (all laugh) Oh, gosh, and then about five o'clock, I got a phone call that said Mum had passed away. So that was the end of that. But we had talked uh, about burials uh, a little, shortly before that,

M: Yeah.

G: Before she got sick, and uh, we, we said that, we had hooked up with the, the uh,

M: Neptune? [Neptune Society, cremation service]

G: Neptune, yeah, and we wanted to be cremated and sprinkled wherever, and so, Mum said, "I want that, too." So see, this is what she wanted, but I know very well Dad had made arrangements for her to be beside him.

M: Yeah.

G: Back, back in Canada.

M: Yeah.

G: I said [to G. G.], "Well, aren't, aren't the arrangements ready for you if and when you do go, up in Canada?" "No." But I know damn well they were.

M: Yeah.

G: But anyway uh, so we, we uh, gave her her wish and that's what, what happened.

M: Yeah, yeah.

G: It was no problem.

M: Yeah.

G: It costs an awful lot to uh, ship a body back there [Canada]. I think it's $400.

D: So, she died in California?

G: Yeah.

D: And what year was it that she died?

G: Uh, in uh, '78.

D: Seventy eight?

G: She was 88. She'd just turned 88. She died the first of February. So, her birthday is the 24th, the 24th of January.

D: When I'm sitting by your hospital beds crying because you're going to die, do you want me to go buy something?

M: Absolutely!

G: Yes! Oh, it's just like, (laughing)

M: Commemorate the occasion!

G: It'll make you feel better.

M: It's just, ya know, different people react in different ways.

D: (To G) How come you didn't want to sit there with her?

G: With who? With Grandmother [G. G.]? I knew she was going to die, I didn't want to see it. And uh, 'cause uh, she had nothing left, I think they could have picked her up with one hand, ya know? But uh,

D: So, she never did have breast cancer, right? She had a lump, and your brother [grandmother's brother] had it.

G: Yes, she did.

M: She had lumps, though, but it was never diag,

G: Well, she had, she had what they call cysts.

D: Cysts.

M: Yeah, but they, it wasn't,

G: In, in one [breast].

M: Yeah.

G: And, and uh, she went into the hospital to get uh, a biopsy taken, and
    they said that, "She has lumps, or cysts, and they could turn cancerous."
    They weren't cancerous at the time.
M: Yeah.
G: And they took it [G. G.'s breast] off!! Boy, was she mad, too, she didn't
    have any say in it.
D: She was out, and they removed her breast?!
G: Um hmm.

9

FILMMAKING

Deborah Fort and Ann Skinner-Jones

When a problem exists, there's always a solution
to stop AIDS, we need a new contribution.
Responsibility from everyone that's livin'
responsibility, caring, and a little bit of giving.

This last stanza from a rap that filmmakers Ann Skinner-Jones and Deborah Fort commissioned for their film about sex and AIDS also is an excellent statement about what they hope to accomplish with the film. Titled *Ya Like Totally Have to Talk About Ya Know, It (Sex)*, the women were interested in producing a film that could be a catalyst for helping young people talk about the range of issues around sex education, AIDS, and the treatment of people with AIDS. It is a way of conveying their caring about young people and contributing to the conversation about sex and AIDS.

The impetus for the film came in 1988, when Ann learned that a family member had AIDS; at the same time, a filmmaker friend of Deborah's had died of AIDS, and she learned that another artist friend was HIV positive. Upon returning to Humboldt State University, where the women teach, after Christmas break, they learned that a colleague in another department had died from AIDS. Skinner-Jones began to read everything she could about AIDS and attended a presentation about AIDS in a psychology class; talking to panel members after the presentation, she announced, "I'm going to make a film about AIDS." The project seemed a way for Ann and Deborah to take positive action in response to their own experiences with AIDS. It also seemed essential because of the gap Fort and Skinner-Jones sensed between the proximity of AIDS—knowing people who were ill or had died from the disease—and the attitudes of their students, for whom AIDS was "some strange disease that belongs in some urban center."

In preparation for making the film, Ann and Deborah viewed existing films about AIDS; they were struck by how distant these films seemed from their intended audiences. They wanted to make a film *with* people, not for people, and they wanted to involve their audience directly in the film. Thus, they decided to use young people talking as the basic content of the film. The two women distributed questionnaires about AIDS awareness to their students, asking what they knew about AIDS, what they wanted to know, and what they were willing to talk about with their sexual partners. The last item on the questionnaire asked whether the student was willing to participate in a film about AIDS; students who responded affirmatively later were invited to be part of the film.

The first group filmed was students in a college human sexuality class who had an interest in talking about AIDS. Skinner-Jones describes the next step this way: "After that shoot, we discussed the important points brought up by the students and how we could film situations that would further develop these points." Fort, who has more experience with the technical aspects of film-making, coordinated that part of the project; Skinner-Jones, who has more experience with documentary work and interviewing, facilitated the group discussions.

Ann and Deborah then brought groups of students together and asked questions based on the issues raised in that first group discussion. They primarily were interested in encouraging the young people to express their opinions and points of view rather than in steering the conversation in particular directions. When making choices about which segments of the conversation to include in the film, they looked for patterns that recurred in the talk and used those that seemed representative. In addition to filming groups of young people, they also filmed a woman who was a colleague and friend of the professor who had died from AIDS; she talks in the film about her reactions to learning he was HIV positive and to his death. Interspersed with the conversations in the film are collages of media images depicting sexuality. The film begins and ends with scenes of teenagers and animation that illustrate the lyrics of the rap-music sound track.

The result is a film that is about choices, empowerment, responsibility, and compassion more than it is about the details of protection from AIDS. Skinner-Jones and Fort hope to distribute the film for use throughout the California State University system and in Planned Parenthood offices, other local clinics, and private schools. They are not targeting high schools because "we know we'll have trouble in public high schools; we don't stress abstinence."

In addition to personal funds, the film was funded by the Bertha Russ Lytel

Foundation, the Humboldt Area Foundation, a Humboldt State University
Affirmative Action faculty development grant, a Humboldt State University
Foundation small grant award, the Humboldt State University Public Relations
Office, Transamerica Corporation, Robert Fort and Phyllis Fort, and William
H. Skinner. The Northcountry Clinic for Women and Children served as fiscal
agent, providing the non-profit sponsorship needed when a targeted funding
agency did not fund individuals.

Ya Like Totally was not the first film Ann and Deborah worked on together;
they began working on collaborative projects while in graduate school. In 1982,
they started a film about decoy carving, with the working title of *The Uncarved
Block*, a film also motivated by personal experience. Skinner-Jones' father,
who carved decoys, had drowned in a hunting accident, and a film about his
hobby was a way for her to examine her relationship with her father as well
as to commemorate his life. Fort had completed an autobiographical film, *My
Mother's House in Albertville*, and was interested in collaborating on the film
about decoy carving because it, too, explored family dynamics. *The Uncarved
Block*, still in progress, took them to Humboldt County, California; living
in San Francisco at the time, they went to Humboldt to interview a local decoy
carver. They liked the area and decided to look for jobs there. Fort found a
job first—teaching film in the Theatre Arts department at Humboldt State
University; she moved in the fall of 1984. Skinner-Jones followed in the spring
of 1985, when she also became an instructor in Theatre Arts.

Ann describes her primary interests as media arts, and she teaches courses
in visual communication, photography, and film studies. Her original career
goal was to become a veterinarian, but in 1962, the dean of the veterinary
school in which she was interested said veterinary school was no place for
girls. She also had wanted to go to art school, but her parents told her it wasn't
practical. So she earned B.A. and M.A. degrees in Speech Pathology and
Audiology in order to have a profession at which she could make a living.
Her interest in visual communication began when her father died in 1968;
she picked up his camera and started taking pictures. When Skinner-Jones
traveled with her future husband, a Vietnam veteran, to Southeast Asia, she
realized she had a real interest in visual anthropology—the documenting of
other cultures through photography. After her divorce, Ann returned to school
at the age of 35 to get a Master's of Fine Arts in photography at the San Francisco
Art Institute. After finishing the program, she stayed on as the director of
Media Services, where she pursued her interest in film and filmmaking.

For Skinner-Jones, her art—whether in the form of photography or film—is
"sustaining." She adds, "If I didn't do it, I feel as though I would shrivel up
and die." She describes herself as two quite different people, depending on
whether or not she is taking photographs. In everyday settings, she sees herself
as a bit shy and reserved, but "give me a camera, and I'll go anywhere and

do anything."

Ann's most frequent photographic theme is women in different cultures in their everyday settings—gathering and preparing food, doing laundry, bathing children, sewing and weaving—"tasks that often are not seen as significant but which are important for the continuation of a culture; women are the real preservers of identity." Another theme is objects that illustrate lifestyle; she has photographed a series of interiors that depict personal space as portrait. Interested in reducing the impact of the camera and photographer on those she studies, Skinner-Jones works in collaboration with the women she photographs, asking them to direct her and to indicate what they consider to be important to photograph. She also uses polaroid film to produce "fast" photographs for the women; these also serve as the impetus for further discussion. Her field work in visual anthropology has taken her to Japan and Vanuatu, in the South Pacific, as well as to Europe and throughout the United States. She is currently working on a book of photographs of Vanuatu.

Like Ann, Deborah's early interests gave no indication that she would become a filmmaker. She considers one of the significant aspects of her life the fact that she was six feet tall by the time she was 15. She grew up among independent farm women and never planned to marry; she believed it would limit her options. She majored in therapeutic recreation at the University of Iowa and worked for several years in a psychiatric hospital in New York. While there, she started taking film classes as a way of coping with job stress. When laid off from the hospital, she got a job with an "Artist in the Schools" program, teaching filmmaking in the first, third, sixth, and high-school grades. When she decided to pursue her film studies, she moved to San Francisco to earn her MFA degree at the Art Institute, where she worked as Skinner-Jones' assistant in Media Services. Filmmaking, film installation, and performance art are central to Fort's life. She explains: "It's hard to think of why I do it because I can't imagine not doing it."

Deborah has specific goals she hopes to achieve in her filmmaking. She is committed to creating experimental films—not the kinds of films coming out of Hollywood. Hollywood films, for Fort, embody the patriarchy. Not only is the structure hierarchical—the director is the dominant voice controlling everything that happens with the film—but the outcome is the embodiment of the male voice. She is interested in getting outside the patriarchal voice both in terms of content and format. In addition, film, for her, is a way of making the personal political and should explore socially significant issues.

Deborah is particularly interested in the use of film to encourage individuals to come to know and express their own voices. She tries to work *with* subjects to help them convey their feelings and ideas and is especially intrigued with the autobiographical voice in film because it is a personal reflection translated into a generalized medium. She is preparing a class on the female voice in autobiographic film and literature that will deal with the different treatments and functions of autobiography in these two media.

Skinner-Jones and Fort plan to finish the film about decoy carving and are researching a film about the right to die. They also would like to do a series on "amazing women," women who have made unusual and important contributions that largely have been unrecognized.

Below is the transcript from the film, *Ya Like Totally Have to Talk About Ya Know, It (Sex)*. The rap lyrics with which the film begins and ends were written for and performed in the film by Ethan Marak of the Freshboys, students at Eureka High School. The "M" and "F" refer to different male and female speakers that change from scene to scene. The 20-minute, 16-millimeter color film consists of scenes of young people, in high school and college, talking about sex. The settings for the discussions include a high-school parking lot, classrooms, and what appears to be a family room. The photographs that follow are frame enlargements from the film. The first two show the title frames of the film, and the third is used to illustrate the rap lyrics in the introduction of the film. The remaining frames show young women talking.

Transcript

Ya Like Totally Have to Talk About Ya Know, It (Sex)

Rap

Well it's easy to see if you investigate
that we're troubled by problems causing crime and hate.
But of all the issues we need to resolve
AIDS is the one that you can help dissolve.

Now I know that the subject is kinda taboo
but I'm only sixteen and I'm comin' to you
And I'm not just talkin' about a gay disease
I'm talking about the new plague that can bring you to your knees.

It's the acquired immune deficiency syndrome
and believe me, you should leave it alone.
And that's simple—protection is an easy measure
so why kill yourself in that moment of pleasure?

Responsible sex is the simplest answer
it could save your life if you're a young romancer.
If you're sleeping someplace new every day of the week
I'll tell you what, man, you might be up a creek.

You can't catch it from a dog or a cat or a bug
you can't catch it from a spoon, a fork, a plate, or a mug.
And just to put you at ease, I think I'll repeat
that you can't get AIDS from a toilet seat.

But if you're doing drugs, that's dumb enough
and if you don't clean your needles then you've got it rough
Because whoever used it last could've had *it* in their blood
and when you use a dirty needle, your name is mud.

So what you're straight, it doesn't matter, man
don't think you can't get AIDS because I know you can.
You're sleepin' here, you're sleeping there, it's different every night
but while you're living in lust you should be living in fright.

Take it easy—consider one steady lover
and if not that, then at least consider cover.
A rubber? Yeah, you might think it mean
but it's an inexpensive way to stay clean.

Now there's another aspect to this whole persuasion
there's one word in my head—*evasion*.
Why should we treat the infected so bad
evasion of these people makes them very sad.

You won't catch the disease by just saying "hello"
you'll make them feel much better—so
Before you evade them, put yourself in their shoes
and figure out how you'd avoid the blues.

Now I been rappin' for a while—you might think I'm a bore
but all I wanna tell you is the choice is yours.
You know the facts and the statistics, but that won't even solve it
be safe, be smart, and you'll help to dissolve it.

When a problem exists, there's always a solution
to stop AIDS, we need a new contribution.
Responsibility from everyone that's livin'
responsibility, caring, and a little bit of giving.

                                              Ethan Marak (Freshboys)

M: I don't talk about sex until I really get to know, know who they are, what they're like and everything. And then, once I feel it's time to, just, you know, pop the question. So! What about, uh, you know — (inaudible). Well, uh, not — not like we have to soon, or anything, but I mean, later on in our relationship, do you think you would — be possible, uh, we should talk about sex.

F: I'll have things to say — I feel as though they — they get stuck there, like they're going around and around, over and over again in my head, like — just waiting to be communicated to this person, and, for some reason, they're — they're just — they feel stuck there. I felt attracted to him. All of a sudden, I didn't know what I wanted. All these things were coming up into my head that I hadn't even thought about. You know, if he's feeling attracted to me, then that's a completely different thing.

F: He's making it like a dare, like, you know —

M: Uh, huh.

F: You're being come onto as if, like, something's trying to be gotten, from, you know —

M: Right. That's the problem I have, too. But it's always just the male/female relationship, though — I never really — I — I think so, at least, I mean — I don't think that's the way it should be, I'm saying that's the way it is. That's what really gets me all bottled up is that —

F: That's not the way — that's not the way it always is.

M: I feel that men have to come on to the women and that it's always that role playing.

F: But don't you think —

M: It's the male using the lines and the female either accepting them or fighting them off, basically.

F: Uh, huh, but —

M: It happens all the time. You never, you never decide that I'm going to have sex with this guy? It just happens? Is that —

M: How else are — are the one-night stands here, among strangers, if women aren't attracted to men? Do men just go in and push them around the bar and then push them out the door and home? Eventually — I'm lost, this is all new to me.

F: It seems like maybe women are — slightly more emotionally motivated and men are slightly more physically motivated.

M: It's wrong to just get in bed together.

F: No, no, it's wrong to — to get physical and expect that you're going to have sex as well.

M: Instead of a fun, good-feeling, comfortable thing — it's a fun, good-feeling, bad thing? It's like if you're with a partner you don't really know, whoever that may be, it's like instead of saying, "Wow, this is — this may be on a whim, or whatever, but it feels really good and it's fun"; instead, it'll be like, "I hope, you know, everything's OK after this time." If sex ever was casual, it's not—it's not casual anymore. I mean, just as far as the mental feeling afterwards. I mean, it's just not quite as free loving. I really do try and be safe. Before, I'd definitely just be safe, you know, as far as pregnancy wise, but I think now I'm beginning to realize that it's not just—it's not just a baby you've got to worry about, but AIDS, too. It takes months to really get to know somebody. But, if you're going to start a relationship, it's not going to be months before you have sex with them, but, just, I don't know, when I talk to—I mean like—I'll take a girl, for example, now. It was just through talking with her and being with her that I realized that it wasn't going to be that open. That's what I'm looking for, something that's open, and something that we both relate with each other on just, like, a friendship level.

M: In the locker rooms, it's a lot different situation with the peer pressure, and some jock will sit there and say, "Yeah, I'm always getting some," and everybody else in the locker room is just saying, "Uh, yeah, sure you are," and grins.

M: They don't know about sexual encounters themselves; they'll—they'll just kind of agree. And say, "Yeah, I know what you're talking about." So they don't look bad, because it's kind of an ego thing. But then they might zero in and start picking on you like, "Hey, have you had sex lately?" And then get really embarrassed and, "Well, uh, no." And if you have a certain girl and everybody's all, "Hey, you know, have you got her, yet?"

M: Yeah.

M: "Well, no, you know, I'm still working on it," and you don't really want to admit that she said no and you got major rejection and got slapped in the face. You just kind of shrug it off and turn your back.

F: It's a lot different with girls, if they go out and people find out that they've had sex the other night, they're considered a slut. It goes around school really fast. That they are sleaze. Girls don't go into the locker room and say, "Hey, guess what I did last night?"

M: I think that a lot of guys, even if they don't feel like they're ready, will, if the chance comes up, do it. Just to be able to have done it and be like, "Guess what I did last night?" And I think the only way to prevent that kind of pressure is within yourself and to be, like, well, I'll do it when I'm ready.

F: It seems like sex should be something that you, like, lead to; it's not like the way it starts. Yeah, I'm embarrassed to talk to my partner about sex, you know, especially when we're, you know, right in the middle of it. So, it's important for me to realize and to remember that, you know, maybe, right, you know, when you're having sex is not the best time to talk about it. And, also, you know, that it is not—that right then is not the best time to talk about protection.

F: Well, there probably isn't any best time to talk about it.

F: That's right.

F: And, we probably just need to start talking about it, and maybe we'll learn when's the best time.

F: I felt rejected and, it—I mean, it was the worst thing. It was terrible, it was horrible, but—and then, you know, a couple of months later, even, I can look back on it and just—I mean, not laugh, I mean, but I'm taking it in as an experience in that I'll go on, I mean.

F: Well, you know, another thing about rejection is that, you know, if you—it doesn't have to be such a painful thing if you say to yourself, "Oh, you know, well, at least I tried," you know, and give yourself credit for what you have done that's good, instead of saying, "Oh, God, I'm such a dumb person," you know.

F: I don't really think there are any role models for how to talk about sex.

F: I know when I first started having sex, I felt like there was no one that I could talk to about it.

F: When I was going through high school, a lot of my friends would come and tell—my girl friends would come and talk to me about problems that they were having with their boy friends or just people who they'd have sex with, and—and then I would wonder, you know, I know they didn't like most of these people, I would just wonder—I wanted to tell them that they had the choice of saying no if they wanted to and why were they bringing this onto themselves?

F: I know, like, I do feel now that I have a choice, that—that it's possible that I can say no.

F: I just can't help thinking that if—if as often in television and movies and commercials and everything else is that people were engaging in sexual activities, that there was a condom somehow in the picture, or someone brought it up. Because it is such a mixed message. It's—here's all these people being loose and wild and free and having a great time on television, but—

M: Hold it, let's put this on.

F: No—yeah, nobody's talking about using protection and it—and so when people do talk about it, it's almost estranged from—from what you usually think of in terms of sex or love or romance. And it seems almost like, maybe, like pressure, something to rebel against.

F: When I hear commercials that tell us to have safe sex, I just get this feeling like it's a parent telling me to abstain from having sexual intercourse. And it just makes me feel like turning it off. I try to have safe sex, but I try to think of it instead as protecting myself, instead of just don't have—

don't do this and don't do that. Nowhere in the media would they ever give the impression that it's not great every time. And I've learned it's just not that way. I think there's this myth about having sex that two people can meet up and go off into a corner and have really good sex, and I don't think that's true. I think that each person needs to know what they're looking for.

F: Well, you know, like, I guess this whole sex deal, it's like, you know, sometimes I want to talk to the guy about it, or something, but it just seems like it's not cool, or whatever. But I do think that the best way to talk about it is just by laughing about it, and, you know, not necessarily, you know, cutting on it, but just, you know—

M: And when you tend to be all serious about it, it's more of a—

F: It's stressful—

M: Yeah.

F: It seems so totally dumb, if you're totally aware of AIDS and these others, like chlamydia and gonorrhea, that you can totally get, and that if you're aware of it, it's just like—then you should—

M: Defend yourself—

F: Right. Then why aren't you using condoms, you know.

M: And I don't believe I can get AIDS because I think of myself as a little smart and intelligent for using prophylactics or whatever that's necessary.

M: Yeah, but even though you think, "Well, I can't get AIDS because I'm using protection," there's always that fear in the back of your mind, but— well, it's a possibility.

M: It's a scary thought, just thinking that AIDS are, like, all around you.

M: If there's a person who's got AIDS and you just meet them and you don't know who they are, you're going to shy off from them; you aren't going to be, you know, compassionate. You're probably going to reject them, sort of.

M: Things start running through your head, you know. Is this person homosexual? Do they use drugs? You know, are they sexually loose? That's when you hear the word AIDS. It's like you think of the person as strange, that's it.

M: And I'll tell you right now, that's why that camera's not on me. 'Cause I'm HIV positive. I am worried. I am afraid about, you know, what's going to happen. I have to work here, I have to go to school here, I have to live here. I really didn't believe it was me. 'Cause I was from a small town, and I always thought I was, you know, I worked all the time, and I thought I was pretty clean about what I did. But, lo and behold, what a surprise. I'm healthy, and I know I'm going to get sick. You know, when you've got to face your own mortality, when it's right there and you've got a definitive time, you know, then it changes everything. It just changes everything.

M: It's happening another time and this is only, like, the second time. It's going to happen again, most likely.

M: What, that you've met, that somebody —

M: Yeah, someone I know personally is going to die of AIDS.

M: Everybody's safe, and it can't happen here. Wrong. It happened right here in Middle America, you know, like, to me. Being afraid of it is not going to make it different, you know? Just, you have to know about it.

F: I guess the reason I don't think about it, too, is no one close to me has died of it. You see it on TV, and you see it, like, in *Life* magazine.

M: I, I know people that shoot up and stuff, I mean, you know, cheap cocaine and crystals and stuff. You wonder, you know.

F: The disease may be your fault, but why should I take that chance?

M: Put yourself in that position. If you had AIDS, and suddenly you're completely, like, what, excommunicated or something? Ostracized?

M: I'd be afraid to be around somebody if they had AIDS. I wouldn't want to — I wouldn't want to be in the same room. OK, if you had AIDS and if you were my roommate, and I found out that you had AIDS, I doubt if I'd like to stay with you. I wouldn't have anything against you or anything; it's just that I don't think we know enough about the disease.

M: It's so hard to say because, you know, I don't know! Because I don't have AIDS, and I couldn't sit here — and I couldn't tell you guys how I — you know, how it feels, you know. I could just imagine and say, "Oh, my God, you know, I'm dying."

F: After that teacher died of AIDS, they didn't say, "Oh, my God, he was my teacher. He touched my papers, he touched this and that." A lot of people were just really sad. They were really hurt because he was a good person. I don't think anyone really discriminated against him. They were sad. They weren't scared.

F: His most fun thing to do was to talk about ideas, and I think that's one of the things that people always liked about Doug. And I also think that's why, perhaps, in the end, when his dementia had taken his memory away, it was, in some ways, a sad, cruel joke that that would be what his AIDS would turn out to be. When he told me that — that he had tested positive — he then accused me for the rest of the evening that we were together of watching him. And he kept saying to me, you know, "don't look at me like that, I'm perfectly all right. I'm going to will you all my books." And I said, "I think that might be a curse, knowing how many books that you have." But I wasn't thinking I would inherit them quite so soon. Everyone here had said goodbye and had let him go and were waiting for me. And I said, "You're waiting for me to do what?" They said, "You need to be very brave and you need to go in and you need to say goodbye." And I said, "Now, wait a minute, I'm not ready for this person to die. I mean, I just saw him less than a month ago, and he was OK."

F: One of the things that I say is, "I have a friend who died of AIDS, and I'm really concerned about it, and how do you feel about AIDS? And how do you feel about protecting yourself?"

F: Well, do you feel like when you tell people that — that you knew someone that died of AIDS — that, I mean, do you feel you're judged because of that?

F: Well, maybe, but I feel like I still need to talk about it. He was my friend, and I love him, and just because a person dies of AIDS doesn't mean that they're strange. And the more we talk about it, the more people will realize that anybody can get this disease.

F: We have a friend who lives with us who has AIDS. And I know what AIDS is doing to her body. Most people will lose someone that they know to AIDS. That's what, sort of, shocks them into taking care of themselves, wearing a condom, worrying about their friends and their partners. I don't think it's right to make a person feel bad for what they've done before and question them endlessly. "So, you slept with this person. Do you think there's a chance that that person had AIDS?" It just doesn't work. What works is saying, "I'm scared about AIDS. I'm sure you're scared about it. I'm sure you've thought about it, and I'd really feel a lot better if you would wear a condom. For you and for me." I think a lot of people have made the decision not to have sex now. They don't feel comfortable with it. A lot of kids are just coming into their sexuality now, and this AIDS thing scares them, and they think maybe — maybe I should wait for a while before I start something this serious.

[Rap is repeated to end]

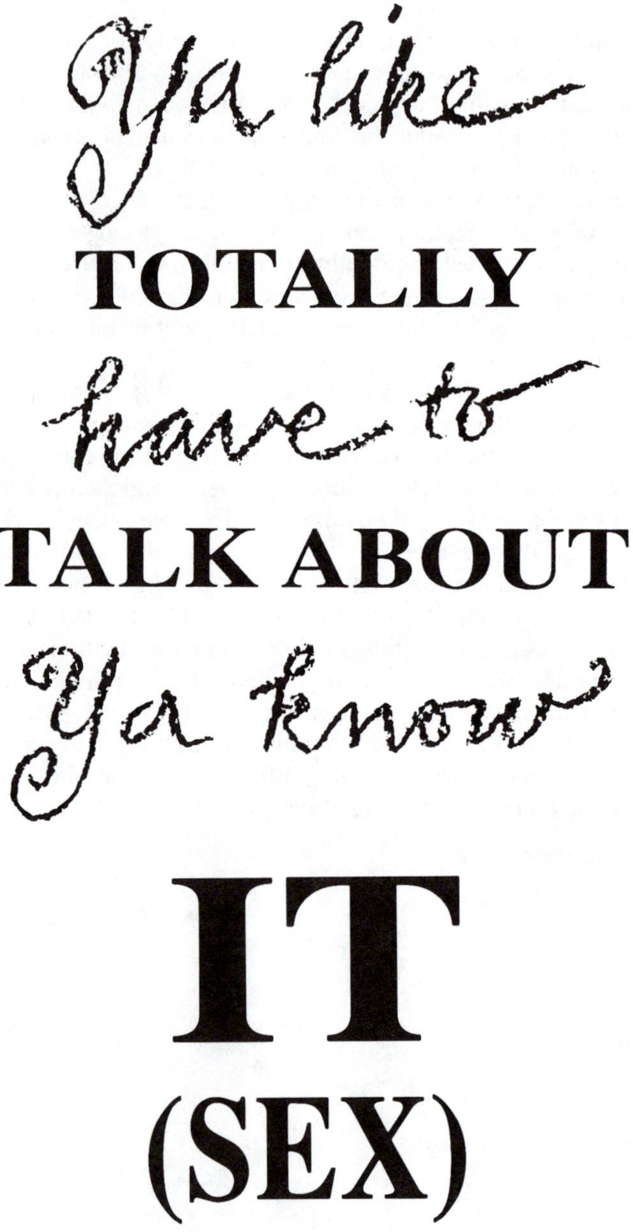

Ya like

TOTALLY

have to

TALK ABOUT

Ya know

IT
(SEX)

Ann Skinner-Jones and Deborah Fort, title frame enlargement from 16-mm film, **Ya Like Totally Have to Talk About Ya Know, It (Sex)**

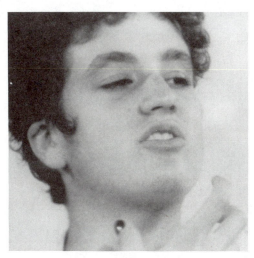

"I'll have things to say—I feel as though they—get stuck there, like they're going around and around, over and over again in my head, like—just waiting to be communicated to this person, and, for some reason, they're—they're just—they feel stuck there."
—Sara Martin
Ann Skinner-Jones and Deborah Fort, frame enlargement from 16-mm film, **Ya Like Totally Have to Talk About Ya Know, It (Sex)**

"I try to have safe sex, but I try to think of it instead as protecting myself, instead of just don't do this and don't do that."   —Connie Stewart
Ann Skinner-Jones and Deborah Fort, frame enlargement from 16-mm film, **Ya Like Totally Have to Talk About Ya Know, It (Sex)**

10

GARDENING

Lynn Uhl

"I don't think I've ever bought a flower. I always thought, why not plant one so you get the whole thing?" Lynn Uhl has put her philosophy to work, transforming the gravel parking lot that was the front yard of her house into a country garden with raised beds for growing flowers and herbs. Uhl specializes in "everlastings" — flowers such as statice, strawflowers, larkspur, and baby's breath — that can be dried and made into permanent bouquets; wreaths; and trim for hats, baskets, and other decorative items.

Lynn describes her garden as "casually coordinated chaos," a phrase she likes because it suggests a bit of disarray as well as order. While she plants flowers quite deliberately to get the amounts she needs for her creations, she also combines different varieties in one bed in order to give her garden the wildness she likes. She does not want a perfectly manicured garden; what's important to her is that weeds don't encroach on her flowers, the grass pathways between her beds aren't higher than the flowers themselves, and the dead blooms are trimmed from her flowers.

Visitors to Uhl's home and garden are welcomed by a pathway to her front door that is edged with different kinds of mint, pink yarrow, California poppies, lady's-mantle, and jupiter's beard. To the right of her path is an herb garden, and to the left is a trellis supporting climbing red roses and wisteria. On Lynn's front door is a wreath welcoming friends. An old church, her house has a large central room that is her main living space and the place where she makes her creations. Her walls, tables, and shelves are filled with colorful bouquets, hats, trinkets, and photographs — and "always dried flowers waiting to be used."

One of her bedrooms has been converted to a drying room that also contains flowers hanging to dry. It also contains baskets full of dried herbs, flowers, and filler—plants such as baby's breath, sweet Annie, silver king, and German statice—that provide the foundation for wreaths and baskets and fill out bouquets.

Uhl always liked to garden—something she associates with her grandparents. She remembers seeing strawflowers in their yard as a child and being intrigued by "flowers that last forever." She also remembers her mother having bouquets of fresh flowers around continually—especially camellias and roses. Lynn still appreciates her mother's sense of arrangement; when she comes to visit, Uhl enjoys her mother's help with her creations.

When Lynn first moved into a house with enough yard for a garden, flowers were the first thing she planted. When she rediscovered "everlastings," varieties of flowers that, if dried properly, are hardy and permanent, they became a major part of her garden: "I'm a person who has difficulty letting go," Uhl says. "So when I discovered everlastings, my compulsion was answered!" She had found flowers she doesn't have to throw away.

Lynn's garden consists of about 20 kinds of everlastings, including sea lavender, golden star, Russian statice, larkspur, and strawflowers. She has 45 different herbs, which she uses in live bouquets as well as in her dried arrangements. Her garden also contains about 40 varieties of flowers that are not everlastings, including roses, coralbells, irises, sweet William, and honeysuckle. She grows and dries some flowers that many people don't think of drying, including bachelor buttons, delphiniums, and forget-me-nots. She finds these particularly appealing because they dry to be a pure blue, and she is interested in having available a full range of colors to use in her bouquets. Each year, she looks through seed catalogs for new kinds of flowers and new shades of familiar flowers to add variety to her arrangements. She saves seeds or cuttings from each year's garden, so she is always increasing the variety, texture, and color of her garden.

For Uhl, the gardening process begins in early spring, when she plants the seeds and cuttings for that year's gardens in her growth room, a small room with many windows, to which she has added grow lights. In the meantime, she weeds and amends the beds, getting them ready for planting. Once her seeds and cuttings have been transplanted, there is still much work involved. Lynn spends up to four hours a day watering her garden, which she does by hand; she hopes to add a drip-watering system to reduce the time she spends at this job. She also spends time weeding, picking off bugs, cutting up slugs with scissors, and fighting gophers.

When the flowers mature in the summer, Uhl picks them and hangs them in her drying room, where they remain until they dry and she can use them in her creations. Much of the satisfaction for her comes from the full cycle involved in starting a plant from seed, nurturing it, drying it, and then sharing it with others in the form of beautiful arrangements. Lynn also delights in friends and passers-by who stop in to enjoy her garden; she likes to share the flowers, the smells, and the colors with them.

Gardening is Uhl's way of keeping in touch with the earth; her sign is Virgo, the earth sign, and she feels a need to stay connected with nature's cycle. She has come to realize that her dried flowers "let me be as close to my garden as possible in winter," so even when she is not tending her garden, she is involved with it as she works with her flowers, turning them into arrangements.

Lynn also sees her garden as a means of connection to the past. She especially likes herbs for this reason: "Herbs have such a history because they've been here forever." She tells, for example, of how, after having their tea dumped at the Boston Tea Party, the settlers learned from the Indians about making tea from the herb monarda (also called wild bergamot and oswego tea)—an herb Uhl has in her garden. She feels a special connection to women's collective history because women have been the ones who most often work with herbs. She follows in that tradition by making wreaths out of herbs using their special properties; she made a wreath out of rosemary, camomile, fleabane, wormwood, and thyme, for example, for a friend who was having nightmares. A protection wreath consists of horehound, hyssop, mugwort, and southernwood; for a love wreath, Lynn uses lavender, roses, lady's-mantle, marjoram, and yarrow. The wreath form itself also provides a historical connection for Uhl. Because a wreath is an eternal circle, it is a symbol of "everlasting life." Wreaths have a long history—they have been discovered in Egyptian tombs, for example—and suggest important celebrations and special events that have held significance for people throughout history.

Lynn uses mugwort and oregano as the main form for her wreaths; this was not always the case, however: "When I first started making wreaths, I picked the tall dried grass from across the street, formed it into a circle, and wrapped it with wire." She did this for two years until she discovered that oregano and mugwort "work much better." To make a wreath, Uhl cuts a large quantity of one of these herbs; picks a nice spot to sit; gathers her wire, wire cutters, and scissors; and begins work. She makes three different sizes—small, medium, and large—and even a small one takes quite a bit of material because it shrinks as it dries. After bending the herbs into a circle, wrapping it with wire, and attaching a hanging wire, she slides a pole through the wreath and hangs it to dry. When she's ready to make a wreath, she wires on a filler, such as German statice, baby's breath, silver king, or several kinds of herbs, depending on the effect she wants to create. She then places flowers into the wreath until she has the arrangement she wants, at which point she glues each flower in place. In an all-herb wreath, which people can use for cooking, however, Lynn wires on all of the herbs. Ribbons and bows, if they are to be used, are added last.

Uhl sells her finished products at a local crafts store, although she does not foresee her hobby turning into a self-supporting business anytime soon. Her "ultimate dream," though, would be "if I could support myself by working in my garden, take what I've grown and made, and sell it." She took two days off from work before Mother's Day because her creations were in such demand at the shop where she now sells her things. She hopes to be able to do the same at Christmas—at that time of year, Lynn can't make enough wreaths to fill demands. In her Christmas wreaths, she likes to combine blue, silver, and white, which she gets by combining silver king, dusty miller, larkspur, and statice. She also uses the more traditional colors of red, white, and green. Uhl is planning to begin selling cut flowers as well, so her garden probably will have an even greater variety of flowers in it in years to come as she expands this part of her business.

Lynn also does custom arrangements, matching bouquets, baskets, and wreaths to customers' bedspreads and wallpaper samples. The most elaborate project Uhl has done to date was the flowers for her daughter's wedding. Using all everlastings, she made the head wreath, boutonnieres, corsages, bridesmaids' baskets, flowers for the arch under which the bride and groom stood, flowers for the flower girl, huge bouquets in baskets for the front of the church, and two bouquets for her daughter—one to throw and one to keep. Pink was the dominant color at the wedding, and Lynn interspersed blue, white, purple, and yellow with the pink for the summer wedding: "It wiped me out of pink flowers for the year!" She would like to do the flowers for other weddings— especially if she does not have to be in charge of the entire wedding at the same time.

Uhl admits that because of her perfectionism—"being a perfectionist is part of the Virgo sign, but it's also something I got from my father"—it takes her longer to do a project, "but the end result is worth it." When she finishes an item, she will set it on the kitchen table and continue to look at it and "fix it" for several days: "I can always find another flower to add or something different to do to it." Sharing her work with others has given Lynn a sense of confidence about what she can do: "I'm willing to take risks I might not have before because of the positive response to my creations."

For Lynn, her garden provides her with a balance in her life—something very different from her work and her concerns for her family; she cleans houses for a living and has a teenaged daughter still at home. She admits that the balance is hard to maintain because "I'm a workaholic," and she easily can become consumed by her garden: "It's a lot of work, but it's also such a pleasure and joy for me to be out there. I spend as much time as I can in my garden." She recently thought about what her priorities would be if she had only a short time to live. She realized that people come first for her—her best friend, Pat; her new grandson; her two daughters; her parents; and her brother and his family—"and that helped me put my garden in perspective."

Uhl has talked for years about putting in a few vegetables, and she finally planted one bed with zucchini, radishes, lettuce, chives, and cilantro: "I usually end up using all the space for my flowers," she says, "but I do enjoy eating from the garden, too." She also has planted nine fruit trees in her yard—plum, apple, pear, and cherry—and also grows raspberries and grapes.

Each winter, when Lynn contemplates the process involved in her gardening, she sometimes thinks, "Oh, I just can't do it again." But once spring comes, she is out there again, working with her flowers and herbs—unable to avoid their appeal. Her garden is a metaphor for life, and in tending her garden, Uhl realizes the lessons she needs to learn are right there among her flowers and herbs. When she sees weeds crowding out flowers, for example, she is reminded of how easy it is for negative thoughts and attitudes to crowd out the positive in life. When she looks out at her garden in early spring and gets discouraged by all the work there is to do, she tackles one box at a time—just as she approaches problems in her life one step at a time. "If I'm working on something in my life," she says, "it's amazing how often I find the answer in my garden."

Lynn's garden, in late summer, is shown below. In the first picture, cone-flowers, lythrum, mint, and jasmine form the back row; feverfew, lamb's ears, and dusty miller are in the center section of the photograph; and santolina, southernwood, and wormwood are in the foreground. The second photograph, of Lynn's drying room, shows statice, tansy, strawflowers, ammobium and agera-tum immediately in front and more strawflowers and tansy hanging from left to right. Yarrow and baby's breath fill the baskets in the chair and on the floor.

Lynn Uhl, flower and herb garden
Photograph: Diana Schoenfeld

Lynn Uhl, flowers and herbs in drying room
Photograph: Diana Schoenfeld

Inventory of Lynn's Garden

Everlastings

acrolinium
ageratum
ammi majus (bishop's weed)
ammobium (winged everlasting)
baby's breath (pink and white)
carthamus tinctorius (safflower)
caspica spangle
catananche
craspedia drumstick
golden baby

golden star
larkspur
nigella (love-in-a-mist)
pentzia
rhodanthe
sandfordi
sea lavender
statice (sinuata, soiree, German, Russian)
strawflower
xeranthemum

Herbs

anise hyssop
borage
chive
cilantro
comfrey
costmary
dill
elecampane
feverfew
fleabane
horehound
hyssop
lady's-mantle
lamb's ears
lavender
lemon balm
lemon mint
lemon verbena
marjoram
marshmallow
meadowsweet
mint
monarda (oswego tea, wild
    bergamot, horsemint)

mugwort
oregano
parsley
pennyroyal
pineapple sage
Roman camomile
rosemary
rue
sage
santolina (lavender cotton)
scented geraniums (apple, coconut,
    rose, lemon rose, sandalwood)
silver king artemisia
southernwood
sweet Annie
sweet woodruff
tansy
thyme
valerian
vervain
winter savory
wormwood
yarrow

Flowers

astilbe (false goatsbeard)
Australian tea rose
bachelor button
California poppy
campanula (canterbury bell)
columbine
coneflower (yellow and pink)
coralbells
dusty miller
forget-me-not
fuchsia
geum
godetia
hollyhock
honeysuckle
iris
jasmine
johnny jump-up
jupiter's beard

upin
lythrum
marigold
nicotiana (flowering tobacco)
Oriental poppy
painted daisy
penstemon
petunia
primrose
rose
salvia
scabiosa
snapdragon
stokesia aster (Stokes' aster)
sweet William
veronica
wallflower
wisteria

Trees

apple
cherry

Pear
plum

GRAFFITI

Blueberry Hill

Women's talk together is done in a variety of settings, many of them private, as in the case of women's reading groups or the sharing of stories by women within a family. In the case of graffiti, the talk is public and assumes the form of an unending conversation, in which the communicators remain anonymous, contribute or not, respond to topics already under discussion, or initiate others of their own. The graffiti that follows is from the walls of the women's restroom in Blueberry Hill, a restaurant and bar in the University City area of St. Louis, Missouri.

Blueberry Hill, owned by Joe Edwards and Linda Edwards, features collections of lunchboxes, comic books, vintage beer bottles, and vintage jukeboxes; an Elvis Room lined with Elvis Presley memorabilia; and its own brand of beer, Rock and Roll beer. The bar is famous for its annual national dart tournament and its annual Elvis birthday party, which includes an Elvis-impersonation contest.

Outside the bar is the St. Louis Walk of Fame, which honors famous St. Louisans with stars embedded in the sidewalk. Among those immortalized are Vincent Price, Chuck Berry, Tennessee Williams, Scott Joplin, Marlin Perkins, and Betty Grable. Another feature of the bar's exterior is a 70-square-foot display window used to present conceptual and performance art that Linda Edwards designs and decorates and in which she sometimes acts. Windows have been done on themes such as Superman, sleep research, the Dionne quintuplets, and Rosemary's baby shower (a Halloween theme).

Blueberry Hill's owners recognize the creativity evidenced in the graffiti on their restroom walls, some of which dates back to 1972, when Blueberry Hill opened. They have compiled 50 or 60 of what they consider to be the wittiest sayings from both the women's and the men's restrooms and have made them into a "graffiti T-shirt" that is available for sale at Blueberry Hill.

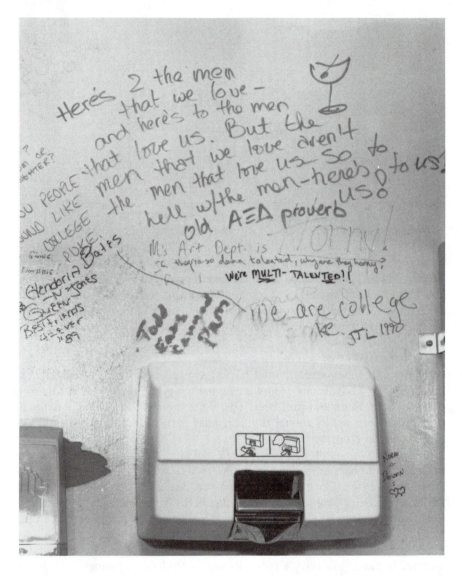

Graffiti, women's restroom, Blueberry Hill
Photograph: Thomas Lanham

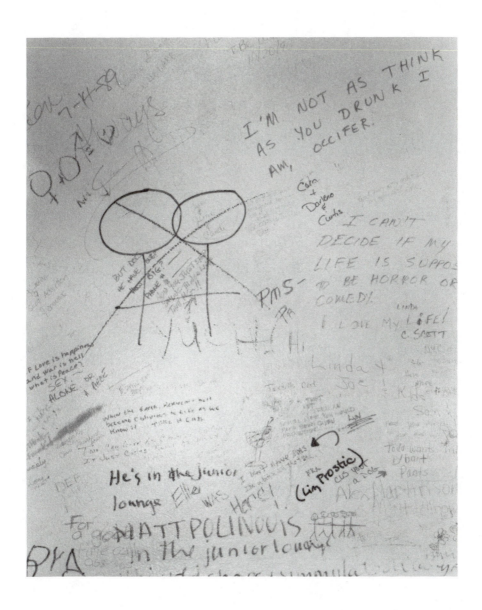

Graffiti, women's restroom, Blueberry Hill
Photograph: Thomas Lanham

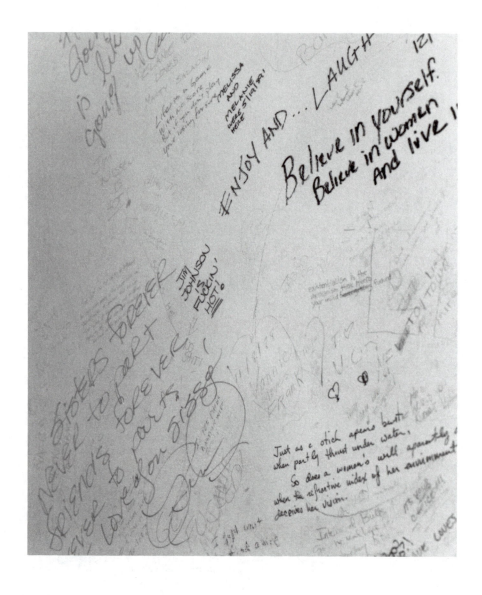

Graffiti, women's restroom, Blueberry Hill
Photograph: Thomas Lanham

12

HERBOLOGY

Jane Bothwell

Jane Bothwell's work with herbs is motivated by a love of plants: "Plants speak a place in me that brings me alive, an ancient place, a re-remembering of the ancient healing ways and of my connection to the earth." According to Bothwell, "separation, more than anything else, creates imbalances within people. We begin to feel that we are separate from our environment, separate from each other." An herbalist in Arcata, California, Jane offers classes and workshops on herbs and works individually with people interested in using herbs as remedies, helping both them and herself "get more in tune with the earth and with the place in which they live."

A teacher and practitioner of herbology, Bothwell regularly offers classes in herbology and conducts a 10-month apprenticeship program, in which participants "dive into the world of plants, doing as much as possible in that amount of time." She also offers herb walks and special one-day workshops on healing through flower essences, women's celebrations, and herbal holidays. Much of her work involves consulting with people seeking advice about herbs and various herbal remedies: "I found a lot of what I was doing when people came to me for herbal formulas was being a counselor. Listening, and talking, working with them, . . . allowing them to come up with what actions they needed to take, or what conflicts they needed to resolve. This feels a lot better to me than feeling like I have the responsibility to give direct guidance."[1] She uses hypnotherapy as well as herbs and flower essences to help people take care of themselves.

---

[1] Crawdad Nelson and Beth Bosk, "Stalking Herbal Remedies: Jane Bothwell," *The New Settler*, 34 (September/October 1988), 9.

Jane's philosophy is reflected in how she collects, dries, and uses plants. She tries to gather as much of the plants she uses personally and uses the search for a particular plant as a ritual or ceremony because "that's when the healing begins." [2] She believes "the energy that's created when you're harvesting a plant has a lot more to do with how that plant is going to work." [3] She prefers wild-crafted herbs—herbs grown in their native environment—and is careful, in harvesting, to "tune into how vital that plant is, how much life force it contains, and at what stage in its growth process it is—as well as, of course, asking if it is appropriate if you take from this patch." [4] She does not pick the leaves of plants when they are still tiny in the spring, for instance: "You wait a while, and they get to what I term 'the teen-age' stage, which is where there is optimum vitality and life to the plant. They are just vibrating with full body and full element. . . . I look for plants that seem to be healthy. The ones that speak to me of being the ones willing to give up their life for our medicine." [5] She also tries to find either "the Grandmother or the Grandfather plant and goes to that plant to ask if it is appropriate to harvest the children." [6] Bothwell used to try to harvest all of the plants using only her hands, but she "realized most plants really appreciate a sharp, clean cut." [7] She now uses a garden shears or knife for blossoms and leaves that don't come off easily with her fingers.

Jane believes that "generally, you have the plant around you that you need. The more I study plants, the more I begin to acknowledge that what you need generally grows right outside your door." [8] She tells the story of going over to her neighbor's house and noticing that she had feverfew growing everywhere. When she told her neighbor it was excellent for migraine headaches, the woman exclaimed, "I can't believe it! I get headaches all the time." [9] Bothwell believes that "herbs are very wise. They know what kind of environment is ideal for both their constitution and contribution, and that they will choose those sites." [10]

Jane's interest in plants and herbs did not develop until she was an adult. While she says this interest "was probably way back in my blood—it's in all our blood"—her parents did not cultivate her interest in natural healing: "My parents were the frozen-vegetable types, and we didn't go camping, although my family spent summers at the ocean so there was an interest in the outdoors."

[2] Nelson and Bosk, p. 7.
[3] Nelson and Bosk, p. 7.
[4] Nelson and Bosk, p. 9.
[5] Nelson and Bosk, p. 14.
[6] Nelson and Bosk, p. 14.
[7] Nelson and Bosk, p. 9.
[8] Nelson and Bosk, p. 14.
[9] Nelson and Bosk, p. 14.
[10] Nelson and Bosk, p. 15.

Bothwell always had enjoyed growing house plants and felt "a real communion going on between a plant and myself." She also started vegetable gardening and took her first backpacking trip when in her early twenties — "and I started opening up to nature and to plants."[11] She then became interested in vegetarianism, meditation, and yoga.

Jane became interested specifically in studying the medicinal values of plants when "I took an herbal remedy for a cold and it worked." Her colds typically took a week to run their course, but friends who ran a health-food store told her she could get rid of it more quickly by taking capsules containing garlic. As a consequence of this experience, Jane began a correspondence course from Dominion Herbal College in Canada. Realizing that she learns best by "touching and seeing and doing," she went on to attend the California School of Herbal Studies in Forestville, California. She had planned to take an eight-week course, but she stayed at the school for eight years — taking classes, serving as an apprentice to other teachers, and finally teaching classes herself. Bothwell moved to Humboldt County, California, because "I felt like it was time to move on from the womb of school and wanted to live in a less populated, greener area." She also knew the owners of Moonrise Herbs, a shop in Arcata, that sells herbs, teas, potpourris, and new-age books and tapes; her office now is located in the same building as Moonrise Herbs.

Jane does not believe herbs are the only means for healing or staying healthy; it is one way, she believes, to connect to the planet and to other living creatures and "by bridging that gap, we can begin to feel more whole." She encourages those who have not made use of plants and herbs to start simply: "as simply as picking rose petals and making a simple tea; as simply as picking a peppermint leaf and pouring hot water over it and letting it steep; . . . making some solar teas (putting some blossoms in water and letting them sit out in the sun); eating a few pansies — gathering and processing in these simple ways and feeling what that can do for your being."[12]

The brochure Bothwell uses to advertise classes, workshops, and special events is included below. It suggests the diversity of her work as an herbalist.

[11] Nelson and Bosk, p. 5.
[12] Nelson and Bosk, p. 16.

Nature's Healers
Summer
Early Autumn
1990

Photo:
Kathleen T. Carr

Herbal Classes
with
Jane Bothwell

Her office is adjoining Moonrise Herbs,
1068 I Street, Arcata, CA 95521
(707) 822-0506

Welcome...

...to the world of herbs. A magical world, a healing path, a way to touch into our roots.

Plant medicines have always been and will always be. They are happy to nourish our bodies, feed our spirits.

Come join us as we explore the ancient wisdom of the plants and each other, our interrelatedness and our journey for a more peaceful path.

Jane Bothwell is a practicing herbalist, Alchemical Hypnotherapist and Bach and California Flower Essence Practitioner. She speaks strongly from the heart with over a decade of herbal experience.

10 Month Herbal Studies Program

February–November 1991

This course is designed for those students who desire a more in-depth experience with herbs. We'll meet the second weekend of every month, February through November, beginning with the first winter wildflowers and progressing with the deep roots of autumn. Each weekend we'll explore different aspects and applications of herbology.

Classes will focus on plant identification and uses, medicine making, wild foods, herbal first aid, flower essences, herb gardening and generally delving into the magical world of plants. Song, ceremony and celebration will be very much a part of our days.

Classes will be taught by Jane as well as occasional visits from other well-known herbalists.

Field trips include canoeing and camping at Stone Lagoon, a visit from Ed and Sara Smith of Herb Pharm, hiking at Fern Canyon and more!

Tuition for the entire program is $888

Upcoming Special Events

Special Guests Jeannine Parvati Baker and Rico Baker will include Arcata in their Autumn tour. We are blessed to have time with these gifted and inspirational teachers. Mark your calendars now for these special events. More details will be announced on an upcoming flyer.

Full Moon Ritual *with Jeannine*
October 4, Thursday night, (Harvest Moon)

Shamanic Womancraft *with Jeannine*
October 5, Friday night

(Men's Circle)
Finding and Freeing the Millenial Man *with Rico*
October 6, Saturday afternoon

Shamanic Midwifery *with Jeannine*
October 7, Sunday

Jeannine is the author of Hygeia: a Woman's Herbal and Prenatal Yoga and Natural Birth. Together, Jeannine and Rico are authors of Conscious Conception: Elemental Journey through the Labyrinth of Sexuality.

Personalized Herb Walks

At your location. Learn to identify the plants in your own backyard and neighborhood.
Tuition:
$40 for 1-1/2 hours
up to 5 people
$10 per person
over 5.

Beginning Herbology

October 11 – December 6
Thursday Evenings, 7–9 p.m.
Field Days: Oct. 27 & Nov. 17, Saturdays

An excellent introduction to the world of healing plants for the beginner and those with more experience, as well. Included will be field identification, herbal first aid, demonstration and use of medicinal preparations, formula making and more, with lotsof "hands on" activities.
Tuition: $135.00
includes samples
Location: 1068 I Street, Arcata

Herbs and Message

A Healing Day for Women
Saturday, August 4
10:30 a.m. – 4:30 p.m.

Pamper yourself with a soothng, nurturing day of herbs and massage. Relax with an herbal facial and massage, foot bath and foot reflexology treatment. We will also be preparing and using exotic herbal oils and teas to nourish and heal our skin. This class will be co-taught with Barbara Browning, professional masseuse for the past ten years.
Tuition: $30 includes samples.
Location: 6791 Greenwood Hts. Dr., Kneeland

Printed on 100% recycled paper. PLEASE RECYCLE

13

HOLIDAY GREETINGS

Audrey Nelson-Schneider

In November of every year, Audrey Nelson-Schneider receives phone calls from friends who ask: "What have you planned for your Christmas photograph this year?" They are referring to the holiday greetings Nelson-Schneider sends out each Christmas to approximately 125 friends and relatives. The format of the greetings remains the same: A handwritten, oversized letter, often as large as one by two feet, printed in red or green ink, in which Audrey tells the news of her family. But what the callers are most interested in is the color photograph of the family that she fastens with a paper clip to the letter. It is a photograph of Nelson-Schneider, her husband, and their daughter and son, always dressed in unusual, matching attire. One year, the family was featured in formal wear; in another, in hats; and in yet another, in cowboy outfits. "I never tell my friends what this year's picture is," says Audrey. "They have to wait until it arrives."

Nelson-Schneider, a communication consultant in business for herself in Boulder, Colorado, began to send a holiday letter when her children were born. As a working mother, Audrey found she simply did not have time to write or call friends and relatives as frequently as she had been able to do before. Her husband's large extended family, in particular, wanted to know what the family was doing, and Nelson-Schneider developed the newsletter as a way to provide an "annual fix" of information for friends and relatives.

For Audrey, the holiday letter is an extension of the journal she keeps on each of her children, a practice she began before her daughter was born. Bedridden for a month when she went into premature labor, Nelson-Schneider began writing to her unborn daughter. She now writes in the journal three or four times a year, and the letter at Christmas is a way of sharing some of her observations about her children with others. She also is proud of her children and sees her letters as a "way to show them off."

As Audrey thought about how to provide information about the family to others, she felt a letter alone was not enough. "I'm more of a visual person," explains Nelson-Schneider; "I want an image." The photograph of the family that accompanies the letter grew from this desire. It also serves as an efficient means for Audrey to be creative. She wants her holiday greetings to be unusual but doesn't have the time to spend creating a totally new format each year; she simply plans a photograph with an unusual theme and is confident that her greetings will be unique.

Nelson-Schneider is guided by several principles as she writes her letter each year and develops the theme of the accompanying photograph. She talks more about the children in the letter than about herself or her husband. In fact, she estimates that 85 percent of each letter is about the children, and only two or three sentences are about the adults in the family. The reason, explains Audrey, is that "so much more is happening with them than with us. Significant things happen in children's lives simply because of the developmental process. In contrast, I'm still doing consulting, which I've been doing for several years. Not much is new there." Nelson-Schneider elaborates: "Plus, it feels too self-centered and self-conscious to write about myself."

In addition, Audrey's holiday greetings are guided by her intent to communicate something about who she is. "I believe in a lot of activity and doing a lot of things," says Nelson-Schneider, "and the letter and photograph, I hope, suggest that—not only in the activities I document in the letter but in the extra effort shown in my choice of a format for the greetings." Audrey also hopes that the form of the greetings reflects how organized she has to be as a working mother: to prepare these kinds of greetings takes thought and planning. Nelson-Schneider enjoys being different, approaches her work and life with an appreciation for originality, and has a confidence in her own unique style. All of these qualities are expressed in the holiday greetings she sends.

Nelson-Schneider's intent in the photographs she sends is to capture her family in a fun and unusual way. She has all sorts of ideas for future photographs; the family might wear tights, angel wings, or bathing suits in front of fake snow. Her selection of the theme for the photograph is tempered, however, by Audrey's awareness of the audience for her holiday greetings. Some family members do not appreciate themes "that are too outrageous," so Nelson-Schneider takes their attitudes into account in her selection of themes.

Audrey is aware of the negative reaction many people have to Christmas letters and addresses such negative responses by trying to personalize hers as much as possible. She uses oversized paper; handwrites the letter, "even though my handwriting isn't the best"; and has the letter printed in red or green ink. She also tries to personalize the letter by including not just facts about the children's activities but everyday "tidbits and anecdotes" about them. "In one letter, for example," explains Nelson-Schneider, "I told about how Armand [her son] hid from me when I went to put him down for a nap. That's not an earth-shattering event, but it gives an idea of the texture of our lives in ways that a recounting of special events and activities doesn't."

Audrey's friends and family have responded well to her greetings — particularly the photographs. Many of her friends collect the pictures of the family because they are unusual, and her pediatrician has the photographs displayed on an office wall. Some of her friends have been inspired by Nelson-Schneider's greetings to do similar letters and photographs. One friend, for example, had a Christmas photograph taken of her family all wearing hats, a theme borrowed from a Nelson-Schneider photograph. "Of course," admits Audrey, "now I've created an expectation that I must live up to each year."

The holiday greetings are important not only to Nelson-Schneider's family and friends. The design and taking of the photograph constitute a ritual for the Nelson-Schneider family. "I'm a firm believer in family rituals," asserts Audrey. "For example, we go as a family twice a year to Glenwood Springs [a resort in Colorado]. The Christmas photograph has become another such family ritual for us." Talking throughout the year about the photograph to come is part of the ritual, and as the children grow older, they offer more and more input. Securing the clothing or accessories necessary is the next step. Then the photograph is taken — usually in September or October — an event everyone enjoys. After the holiday greetings are sent out for the year, the photograph is framed and hung on the wall by the staircase in the Nelson-Schneider home.

Following are two of Audrey's holiday letters — one from 1985 and one from 1988 — and four of her holiday photographs. Included in the photographs are Audrey; her husband, Adam Nelson Schneider; their daughter, Alexandra Nelson Schneider; and their son, Armand Nelson Schneider. In the photograph for 1984, Audrey and her husband are dressed completely in white, and Alexandra is in red; this photograph was taken before the birth of Armand. The photograph for 1985 features the family of three in formal attire. In the 1986 photograph, the family members all wear hats, and the 1988 photograph shows the family in black turtlenecks.

December 1985

Dear family and friends,

It has been another eventful year. Alexandra is three now and began pre-school. It is a Montessori school called Jarrow. She is thrilled with it—often in the car she will sing, "Here we go to Jarrow." Her favorite activities include drawing and singing songs ("I am a little apple tree" ranks one of her favorites). We also began dance—she is something else in her tap shoes. Adam and I have a sentimental connection with her dance lessons—our first date was attending a dance recital at "Debbie's Dance," which is where Alex is taking her lessons. As a matter of fact, she will be in the same recital in spring of 86!

Alexandra also took her first plane ride in our plane (which we have had for 5 years). Once in the air, the engine failed. Adam managed to put the plane down safely. For a few weeks that followed, she would say, "Is everyone OK?" (Adam's first words to her after they landed).

Adam is still loving his flying and doing lots of it. My consulting-training is doing very well. I have a seminar in Honolulu the first of December so we all are going—one week to Maui.

We look forward to the New Year—we will start our addition on our house. We wish you all a peaceful holiday. Peace to you and a wish for *world* peace. From us to you—the very happiest holiday!

Alex   Adam   Dee Dee

December 1988

Dear family and friends,

Adam has just emerged from his shop and he has crafted a wooden star
for the top of our "live" Christmas tree (we planted it our 1st year in the house).
And Alexandra and I attended a performance of the "Nutcracker." Now I *feel*
in the Christmas spirit.

Alex turned 6 this year and she is in kindergarten. Her school is two blocks
away. I really enjoy that morning ritual of walking her to school. She and I
had a 6 day Sierra Club backpack trip planned (in the Texas Hills) but the
day before she came down with the *chicken pox*! Oh well! We did take a pottery
class together this summer.

Armand is almost 2 1/2. This fall he began a morning pre-school program.
We have named him "wild thing." And what a character—he really knows
how to use those *big brown* eyes—he is so animated.

Adam is flying a Dash 7 (50 passenger aircraft). His routes are still in the
West.

I had a pleasant surprise! I was named "Business Woman of the year" by
our local chapter of Business and Professional Women.

We are all taking cross country ski lessons this winter (Alex too!) Armand
will ride on Adam's back. Wish us luck! Love to you all!

Dee Dee

Nelson-Schneider family photograph, 1984
Photograph: Jan Oswald

Nelson-Schneider family photograph, 1985
Photograph: Jan Oswald

Nelson-Schneider family photograph, 1986
Photograph: Jan Oswald

Nelson-Schneider family photograph, 1988
Photograph: Jan Oswald

14

INTERIOR DESIGN

Jeannette Reinholtsen

Jeannette Reinholtsen, an interior designer, recalls a favorite aunt who influenced her own sense of design. "Not afraid to break the rules," her aunt had a natural talent for making a room come together. She could combine patterns and stripes or the old and the new in ways that today would be called eclectic. Reinholtsen remembers her aunt combining parts of three different lamps, for example, to obtain just the look she wanted. This does not mean that any kinds of patterns and combinations can be put together, explains Jeannette; "it has to be done by a trained eye." But her aunt inspired Reinholtsen's own sense of creativity by introducing her to the range of possibilities in design and to using objects for functions other than those intended.

Jeannette, an interior designer in Eureka, California, was interested in art in high school, but she didn't want to be a "starving artist." She applied for a work-experience program through her high school and was assigned a job with a local florist, which gave her first-hand exposure to principles of artistic design. Reinholtsen kept the job while completing an associate's degree, taking as many art classes as possible.

Jeannette's decision to move into interior design came from a desire to apply to home environments the principles of arrangement she had learned in florist shops. She took classes in interior design at American River College in Sacramento, which offered a certificate of achievement in design. Her art background helped her considerably in her classes: "I found out I was doing a lot better than many other students because I had my art background, and

149

I seemed to be raising my hand a little bit more than anybody else." An internship with a local designer in Sacramento led to the discovery that design "wasn't as glamorous as you'd think. I got stuck doing a lot of filing and sample work. But being around all those designers—that exposure reinforced how much I wanted to do it."

After completing her certificate, Reinholtsen accepted a position with a Sacramento wallpaper store, a store all the designers frequented because of the attention the owner gave them. Jeannette "had the best of everything" in this position, she felt, because the designers did not know what the others were doing, but Jeannette did. She was able to see what they all were working on, "and I could see what clients liked and what they didn't like and how the designers worked with them." She worked there for three years until she and her husband moved back to Northern California and settled in Eureka. After working for a couple of years in a local furniture store to establish herself, she explains, "I got brave and decided it was time to head out on my own." She has been in business for herself since 1984.

When working with clients, Reinholtsen's most important goal is to help them create a room with which they are comfortable. While the designer she worked with in Sacramento had an obvious style that was identifiable as hers— and that she would incorporate regardless of her clients' preferences—Jeannette wants the rooms she designs to be a collaboration between her sense of style and the lifestyle and tastes of her clients.

When beginning to work with new clients, Reinholtsen asks questions to determine what her clients' initial preferences and needs are. She conducts, essentially, a case study, asking questions about the kind of look the clients want in a room—homey, sophisticated, or showcase, for example. She also looks at the general ambience suggested by their present style and considers the kinds of spaces with which she'll have to work, the furniture present in the house at the time, and what pieces her clients are committed to keeping.

Jeannette also attempts to determine her clients' goals: Are they trying to get away from a "cluttered look"? Do they know they want to update a room but don't have specific ideas on what they want? How will the space be used? What she designs varies, depending on whether clients entertain heavily, for instance, or whether there are children in the house. Reinholtsen also asks very specific questions about whether her clients are allergic to wool, if they have colors they particularly like or dislike, and any other factors of which she needs to be aware. She encourages clients to thumb through magazines that feature household designs, arrangements, and furniture and to show her the kinds of things that appeal to them.

One of the principles of design that Jeannette is "a real stickler about" is that a house should "flow and coordinate as you move from room to room." She often achieves this goal through the use of color; color can pull a house together, even when the furniture is of different styles and periods. She particularly enjoys designing interiors in which she can create an eclectic look, coordinated around certain colors. This approach does not mean, however, that every room is identical. Two colors from living-room chairs might be carried over into a bedroom, for example, where a different color is added for interest. Jeannette uses the metaphor of assembling an outfit to explain her approach to color: "If you put on a blue-and-beige skirt with a beige blouse, you can add a scarf with a touch of another color. Your earrings might have all three colors—and maybe even a fourth." Not only do coordinated colors help unify a house, but they add longevity to furniture use. A living-room chair, for example, might be moved later to the bedroom to change the look without having to buy an entirely different piece—something not possible when each room is done in a single color.

Providing people with comfortable home environments is one of the biggest rewards Jeannette receives from her work. She believes the environment affects our mental states: "I've seen people re-energized by a new look with updated colors. Their attitudes change, they want to spend more time at home, and they want to entertain more." She also enjoys the "process of seeing the package unfold." For her, it is similar to painting on a canvas: "As you go along, you see a room develop more and more. It's a slower process than painting, but it's three dimensional and not so flat." In addition, she enjoys the process of visualizing the project in the beginning and seeing the end result. She often gets up in the middle of the night, when she has no distractions, to consider different options for a room on which she is working: "I visualize the whole room and tear it apart and put it back together again; in my mind, I introduce a new color, add a piece of furniture, or vary the room arrangement."

While Reinholtsen enjoys the freedom that owning her own business offers, she also experiences frustrations. With two young children, she is, at times, frustrated that her house isn't always exactly the showcase some clients might expect. On the other hand, she wants her clients to realize that she does live in her house and that "having things out of place is normal." The interiors pictured in magazines, she reminds clients, are showcases—not places to live— and she wants them to think about how their homes really will be.

Reinholtsen's long-term goal with her interior-design business is to have a small studio, "where I can meet with clients," and not have the distractions of home. She can be distracted by household chores if there's something related to the business she wants to avoid: "There are times when you don't want to do your books, and you run to the laundry basket. Is there any laundry in the basket? Oh, there you are, one sock. I'd better bleach it and darn it and whatever else!" Jeannette also hopes to get back into her art and comments that she has been feeling "an awful urge to paint" lately.

The photographs below of Reinholtsen's work in interior design show two very different styles of homes. The first photograph is of the living room of the home of Mary Hosley and Jim Hosley in Arcata, California. Jeannette was involved with the Hosleys' decorating needs even before the house was built—"the best time to do it" because the house then can be built to suit the furniture. The Hosleys ended up pushing out one dining-room wall, for example, to accommodate a sectional sofa and the dining-room table they had chosen. The Hosleys first had planned on a brown carpet because it's the most common neutral color and is "something to which most people are accustomed." Reinholtsen, however, suggested a gray carpet, a color picked up in the white-washed cabinets in the kitchen.

The living-room sofas were among the first items of furniture chosen, and the rest of the color scheme was developed to pick up the colors in the sofas—a light blush background, peach-pink flowers, and touches of mouse gray, gray blue, and fawn brown. These colors are repeated in the ceiling border, which suggests granite with speckles of brown, peach, and blue. The wall behind the large sofa is painted a dark peach, as is the parallel wall in the dining room; the remaining walls in these two rooms are a lighter tone of the peach color. The overall effect is what Jeannette calls a "soft, contemporary look," achieved through the simplicity of the decor and the muted colors.

The second picture shows a portion of the master bedroom in the Hosley house. Reinholtsen carried the peach colors into this room but in shades that are more intense than in the living room. She intensified the colors here because the room is darker and needed some brightness but also to keep the color scheme from becoming boring. The bedspread was found first; it contains peach, apricot, light and dark green, and blue—similar colors to the living-room sofas. In this room, however, Jeannette added a sea-green—an additional color picked up to add interest. A sea-green wallpaper covers the entire wall behind the bed; this same paper runs 36 inches up the other walls to form a wainscoting and is topped with a decorative chair rail. The paper above the wainscoting is a print is peach, blue, and green. Padded valences on the windows, not visible in the photograph, match the bedspread.

The two remaining photographs are from the house of Michelle McKeegan and Ed Olsgard in Eureka, California, a house done in what Reinholtsen calls an "English cottage country style." When the couple married, McKeegan moved into Olsgard's house and brought her furniture with her, so the couple had a variety of styles and types of furniture to be incorporated into the home. They wanted a warm, comfortable look that still had some interest and class.

The project began when her clients found a fabric they liked for the sofa; it has a background of royal blue, with peach and green the dominant colors in the flowers. They then chose new carpet—a champagne color—with an interesting texture that produces a "nice glow" when the sun comes into the room. The walls are a neutral shade, similar to the carpet. McKeegan has several Oriental pieces she wanted to include in the room, so Jeannette incorporated touches of red to highlight them. The vase in the photograph above the flowered sofa, for example, is red, and there is red in an Oriental carpet in another part of the living room. According to Reinholtsen, the red "gives the room the punch it needs" to create an adult version of an English country house—"not overly cutsey and sweet."

The second picture of the McKeegan and Olsgard home shows a corner of the master bedroom. To begin, Reinholtsen suggested vaulting the flat ceiling, which her clients were willing to do. The ceiling was done in a whitewashed pine to match the color of the furniture in the room. The fabric on the wicker chair matches the bedspread: it is a sweet-pea green with accents of peach and rust. The design in the fabric is suggested in a design painted on the armoire. The wallpaper has a peach background with a small, white, fleur-de-lis pattern, and the balloon valences match the dust ruffle on the bed.

Jeannette Reinholtsen, living room designed for home of Mary Hosley and Jim Hosley
Photograph: Diana Schoenfeld

Jeannette Reinholtsen, bedroom designed for home of Mary Hosley and Jim Hosley
Photograph: Diana Schoenfeld

Jeannette Reinholtsen, living room designed for home of Michelle McKeegan and Ed Olsgard
Photograph: Diana Schoenfeld

Jeannette Reinholtsen, bedroom designed for home of Michelle McKeegan and Ed Olsgard
Photograph: Diana Schoenfeld

15

JEWELRY DESIGN

Holly Hosterman

"Holly Yashi" is a label familiar to many women who appreciate unusual jewelry. It belongs to a jewelry design and manufacturing company in Arcata, California, begun in 1981 by Holly Hosterman and Paul Lubitz, whose nickname is Yashi. Hosterman brought her artistic talents to the business, while Lubitz brought his technical expertise as an industrial arts major. The company began in the couple's garage and, when it grew too big for the space, moved to an old creamery building. In 1988, Holly Yashi moved to a new building, designed and built for the company. Approximately 40 employees work in production, and another 14 are employed in marketing across the country. In the spring of 1990, Holly Yashi was represented at a trade show in England, the first time the jewelry was marketed overseas.

Holly always had been interested in jewelry design and had made it the focus of her art major in college: "I've always loved to work with little things and metal." But she did odd jobs for several years and did not seriously pursue jewelry design as a career until she and Paul decided to start a business. As she explains, "I had done some earrings for a craft fair around the time we decided to go into business, so that's how we decided to make jewelry. I wasn't really set on making my living as a jewelry designer or anything like that." When the business began, Hosterman did not have a vision of where it might go: "I just liked what we were doing. And we stayed with it because it was so much fun. It was a challenge, and if we could make money while we were doing it, that was an added bonus." Lubitz, on the other hand, "always had the big picture in mind. We complement each other and keep each other

157

motivated and in line and balanced."

The first Holly Yashi pieces were primitive animals in brass and sterling. The colors for which the jewelry now is known began to be incorporated when Holly and Paul discovered a process of creating color by running electrical voltage through certain metals (they use niobium most often) so that a colored oxide forms on the outside of the metal. By changing the voltage of the electrical current, different colors are created; Hosterman has learned which voltages produce particular colors and thus can control the colors that form. The colors, Holly explains, are what "caught on and made the business go."

When designing jewelry, Hosterman says it first "has to be something that I would like to wear." She also wants the designs to be enduring: "I don't want them to have a certain look that people will get tired of." While she is influenced by fashion trends, she is not "dictated" by them: "I don't follow them in order to come up with new things. I just can feel what's changing or what's happening in our market—which way trends are going. I don't see something that's really hot and think, 'OK, we're going to do this.'" Her choice of colors in her designs is influenced by her appreciation for the tropics: "I really like going to Hawaii, and the colors we use are vibrant, similar to what you'd see in a tropical climate. I like the feeling that those colors suggest— they're lively and bright." An Oriental influence is evident, as well, in Holly's designs, particularly in the designs' simplicity: "I like the simplicity; it's trying to get it down so the design works in the most simple way and still looks elegant." A final consideration in her designs is whether and where a design fits into the Holly Yashi line. Hosterman experiments with many designs that never get produced; "they look too different or are too off on another tangent."

Holly is beginning to design larger and more elaborate earrings than she previously has done. She and Paul are interested to see what kind of response the larger pieces receive. They foresee a time when Hosterman will design one-of-a-kind gallery pieces in addition to catering to the "gift-shop" market to which her regular line appeals.

Balance is important in everything Holly does—from her artistic designs to her home life to her business partnership: "I think that women are always having to balance things in their lives." Married and the mother of a young daughter, Hosterman brings her daughter to work, and her mother and father come to the shop to help care for her. Hosterman realizes that for her to be able to work and care for her daughter simultaneously is unusual: "I get to have her with me most of the time, and a lot of women don't. They have to give her to day care—that would be really hard. I don't think I could do that, at least not until she's a little older." While she currently feels a pull toward the domestic side of her life because her daughter is still very young, she values the possibilities offered by the juggling of domesticity and a career: "I'm definitely pulled toward the domestic side right now. But I have such a big thing going here that it pulls me back into the business. If I didn't have such a commitment or investment into such a big business right now, I might slip more into the domestic side. But I'm feeling another spurt of creativity coming about, and I want to start working more in that respect. So I think it's taking a turn back to getting in balance. I feel really lucky."

Some of Holly's jewelry designs are featured in the following photographs. The first depicts three prototypes for earrings that may or may not become Holly Yashi designs. The second shows a necklace and earrings as they are marketed for retail sale.

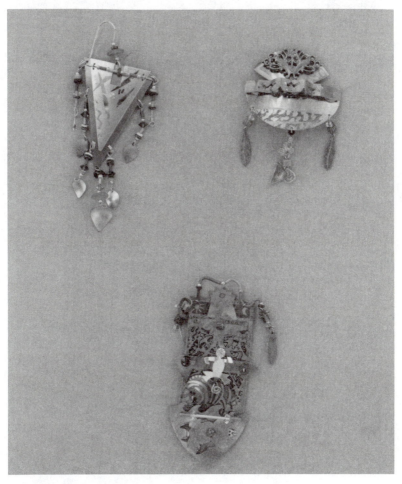

Holly Hosterman, prototypes for earrings
Photograph: Diana Schoenfeld

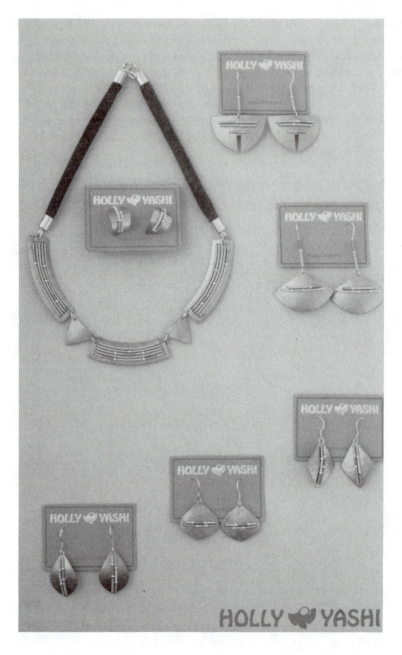

Holly Yashi jewelry
Photograph: Diana Schoenfeld

16

JOURNAL WRITING

Joan Carpenter

"What I write here is nothing more than How It Appears to Me—Nothing more, nothing less. This is not necessarily true or honest or real—but merely—how it all appeared to me. And more important—how it *felt* to me." This excerpt from Joan Carpenter's journals suggests her use of journal writing as a way of helping her record and work through issues in her life. The birth of her journal writing coincided with the birth of her first three grandchildren: "My journals began with a series of letters that I wrote home when my second daughter and my third daughter were pregnant at the same time with their first children. My first daughter had just had a child. . . . I wrote a series of letters of what was going on at the time and years later went back and looked at those letters, and it was such a metaphor for birth—the whole thing—so that's really when my journals began."

Carpenter's journals date back to 1974, but they became increasingly important to her when she started back to college at the time her youngest son (she has six children) entered high school: "A lot of things started happening with me—a lot of change stuff. So I started writing. And it became my salvation. You know, my place that was totally mine." In addition to returning to school, Carpenter went through a divorce, remarried, and moved from Southern California to McKinleyville, California, where she has a private counseling practice. She also teaches classes in journal writing and dream interpretation through the Extended Education Program at Humboldt State University. She uses journal writing extensively in her counseling practice and her teaching and has shared portions of her own journals with clients and students to illustrate various journal-writing techniques. She believes that "the more you write, the more open you become to your own words and the more you're willing to share stuff you wouldn't have shared before."

Joan sees journal writing as serving several important functions in her life, although "why I write in a journal changes — the answer I give today will not be the answer I give six months from now." One of the reasons she keeps a journal is that writing allows her to process the experiences of her life. She sees it as valuable to "write in a journal, but it's even more beneficial to go back and read it" because of the insights and patterns that are revealed. She also has found that writing helps her remember earlier events that she thought she had forgotten: "I couldn't remember a lot of what went on in my childhood, but once you start writing, it all comes back. So it's really like recreating my life." For a time, her journal writing brought up things she didn't want to deal with in her regular journal — she did not want to contaminate it — so "I went out and got another notebook that was a real dark blue, and I took a black marker and made it even blacker. And I said, 'Now, this is my black book.' I started putting things in there — issues I didn't want to deal with — but over the course of years, I've incorporated it into the regular journals." Furthermore, journal writing is an important resource and inspiration for Joan's own writing: "There are a million stories in there, and so if I ever do settle down, sit down and retire, then I do have that resource to work with."

Another reason Carpenter writes is to merge the external God with the Goddess within: "The early journals, back in 1974, were written as letters to God — out there. Then, through time and the journals, I discovered the Goddess inside me. Hopefully, through continuing to journal, the writing will lead to a marriage of the two. Or has it already? I must go back and read and see. Because if it has happened, that's where I will find it — in my diary." Her journals have been a way to explore her evolving understanding of her spiritual self.

One of the most important functions of journal writing for Joan is that it is a way of preserving women's voices: "I feel very strongly that women need to leave a record — that women's voices need to be heard, and we need a history that we haven't had. I know when my mother died, there was just a tremendous amount of anger in me about many things, and I didn't feel like I knew her at all. And I swore at the time that I was going to leave me for my kids to read whether they wanted to or not." As part of the preservation process, Carpenter has begun putting her journals on computer disks: "I like to go back and refer to them, and they get threadbare; they start looking a little sad. So it's much easier to have them on disk. They're easier to read that way."

For women, too, journal writing is a means of translating women's internal lives into the external world. As Joan explains, "Traditionally it has always been men who had more active external lives than women; writing, though, is a way that you can translate your internal to external and it's OK. It's validated." Journal writing also is a form of expression that is "perfectly all right for women." Carpenter sees major differences between the kinds of journals men and women keep and cites herself and her husband as examples: "Before we got married, we went on a bicycle trip around Northern California. We both kept journals and then in the evening, we would exchange journals and read each other's. His journal was so different from mine—he had where we had gone, what we ate, those chronological things, where mine was what was going on inside of me."

Joan has shared her journals in various ways, although she admits that reveaing intimate thoughts and feelings to others is not always easy. She has encouraged her children to read her journals, although they haven't shown much inclination to do so yet, perhaps because they're afraid of what she has written about them or they just "didn't want to get into who I really am." She recognizes that there are parts of her journals—and therefore parts of her—that her children will not like: "That's OK. There are parts of them I don't like!"

The following excerpts are typical of Carpenter's journal entries. She writes about relationships with family members and friends, her writing, her health, the process of personal growth, and reactions to events in her life. While she usually uses a stream-of-consciousness format, she also includes poetry and records dreams in her journal. She does not write in her journals as much as she used to, something with which she has had to come to terms: "There's a time for writing and a time for teaching. I used to think that if I don't write, it's going to be gone. But I know that's not true. I think lives seem to go in ten-year cycles anyway, and journal writing seems to be a ten-year cycle. So I'm very curious to see what's going to happen in this decade!"

Journal Entries

April, 1984

4-3

April snuck in over the weekend when I wasn't looking. I'm not sure I can face this morning without my grapefruit.

Obviously not—since it's 5 hours since I wrote that line, then quit. I feel a mite squeezed out. Shot my wad yesterday, writing "Letters From Colorado" in one sitting. Ejaculated all over the page & emptied myself.

A high wall of 3 tiered frothy breakers today. Like a terraced hill. Planted with alyssum. Another thing that snuck up on me, like April, is that I feel like a writer. No. I feel, I am, a writer. And can't put my finger on when that happened. Has something to do with the last 3 pieces—the poem "Spectacles" & "Elegy to a Friend"—and the story yesterday. And all of a sudden, yes, I believe it. Reaction to "Quid Pro Quo" at the HUG workshop Sunday. My story was a success—it provoked violent controversy. I do not write to entertain, to present a fantasy experience to become lost in—I write to force people to think—to discuss—to touch. The 2 women who the world would label Dykes were violently opposed—said it was antifeminist & pro male—wanted me to change the ending—felt the woman was being rewarded with success for right (male) thinking. Suppose that has something to do with their unfinished business & self concept—but I don't feel like getting into that now. One's interesting comments—about wanting to be a boy, penis envy, & always taking the male role in her relationships, sexual play, & even fantasies. But feels o.k. enough about herself as a woman that she can now even become the female in her fantasies & likened it to making love with herself. And then the anger, from another, even carried over to my "Elegy" poem & she leashed a tirade against turning bodily functions into art. But the feeling I picked up was disappointment, in me. As if I had let her down, someway, in the things I wrote. Did I topple off my pedestal? Yes, there was sorrow in her also.

Just went back & read "Colorado"—& it ain't that good.

Christine [oldest daughter] & I do this ritualistic dance along the sharp blade of a sword. Each one trying desperately not to fall into the jagged edges of broken glass below, & at the same time trying compassionately to keep the other from falling—yet dancing & swaying—parry & spar—all the way. Our phone conversations are a delicate balance—not to fall—not to push. And terminate when things begin to get out of hand. This is one of those times.

Yet I will not push her away or desert her this time. No more. I'll stay — but at a distance that's safe, where I can breathe, until this cycle turns.

4-6

Windy, windy white capped water. Such clarity of colors it pinches the senses & soul. Toy fishing boats bobbling, seen then unseen, plowing thru the green/brown soil. Drawing lines back & forth across my window as they check their crab traps.

For a couple weeks a really odd head, pain & electricity & a real space cadet. Massaging my third eye area all the time. Top of the head shooting warm air out the hole. (I see pieces of 6 boats flopping in & out of the waves. That's alot! Just to put crab & red snapper on my plate. Thanks.) Anyhow, back to the craziness. So sitting in psychic growth class Wed I realize what's happening. The meditation every day, the exercises, are opening up my third eye. Grinding those gears apart so the light that comes in at the top can shine out there. I've heard people say how painful the process is — I immediately would think — well, here we have the lunatic fringe, again — but I submit — I'm a believer. Also felt I should ground myself more at this time so I don't go too far out. Like a kite that breaks its string in the wind & lands on some foreign sand. Also, saw a really live green & yellow aura around Mary's [one of the class members] head there.

Right now I feel sorta drained. Closed. Nothing flowing.

Yesterday Judith [writing instructor] laughing at the graffiti on the CPR poster at HSU. Among other things, someone had drawn a penis on the model. I thought that was younger school stuff. Remember in grammar school drawing dirty pictures on the dirt with a stick. I drew parentheses with a slash down the middle. I do remember that. Don't ever recall drawing a penis, tho. Guess even then I was more interested in what's happening in Here rather than Out There. Turned in "Letters" to be discussed next week. We shall see. Grateful to J [class member] for turning in a racy story — gives me permission to turn in "Quid Pro Quo." One woman said she didn't want to write for *Playboy*, but wanted to write children's stories & wondered if she was in the wrong class. Judith handled it very well, said she would have to make that decision herself. I for one care nothing for critiquing children's lit. Waste of time for me — as she probably feels critiquing our soft porn is a waste of hers.

I feel like time is excitingly fleeting. Always as if something, some great & glorious secret is just around the corner & I'm rushing toward it — or as if something excitingly different will come in the mail today — always that sense of ecstatic anticipation. Then all of a sudden I realize what I'm rushing toward is death & I think what in the hell am I doing & dig in my heels & put on the brakes & skid to a stop.

Had it with the poetry class Monday nite. Left in the middle & won't go back. Cannot any more abide the male linear approach to teaching. "They" will no longer own my time.

Sam [brother] called Monday nite about the wedding. I was gone to class. Sounds like I'm supposed to play some sort of role as his only female relative. Can't wear the black Mexican dress I intended. Wedding colors are pink & violet & white. Of course. So once more I'm asked to be what I should instead of what I am. Shit. I'm gonna shave my legs for the damn wedding, what more can he ask? First time in 2 1/2 years. Now *that's* a sacrifice. Maybe I'll go ahead then & get the snake tattooed on my ankle. But not till I get back, tho. I do have some nice girl left inside me.

Notes from the poetry class of 4-2 thru CR [College of the Redwoods] at Arcata High.

subjective: from your own point of view. objective: the way things are. according to the instructor—Can you spit it out, regurgitate it for a spot quiz? You better. This is a class—not a workshop.

metaphysics is an attempt to find the spiritual realm, basis, of things. it means transcendental, to rise above. We (no, not we, the males of this class) are attempting to "f the ineffable." Poetry is a hi realm of writing, the man says. Hi there. We must find the realm of the reasons for what we are studying, Mustn't we men. Our handout by Emerson is full of the male pronoun, for men & about men. And here I am again, out of order. How do you get there, he asks? How do you transcend? Inspiration the man says. Dictionary definition is stimulation of the faculties to a high level of feeling or activity. An agency such as a person or work of art that moves the intellectual. Inside, Inside, I scream. breathe in in spire. Divine guidance that acts directly on the mind & soul of *man* is the religious definition. Great Goddess help!!

As a poet I feel alienated from this group. I cannot fit into a class that speaks *only* by & for mankind. Anarchy is the next word we must define. The man says it means individualism. The boss man doesn't like that. No rules. No system. Non acceptance of roles & systems. The women in this class, including me, do not speak.

Women's poetry is a revolt from being subject to the rule of the object. Is this why so many women are anarchists? We create our own meaning for our own words. And back to metaphor as woman's language, voice, words. He speaks of the birth of modern poetry & says where there is a birth there is a clash, this is *not* a woman's definition of birth. He says the next word we have to know is voice—& I've already gotten there. Me. Personal. What is my song & how I sing it. My individuality. Words in my own style, he says. (Lordy lord I sure wish he would quit yelling at us. Did the guys who came in and sat in the back of the room know something I didn't?) He tied it all in to collective unconscious & Woody Guthrie's remark that we don't write

a poem we run into it. Ooops, tripped on the collective uncon. Poets are seeding
a true reality. He speaks of rhythm & cycles & oceans & waves & is not, I
don't believe, really understanding what he's saying, but we know, we the women
know. Why don't women talk in class? Because they don't have to. They already
know. Why shout it out?

4-9

It's all those "befores" that get to me. Before I can sit down & read & write
I have to put a load of clothes in the washer to wash while I'm sitting. But
before I do that I have to collect the towels from the bathroom. And before
I do that I have to scour the sink so I can use the used towels for that. And
many times, before I can wash, I have to run to the store for forgotten soap.
There has been so much before in my life there is no wonder that there's not
been a large supply of after.

I wonder again why write when there are so many good books out there
that say it all in such a marvelous way. When I've finished one & am ready
to start a new, it's as tho I'm beginning an exciting adventure. Curiosity.
Breathless anticipation. So I picked up *The Four Gated City* just now. And
already she touches & I say "Yeah." "Living in a small town anywhere means
preserving one's self behind a mask" and speaks of the anonymous freedom
of going to a new place. My blessed joy those first weeks up here—& some
of it remains. To be able to go & do what I please—& no one cares. I don't
have to live up to or for anyone. There is nothing one *has* to do. Is that why
Joe [youngest son] went to LA? And stays? Remaining out of contact? And
it's not just to get away from the *bad* you've done—but also the good. To not
have to live up to a reputation—a name you've made. They are all masks—
each identity—as multiple personalities (not taken to the limit of pathology, tho.)

Speaking of a road, Lessing says "no trees—& therefore no roots." That's
what's happened in Ventura County. Road building. They've pulled up the
trees—paved it over. Made roots impossible. So no one there has them anymore.
People up here have an abundance—& logging is handed down from father
to son to grandson. Generations of roots in these trees up here. And alienation
down south. Roots cannot grow thru concrete. And without trees the moisture
in the air isn't dropped. No rain. No nourishment.

Janet [childhood friend] & I used to go to Santa Barbara with her dad. We
were about 11 or 12. Her father was working on a dredge, & they were cleaning
out the harbor, so he was up there all day. We had to leave early, before the
sleep was out of my eyes, so he could get up there in time to start. We curled
under blankets in the back seat & finished our sleep on the way up. Recall
once him opening his door & Jan quickly burying her head under the quilt,
& I, unknowing, not so quickly acting, & ending up with brown spots on my

face. Her father chewed snuff, & had opened the door while driving along
to spit. They both laughed uproariously at my first experience with tobacco
juice. We spent our day at the pool on the beach in Santa Barbara. But of
course, it wasn't open at 8 when we got there. For a few hours there was no
one there but us. It was enchanted. We shared our kingdom with no one. Just
each other. We could play in the wading pool, which wasn't fenced, & had
a large mushroom shaped island you could climb up under & the water dribbled
from a hole in its center. Or we went to the park across the street that had
a clam shell stage where we gave performances, singing our heart & lungs
out to imaginary audiences. Then when the pool opened we went back & swam,
all day. And met boys. And gave out imaginary names and histories. Fantasy
identities. Except we were always slipping up & forgetting & calling each other
Janet & Joan. We went back to the car & ate tuna sandwiches her mother
made. She was an expert at making sandwiches. They tasted like store bought,
uniform, perfect, the expertise that comes from bored experience.

I suppose the reason there's not so much conflict with Gayle [second
daughter]—why I feel so at ease 90% of the time in my relationship with her,
is because she is a person with no expectations. She does not expect me to
be that mother person the rest of them do. Because Gayle has no expectations
of what that mother role means, the duties it holds. She is roleless. Which
is why she does not know how to play the role of sister. Or family member.
Or mother. She never took in all the strings & webs of meaning dangling from
those labels. So I, in turn, can 90% of the time, be roleless with her. Comfy.

I recall my confusion when I left home & went out on my own & Yvonne
[best friend] told me now I would have to get me a basic black dress & my
thinking she did not understand, that that was the life I had run from. Was
that our attraction? Y and I? That we were mirror images. So when we ran,
we ran to where the other already was? I saw her as unorthodoxy and I as
conformity. How did she see the 2 of us?

I suppose that feeling of excitement unknown just around the corner comes
from being in this strange to me place without my roots & roles. Down south
had become predictable. I remember thru the teens I lived with butterflied
stomach. Up until I got married & had kids & then it started to fade—& has
been swept away by the years. That delicious terror that invaded my gut,
frequently for no apparent reason—but was always there for a new date, a
new experience, a dance, a happening—anything, really. But sometimes just
riding along in the car. Or just sitting doing nothing. What I have got is the
essence, but without those fluttering butterfly wings.

When I was younger I could run my hands over my body, my legs, or arms,
or torso, & I'd feel nothing but smooth taut skin. Now I feel lumps & knots
under the skin, and ridges & bones & nothing is smooth & even anymore.
These are indications of so much more substance, so much going on under

the skin that I was never aware of. So much more to this body called me than I ever suspected when I was younger.

4-11

My problem with Lessing is that she is so dark & brooding. Heavy. Pessimistic. English without the necessary wit. Just grinding down coal dust & fog. Her writing says we have fallen from Grace.

So this weekend I'll go to Sam's Jewish wedding. His search for, need for rooted security. The soft lumpy bosom to curl up inside of. I go—even tho Marsh [third daughter] is not because of childhood experiences that are causing her anger, Joanne [fourth daughter] not because of empathy for Marsha & for Chris because of Sam's righteous snub of her, altho Chris doesn't know. (It's neither right nor fair that I did not tell her.) & Chris says she's not going because of time & money. So I'll go for me, to have & enjoy as Joan—no ties, no strings or umbilical cords. As nobody's mother.

Fallen from Grace. Amazing Grace. Grace under pressure. Must write a story about Grace. Amazing Grace has fallen, & lies under the pressure of a male nude body. Becomes pregnant with a daughter (full of Grace) whom she names after herself. She lives in the state of Grace, country of oblivion. Dwelling in the good graces of authority. They all celebrate a Day of Grace. She & her daughter become The Graces.

A character in a story stands out, is remembered because of one deformity, one abnormality in visual appearance, & that abnormality infects, dictates their personality, is the cause of their most minute action. Everything flows from that core source.

Out of the Nowhere: into the Here—or—thru the Years

Just as the dew comes out of the grass
The words are sad glad mad & skedaddle around
I'm not able to uncover myself
Am I trying to remember myself before the world closed in on me?
This intimacy has taken its time
Dynamite must blast away the cavern wall
And I didn't believe him, either
That God is waiting for me
All comes from the same pure matter
Just as the dew comes out of the grass
I come from the brown earth

From the inside out grows the seed
Cell upon cell overlapping & burying
Hiding the deepest parts with gold overlay
Which is real gold & which only plate
Pure crystal center with pebbly overcast
Which will tarnish & what is true
All comes from the same pure matter

I want replacement not displacement
lower the mercantile value & raise the human value
I put a slug in the vending machine dispensing life
Professional power is penetrating pornographically (sexual)
Social servants defend the dependent
Systematization is the death of creation—Thus spaketh Lilly
Luminessence—cold light—no energy is transferred.
Ode to this winter's madness
What are you doing earth?
Just stretching—flexing my muscles
Just telling you that I am still here
You—with all your atomic bombs & nuclear reactors & red
   telephones & itchy trigger fingers—
I am still the boss.

Son of a Deity

Because I am the son
Must I eternally face extermination?
Killed for the father's ambition
So as not to quite reach his height
I did not come to compete with you old man
Nor to sit on your right hand here at the throne
My halo glows
My crown is burning stones
While yours are brilliant gems of heaviness, causing necks to bow
A man has a son so as no longer to be one.

Daughter of a Deity

Listen father, I need to know
Why you've made me illegitimate
By not marrying, nor acknowledging my mother
And she in shame closes up and retreats
I know her now
I know his name
I know mine
I know not hers
So you kill me, abort me, so she will always remain hidden,
   unacknowledged,
Unconscious
But blood will tell
You judge the living and the dead
who is alive and who is dead
Why does a man have a daughter?

To Sam, the Traveling Man, on the Eve of His Wedding

Late born, to a mother who smothered and a father too gentle to
   last
A brother and sister more parental than sibling
Father wanted Arthur, that Noble one of the Welch whose board
   encircles the world
But we turned you into Samuel, the Hebrew 'asked of God,'
Shortened to Good Sam

Flying before your down had become feathers
Confused by your roots, wandering blunderingly thru Turkish baths
   and palaces of Geishas
To settle, sighing, amongst ivy walls
And academic drugs
(Not of the hippie happy wanderer's type.)

Then searching the length of the land in VW bus
Squeezed dry in Orange County
To return to Baghdad by the Bay, spreadeagled
Crown of your treetop in whitewashed halls
One leafy branch reaching out to Tahoe
The other pointing south of the border.

And her to join, as a root seeks toward its water source
Quenching the dying thirst.

Does she know this distressed Presbyterian is descended from the
King of Wise?
And has a sister who burns incense to the goddess in prayerful
entreaty not to be burned once again at the stake?
And has a brother, whose prosperous wall of conformity protects
the soul of the soaring falcon?
And that there is no cure for wanderlust in the immigrant?

4-13

Thru the eye of the hurricane. Seems I get this real spacey far out thing
& sit down & out pop the words. Sorta like the Catholic woman in Monty
Python's *Meaning of Life* who as she stood fixing dinner over the stove plopped
down a baby between her legs & nonchalantly said to her daughter, "Pick
that up for me, will you luv?" And that is what I do, drop these poetic rhetoric
out & let my daughters (& sons) reap the consequences. Happened yesterday
with the poem to Sam. Now all sorts of iffy feelings about if I should give
it to him—but of course I will.

4-18

It's such a joyous relief to get up & know that this is not an exercise day.
That that is one nagging voice that won't keep intruding. That I can just pout
around in my owned body & read & write without have tos.
Bits & pieces too numerous to mention.
R [Richard; husband] was erupting on both ends Thurs nite. In preparation
for his pilgrimage down south this week. Cleansing. Unfinished business with
Paulette [his daughter], his father, a few of his left-behind clients and loves.
His dallying in the motel in San Francisco Monday was indicative. R has trouble
saying goodbye. Prolongs. Hangs on. Or leaves without a goodbye. Is he down
there getting rid of excess baggage, as notches in his belt? Sent him wings
of goddess white this AM.
Thurs. we discussed "Letters" in writing class. No one understood, the least
of all Judith. Felt some discouragement and withdrawal, feeling of doubt in
my ability. Then Friday's seminar helped. L. Crux [seminar leader] & her
talk of the woman's psychic journey. So I wrote an essay yesterday *about* my
story. More explaining. Defining. Naming. My lantern & cross. Always. "Do
you understand?" "Do you hear what I'm saying?" "Do you see what I mean?"
Got out "Quid Pro Quo" to polish up for class and realized just how badly

written it is. But I don't want to mess with it without my typewriter. Easier. Things are stacked up on the typing table.

Sam's poem. Finished it & liked it. Even tho uneasy feelings, decided I really must give it to him, after all, why not? So took it down to his wedding & *really* had hesitation. The poem fits up here & feels o.k. in this environment — but take it down to the city [San Francisco] & it seemed totally inappropriate & out of place. And so did I. The first nite in the motel in the city felt so hemmed in, sides-top-bottom, enclosed in square hunks of concrete so that I could not sleep. Felt panicked. Driving back up Monday was great. As the miles pulled away from the metropolitan area it was like shedding scales of spiked skins along the freeway. Breathing & thinking a feeling expanded. It would be a constant battle between me & me & thee if I had to live there. But aside from that, the weekend was glorious. The dinner. And the ritual & rites of the Jewish wedding. Tactile stimulation. Color & taste & sound. I cried for mom & dad not being there. The son so late in life that they couldn't last for it all. She did for some. He didn't. But altho she lasted — she didn't participate. Didn't taste. She left that to me. It would have been easier, I wouldn't have cried so much, if Sam didn't look so much like Daddy. Oh yes, I miss him & that perpetual scrunched up brow, as if he was trying very hard to peer closer, thru the muck, to understand. One problem with being around Merle & Sam [brothers] is that I too easily fall into the little sister role, which is weird as I'm 18 years older than Sam. Can understand why Joe has to stay away from this family.

And then there's Chris' latest fiasco. Delaying us 45 min. by sending Geoff [grandson] on an errand. And screaming how angry she is at R & I. For accepting the money she owed us. Geez. I don't feel that I owe her anything. But on the contrary, I do feel she owes me. She owes me some typing — & that's all I expect from her. And I'm fervently looking forward to the day that debt is discharged.

Reading *Women Who Marry Houses*. I danced in & out of agoraphobia. Pulling the shades in hysterical panic and standing in the square middle of the kitchen when the neighbor across the street chased Chris home & screamed at me to keep her there [she was biting the neighbor's kid]. Later panic of elevators, confessional, under water, driving the car at nite down the Hwy 1 to get Allen [first husband] after his truck broke down, his making (pressuring) me to stay home from playing cards, then more & more excuses to stay home & not venture out, the life on the farm that made that possible, hiding in the bathroom from people I didn't want to see, all that broken when Allen tried to force it by locking my car in the garage. But it took me 3 days to do it, even when I knew where the key was it still took me 3 days. And the times of not writing were the times of severe agoraphobia — & the writing was/is always an attempt to break thru the block.

So. California is *not* the free & easy anything goes life style its own publicists put out (nor is S. F.). There are too many imperatives. You are *required* to be laid back, or dress for success, or adopt a strict life style (gay). Required to be healthy (body nuts) happy (social whirl) successful & wise. Everyone is grasping & climbing over everyone—a bed of hot & angry & agitated reptiles.

Bargain psychology. Yes, that was/is always part of my marital relationship. I bought nothing unless it was on sale. I attended only rec classes whose cost was minimal rather than the hundred dollar jobies Yvonne went to. I got books from the library rather than bought. And who did he [first husband] give me up for? I was shocked when I heard her discussing that her way of getting bargains was switching price tags on items. I should have realized that kind of dishonesty would have no compulsion in undermining me so she could acquire my husband/home/children/lifestyle.

I tried to make mama fight the battles she *could not fight*, but she was too wise. She left the fight up to me.

It blows my mind that I simply sat & wrote "Colorado Letters" 10 years ago (of *course* that's the title. red letters) without any idea what I was doing or how very much I was saying, how much was in it until I started analyzing. I am amazed at the layers of consciousness & the wisdom that runs in the deeper levels. Symbols.

And I will *still* practice my agoraphobia. I refuse to get out there in the business/professional world where things are unjust & *not* equal. A good example of that was at the block-big Ramada Inn where we stayed this weekend—down in sublime suburbia of Mountain View. It was chock full of suited & briefcased men running around, making deals, checking in & out, attending the myriads of mtgs in multiple meshing rooms—& I saw not one woman. And I know who was inside the gracious lovely old homes that lined all the tree shaded side streets. I'll stay home and write as long as I live in the world not of my making. I make the choice not to be the dancing dog— but I know it's there—& I write of it. Someday out loud. Soon.

I was not raised with boundaries as a child. Wandered all over Hueneme before age 6—all over the farm endlessly—came & went as I pleased—no curfew in hi school. The boundaries came *only after I married*. No wonder I almost perished at the thought of marrying Richard 6 years ago. As a good wife of the 50s, marriage meant restriction & boundaries to me. I had to learn differently. Karma. Had to go back & do it again & try to get it right.

4-22

Think I'll change my name to Joan Condor. I come from Ventura County. I'm a rather ugly old bird, faced with extinction, but with a little help I'm making a comeback. I also feed on carrion—the dead & decaying flesh that writers have cast aside—the words they have finished with. And I do need help matching my own creations—otherwise I'll get in a shouting screaming match with my other (male) half & kick my eggs out of the nest, too soon, to lie shattered & aborted on the rocks below.

I am Joan Condor
I come from Ventura County
I'm a rather ugly old bird
faced with extinction
But with a little help
I'm making a comeback

I feed on carrion
the dead & decaying flesh of writers
I devour cannibalistically words
nourishing my scrawny body

I do need help hatching my own creations
Otherwise I get in a shouting screaming match
With my other half
And kick my eggs out of the nest too soon
To lie aborted and shattered
On rocky pinnacles below.

17

LANGUAGE

Suzette Haden Elgin

Suzette Haden Elgin is the creator of Láadan, a language constructed for the purpose of expressing the perceptions of women. The idea for such a language came to Elgin in 1981, when she was reading Cheris Kramarae's book, *Women and Men Speaking*,[1] and became aware of the feminist hypothesis that existing human languages are inadequate to express the perceptions of women. At the same time, she was reading a series of working papers by Cecil Brown and his colleagues on lexicalization—the assignment of words or parts of words to units of meaning in human languages. In these papers, they suggest that some elements of lexicalization are natural in language. Suzette disagreed: "I kept thinking that women would have done it differently, and that what was being called the 'natural' way to create words seemed to me to be instead the *male* way to create words."[2]

Elgin began to talk about the need for a women's language at meetings, conferences, and with her friends and colleagues, and a common reaction to the idea motivated her to give form to her idea: "People would ask me, 'Well, if existing human languages are inadequate to express women's perceptions, why haven't they ever made one up that is adequate?' And all I could ever

---

[1] Cheris Kramarae, *Women and Men Speaking: Frameworks for Analysis* (Rowley, MA: Newbury, 1981).

[2] Suzette Haden Elgin, *A First Dictionary and Grammar of Láadan*, 2nd ed. (Madison, WI: Society for the Furtherance and Study of Fantasy and Science Fiction, 1988).

say was that I didn't know." [3] She later discovered that St. Hildegarde of Bingen (1098-1179) had constructed a language of 900 words with an alphabet of 23 letters. The language has been lost, and whether St. Hildegarde constructed her language to express perceptions that she felt her own language could not is unknown.

"Somewhere along the way," Suzette explains, "this all fell together for me, and I found myself with a cognitive brew much too fascinating to ignore." [4] She chose to explore the notion of a women's language through the writing of a science-fiction novel about a future America in which a women's language has been constructed and is in use. The book, *Native Tongue*, was published by DAW Books in 1984; its sequel, *The Judas Rose*, appeared in 1987. Elgin currently is working on a third book in the series, which will be called *The Láadan Model*.

In order to write the novels involving a language for women, Suzette felt obligated at least to try to construct the language about which she wrote. As she explains," . . . I am a linguist, and knowing how languages work is supposed to be my home territory. I didn't feel that I could ethically just fake the woman-language, or just insert a handful of hypothetical words and phrases to represent it. I needed at least the basic grammar and a modest vocabulary, and I needed to experience what such a project would be *like*." [5] In 1982, she began the construction of the language that is Láadan. She chose as the name for the language *Láadan*, meaning "language of those who perceive."

Elgin's approach to the construction of her language was to combine features of different existing languages that seemed to her to be valuable and useful, a method specifically chosen for its analogy to the women's craft of patchwork quilting. She drew particularly from American Indian languages, especially the Navajo language. To construct the vocabulary, she created roots and added morphemes to them, guided by linguistic theory on what is universal in human languages. In her formulation of pronunciation of the sounds in the language, Suzette tried for the smallest possible number of distinct sounds consistent with efficient communication and tried to choose sounds generally regarded as easy for non-native speakers.

To emphasize women's perceptions in the language, Elgin used her own experiences of "I wish I had a word for that" and similar items she encountered in reading or listening to women. Translating the very masculine King James Bible into the language also made clear gaps between women's experiences and traditional languages that she tried to correct in the new language. One of her primary goals was the lexicalization of body language, including intonation of voice, to save women work.

[3] Elgin, p. 5.
[4] Elgin, p. 4.
[5] Elgin, pp. 4-5.

Suzette brought to her construction of Láadan expertise in linguistics and languages. She earned a B.A. in French and master's and doctorate degrees in linguistics. Her teaching and research areas include the syntax of Navajo, transformational grammar, application of linguistics to cross-cultural communication, the relationship between linguistics and medicine and linguistics and other contemporary issues, and verbal self-defense. Her experiences as a woman, of course, also contributed to the construction of Láadan; she is the mother of five and the grandmother of six children.

Elgin is the founder, in 1981, of the Ozark Center for Language Studies, located at her home in Huntsville, Arkansas, a resource center on linguistics. She presents workshops, audio tapes, and videotapes on linguistics; provides tutoring on request for local students; provides consultation in linguistics and language-related problems; and maintains a library of sources on linguistics. Among the services she provides is a bimonthly newsletter in linguistics and language studies, *The Lonesome Node*, which covers six research areas: women and language, religious language, language in health care, Ozark language, verbal self-defense, and language and the brain.

Among the ways in which Láadan differs from English (and many other languages) is in its inclusion of language forms and markers that communicate information women regard as important. The language contains, for example, a number of different forms for the names of emotions, rather than a single word. Different words in Láadan for *love*, for example, include *áayáa*, mysterious love, not yet known to be welcome or unwelcome; *áazh*, love for one sexually desired at one time but not now; *ad*, love for one respected but not liked; *am*, love for one related by blood; *ashon*, love for one not related by blood but kin of the heart; *azh*, love for one sexually desired now; *oham*, love for that which is holy; and *sham*, love for a child of one's body. Suzette separated out different dimensions of emotions and gave them individual labels because "women constantly chafe at the inaccuracy of just saying they 'love' someone or something; it's too vague, too broad."

Láadan also includes a Beneficiary marker that is added to a word to indicate for whom or on whose behalf something is done. It can assume one of four forms: *dá*, against one's will when forced or coerced; *daá*, accidentally; and *dáa*, not because of force or coercion but because of an obligation of law or duty that one accepts. In any other situation, *da* is used. The Beneficiary marker is consistent with women's experiences in that women spend their lives doing "for" others; Elgin feels they need a way to indicate why.

The Láadan possessive also is different from the possessive in English; it varies according to the sort of ownership involved. Making such distinctions, Suzette believes, tends to be important for women because women (and children) so often are treated as property, as in *my wife, my child*, and *you're mine*. Such use of the possessive, suggests Elgin, should be distinct from the ownership indicated in phrases such as *my arm* or *my car*. If ownership is because of birth, as with *my arm* or *my mother*, the ending *tha* is used. If it is for no known reason—a task that someone ended up with somehow, inexplicably—the proper ending is *the*. If possession is by luck or chance, the ending is *thi*. If phony ownership is involved, marked in English by *of* but really involving no possession, as in *a collection of books*, the proper ending is *thu*. In any other situation, the ending *tho* is used; this same ending is used if the speaker is not certain of the reason for the ownership but is sure there is a legitimate one.

A few samples of the vocabulary of Láadan suggest its focus on women's experiences and perspectives. Some words feature women's physiological processes and various attitudes toward them: *elasháana* means to menstruate for the first time, *husháana* is to menstruate painfully, *sháana* is to menstruate joyfully, *lewidan* is to be pregnant for the first time, *lalewida* is to be pregnant joyfully, and *zháadin* is to menopause. Other words describe women's common experiences, many of which have not been named in English or other languages. *Radíidin*, for example, is the term for non-holiday, a time allegedly a holiday but actually so much a burden because of work and preparations that it is a dreaded occasion, especially when there are too many guests and none of them helps. *Rashida* is a non-game, a cruel "playing" that is a game only for the dominant "player," who has the power to force others to participate. *Wonewith* is someone who is socially dyslexic, uncomprehending of the social signals of others. *Ralorolo* is non-thunder, much talk and commotion from those who have no real knowledge of what they are talking about or trying to do, something like "hot air" but more so. The selections that follow are from *A First Dictionary and Grammar of Láadan*, published in 1988 by the Society for the Furtherance and Study of Fantasy and Science Fiction. Included are sections dealing with the pronunciation of Láadan; a portion of the vocabulary of Láadan, both from English to Láadan and Láadan to English; and a sample of Láadan in use in the Lord's Prayer.

The Sounds
of Láadan

Láadan was constructed to be simple to pronounce. This description is tailored for speakers of English, because the material is written in English; but the sound system has been designed to present as few difficulties as possible, no matter what the native language of the learner.

Vowels: a   as in "calm"
             e   as in "bell"
             i   as in "bit"
             o   as in "home"
             u   as in "dune"

Consonants: **b, d, sh, m, n, l, r, w, y, h** — as in English

             th   as in "think"
             zh   as in "pleasure"

There is one more consonant in Láadan; it is "*lh*" and it has no English equivalent. If you put the tip of your tongue firmly against the roof of your mouth at the point where it begins to arch upward, draw the corners of your lips back as you would for an exaggerated smile, and try to say English "sh", the result should be an adequate "*lh* ". It is a sound with a hissing quality, and is not especially pleasant to hear. In Láadan it occurs only in words that are themselves references to something unpleasant, and can be added to words to give them a negative meaning. This is patterned after a similar feature of Navajo, and is something so very handy that I have always wished it existed in English

When a Láadan vowel is written with an accent mark above it, it is a vowel with high tone. English doesn't have any tones, but that will be no problem for you, since you can express it as heavy stress. Think of the way that you distinguish the noun "convert" from the verb "convert" by stressing one of the two syllables. If you pronounce a high-toned Láadan vowel as you would pronounce a strongly-stressed English syllable, you will achieve the same effect as high tone. Because Láadan does not use English stress, this will not be a source of confusion.

English to Láadan
Dictionary

a/the-final-one	nonede
to be **able**	thad
above	rayil
absence-of-pain	shol
to be **accursed**, unholy	rahéeda
across	mesh
after	ihée
afternoon	udathihée
against	ib
agriculture	eróo
air	shum
airplane	zhazh
airport	hozhazh
ale	wéebe
to be **alien**	née
an **alien**	née; an alien (noun)=néehá
to be **alive**	wíi

to be **alone**	sholan
all, every	woho
all-power	hohathad (like "omnipotence", but without the feature MALE)
all things, all-that-is	abesh
although	íizha
always	hadiha
to be **amazed**	míi
ambulance	duthamazh
Amen	Othe
analysis	yan
anarchy	ralod
and	i
and-then	id
anesthesia	duthawish
angel	noline; angel-science=enoline
anger[1]	bara; bala; bama; bana; bina
animal, domestic	shamid
animal, wild	romid
anorexia	rayide
ape	omamid
APOLOGY	hoda=pardon me; hóoda=excuse me
apple	doyu
apricot	thuyu
April	Athil
argument, quarrel	rashon (not used of an "argument" in a theory or an equation or proposition)
Arkansas	Arahanesha (a loanword) Aranesha, "pet" name, short form
arm (the body part)	oda
around	o
to **arrive**	nósháad
to **ask**	mime
asteroid	thamehaledal
at last, finally	doól
to **attend**, be present at	ham
attend, pay attention to	hil
aunt	berídan; great-aunt=hoberídan

[1]Many nouns of emotion have a number of forms in Láadan; see Pages 132–133 for an explanation.

Láadan to English
Dictionary

(Based on work done by Karen Robinson; used with permission)

As is true in the translation from any language into another, many words of Láadan cannot be translated into English except by lengthy explanation.

We wish to note that the pejorative element "*lh*" can always be added to a word to give it a negative connotation, so long as it precedes or follows a vowel and does not violate the rules of the Láadan sound system by creating a forbidden cluster. The addition of "*lh*" need not create an actual new word; for example, "*awith*" means "baby"—to use instead "*lhawith*" (or "*awithelh*") means only something like "the darned baby" and is ordinarily a temporary addition. But it is very handy indeed; we are indebted to the Navajo language for this device.

a	love (for inanimates only; to love (inanimates only)
áabe	book
áala	THANK-YOU
áalaá	butterfly

aáláan	wave
áa na	sleep [ina=to sleep]
áa th	door
áa tham	church [áath=door + tham=circle]
áa yáa	mysterious love, not yet known to be welcome or not
áa yo	skirt
áa zh	love for one sexually desired at one time, but not now
ab	love for one liked but not respected
aba	fragrant
ábed	farm
ábedá	farmer [áabed=farm + -á=agent, doer]
abesh	all things, all-that-is
ad	love for one respected but not liked
ada	to laugh
Adaletham	August (berry month) [daletham=berry]
Adol	December (root month) [dol=root]
adoni	to land (as a ship or plane); also a landing [doni=earth]
Ahede	September (grain month) [ede=grain]
áhesh	to be responsible
Ahesh	March (grass month) [hesh=grass]
al	toilet
alehale	to make music
Alel	January (seaweed month) [lel=seaweed]
am	love for one related by blood
Amahina	May (flower month) [mahina=flower]
Ameda	July (vegetable month) [meda=vegetable]
amedara	to dance
an	to know (of people)
ana	food
anadal	meal (lunch, dinner, etc) [ana=food + dal=thing]
anadalá	cook [anadal=meal + -á=suffix for doer]
aril	FUTURE, (time aux) [aril=later]
aril	later
Aril	LEAVETAKING, FAREWELL [aril=later]
aríli	FAR FUTURE (time aux)
ash	star
ásháana	to menstruate joyfully [oshaána=to menstruate]

The Lord's Prayer

Láadan	English
Bíili,	Our Parent,
Thul lenetha Na[1] olimeha.	You are in heaven.
Wil héeda zha Natha.	May Your Name be holy.
Wil nosháad sha Natha lenedi.	May Your Harmony come upon us.
Wil shóo yoth Natha,	May Your will come to pass
Doniha zhe olimeha;	on Earth as in heaven.
Wil ban Na bal lenethoth lenedi	May You give us our bread.
I wil baneban Na lud lenethoth lenedi	May You forgive us our debts
Zhe mebane len ludá lenethoth lenedi	as we forgive our debtors.
I wil un ra Na lelneth erabal hedi	And lead us not ito temptation
Izh wil bóodan Na leneth ramfilade	but deliver us from evil.
Bróo sha, sha Natha	For Harmony, it is Yours,
I hohathad, hohama Natha	Power, it is Yours,
I hohama, hohama Natha	Glory, it is Yours,
Ril i aril i rilrili.	Forevermore.
Othe.	Amen.

Morpheme-By-Morpheme Translation:

Bíili
I SAY TO YOU, IN LOVE:

Thul **lenetha**
PARENT WE(MANY)-OF, BY BIRTH

O **Na** **olimeha**
BE YOU HEAVEN-AT

---

[1]The form "*na*" is a second person pronoun meansing "beloved you/thou"; the capital "*N*" indicates reverence for the deity.

Wil   héeda   zha   Natha
LET-IT-BE   HOLY   NAME   YOU-OF

Wil   nosháad   sha   Natha   lenedi
LET-IT-BE   ARRIVE   HARMONY   YOU-OF   US (MANY)-TO

Wil   shóo   yoth   Natha,
LET-IT-BE   COME-TO-PASS   WILL   YOU-OF

doniha   zhe   olimeha;
EARTH-AT   AS   HEAVEN-AT

Wil   ban   Na   bal   lenethoth   lenedi
LET-IT-BE   GIVE   YOU   BREAD   WE (MANY)-OF-OBJ   WE (MANY)-TO

i   wil   baneban   Na   lud   lenethoth   lenedi
AND   LET-IT-BE   FORGIVE   YOU   DEBT   WE(MANY)-OF-OBJ   WE (MANY)-TO

zhe   mebane   len   ludá   lenethoth   lenedi
AS   PL-FORGIVE   WE (MANY)   DEBTOR   WE (MANY)-OF-OBJ   WE (MANY)-TO

i   wil   un   ra   Na   leneth   erabalhedi
AND   LET-IT-BE   LEAD   NEG   YOU   WE(MANY)-OBJ   TEMPTATION-TO

izh   wil   bóodan   Na   leneth   ramíilade
BUT   LET-IT-BE   RESCUE   YOU   WE (MANY)-OBJ   EVIL-FROM

Bróo
BECAUSE

Sha,   sha   Natha
HARMONY   HARMONY   YOU-OF

i   hohathad,   hohathad   Natha
AND   POWER   POWER   YOU-OF

i   hohama,   hohama   Natha
AND   GLORY   GLORY   YOU-OF

ril i aril irilrili
FOREVERMORE

Othe.
AMEN.

18

LETTER WRITING

Charlea Massion and Lesley Meriwether

"I loved the rose/wave card & it came at a perfect time on Wednesday. I'd really felt like I had taken a break with you." This line, from a letter to Charlea Massion from Lesley Meriwether, suggests the importance of their correspondence in their lives. Major themes that run throughout their letters are families, relationships, work, health, books recently read, and the activities of their cats and dogs. If writing while traveling, those experiences also are discussed. The two women also respond to the previous letter of the other—usually at the beginning or end of each new letter.

A mutual friend introduced Massion and Meriwether in 1981, when both lived in Arcata, California; he thought they would "hit it off" because of shared interests. Charlea is a family practitioner; Lesley is a marriage and family counselor and a licensed nurse who practices with a group of medical doctors. Both list healing as among their primary commitments as well as respect for the planet, its people, and animals. Their correspondence began when Massion moved out of the area in 1982, first to Arizona, then to New Mexico and Texas, and finally back to Aptos, California. While the two women now talk more frequently on the phone since Charlea is in California (and calls are cheaper), they still write to one another with as much frequency as they did before.

Their correspondence serves several functions for Massion and Meriwether. First, their letters are like journal writing; each writes to the other when she wants to think about or work through something. Writing to the other, then, is therapeutic in that the act of writing something down often reveals significant insights to the writer herself. Their letters are therapeutic at another level, too. In their roles as therapist and physician, they can offer one another advice about the issues that arise in their lives. Their correspondence also provides them with the opportunity to make time in the day for a break. Charlea describes the experience of letter writing "as a way to set up and create a situation where I can be focused. It's like a meditation; it gives a time and space where I can focus my energies internally." Because both women deal with patients/clients, where their energies are focused externally on other people, they acknowledge the importance of having ways that allow them to retreat inward. Letter writing primarily serves, however, to maintain and deepen their friendship as they share what is happening in their lives and their responses to their experiences.

Both women treat the arrival of a letter as a special event. Meriwether describes a letter from Massion as a "special part of my life." She doesn't read it immediately but carries it around until she has enough time to enjoy it fully. She often arranges a special time and place for this activity—perhaps going to a favorite restaurant for a cup of cappuccino.

Both Lesley and Charlea value writing, so the kind of correspondence that emerged between them was not surprising. Massion began writing letters seriously around the age of ten or eleven and has several friends with whom she corresponds in the way that she does with Meriwether. She has a couple of male friends with whom letter writing is a primary tie, although the focus of those letters is different. The letters she receives from male friends, she explains, "focus on factual descriptions" of what is going on in their worlds more so than on personal feelings about those events. Lesley does not carry on the kind of extensive correspondence she has with Charlea with anyone else. Unlike Massion, Meriwether keeps a journal, where she also has the opportunity to process what is happening in her life.

Included here are five months' worth of correspondence between Charlea and Lesley, a typical series of letters for them. The letters are reprinted in their entirety except for minor editing to preserve the privacy of family members and friends. Both women feel strongly that the letters included here should be essentially unedited, despite what they reveal about their personal lives or the feelings of vulnerability they generate, because they see value in sharing experiences and in revealing women's voices to the public world. As a physician, Massion has lost some boundaries she used to maintain because she often must violate others' boundaries in her work. As she has become more open about telling people about her experiences and what she has learned from them, she has come to see the importance of doing so, a commitment also shared by Meriwether: "It's good to talk about these things; our joys and sorrows don't need to be so private."

Letters

May - September, 1989

"Moments shower away; the days of our lives vanish utterly, more insubstantial than if they had been invented. Fiction can seem more enduring than reality."

from Moon Tiger
Penelope Lively

May 5, 1989
Santa Fe

Dearest Lesley.   Hello from one of our home towns—the sky is a flawless azure and a small soft dry wind spins through the leaves of the Russian olive trees outside this window. I am especially fortunate—the lilacs are in bloom here and Santa Fe has thousands of lilac bushes—I have had lilac scent drifting through my dreams. I arose before dawn today and drove to Wilderness Gate Road to see the ETA Aquarid meteor shower—saw only two—a long wide silver one and a short spark. Lots of birds twittered before sunrise.

So I guess Pooka [cat] & I are about halfway to Santa Cruz—Today we are driving to Chinle. Pooka has been an excellent traveller. She seems to sleep even more than normal at this higher altitude.

Packing last week went very well. I got plenty of help—esp. when I asked for it. I had about ten days of parties—meeting friends for lunch or dinner or tea (really coffee for me). I will miss my diverse community of friends in Houston—but when I drove past the city limits, I felt no remorse.

In Dallas I had a good night with Tony & Catherine. Catherine looks nine months pregnant but really is only seven. They both are impatient for the birth. The diapers are already stacked to the ceiling in the room.

I am enjoying my life once more. Wanting to live gives life a different perspective. My depression lessened dramatically about ten days prior to the move.

So—I expect to arrive in Santa Cruz next Wednesday or so. I need to do something there for work and also final arrangements for my obstetric work in San Jose. My friend Robert who lives in SF has some days off and we plan to go camping for 4-5 days. And somewhere in the plan I hope to come to Arcata. I'll call you to discuss plans.

I want to tell you again how important your support has been (and still is)

over the past months. I appreciate very much your love and care and devotion—
and your willingness to attend to me when I called at whatever time or whatever
day. Your patience, knowledge, experience and encouragement all were
invaluable in my dark passage.

I'm looking forward to walking with you and your lively canines in the marsh
soon.

A big hug to Jerry [Lesley's husband] and lots of love to you, dear friend,
Charlea

13 May 89 Lakeport   Sunny, breezy, springy

Hello Dear One: I am on a brief holiday at Michael's [first husband] folks
in Lakeport. Mike [son] drove me down Thursday & will return tomorrow
(Sunday) to pick me up. He has gone to Sacramento to visit friends & I am
escaping the activity on 6th Street & getting in a good visit.

Thank you for your letter, it was so good to hear from you Charlea—your
mood is so much lighter: I am so pleased with your progress. I also appreciated
the N.M. postmark—we will return! I think I'd like to celebrate my 50th
birthday there—or in Scotland if I have enough $ (my fantasy anyway).

Glad to hear Pooka was a good companion—unlike her memorial flight to
Arcata & yours truly . . . I'm glad our relationship survived that!

Did you enjoy Moon Tiger? I haven't read it but remember it got good reviews
when I was in England.

Oh the magnificent scent of lilacs in spring—here the most impressive sight
is the iris bed, ablaze in a sea of color—most breath taking—taste wise: the
strawberries: fresh, juicy, sweet, am making microwave jam at the moment.
It retains that fresh picked flavor rather than the stewed flavor of traditional jam.

Later—had a lovely lunch & hot tub with a friend of Mom's (Irene) who
I met in Crescent City at a watercolor painter's workshop in July.

I am reading about Findhorn in Scotland—very interesting place (The Miracle
of Findhorn). I am now on the front porch with a cup of tea, warmish breezes
shaking the leaves lull me. I am finally relaxed—hadn't realized how uptight
I was. I've napped every day here & slept good @ night. Amazing.

Isn't it amazing how geographical locations can alter depression? (you leaving
Houston). I felt a heavy depression when I went to Sonoma near the end of
my parents' lives & after their deaths. I went there later (a year or so) & still
felt bad! By now I could probably handle it—but it started around Santa Rosa
coming & going. It was a physical manifestation: I'm glad you got a better
perspective on your depression from another psychiatrist.

I called Jerry. He'd just finished putting his final grades in the computer
& then was going to graduation then he's all done til the fall. Lucky guy.

Teaching is an attractive thing for me because of the amount of time off.

I selected this card & then saw it came from Texas: small world that it is. The something old/something new caught my eye as a welcome to California for you.

I hope you are well & enjoying being back in California & so near the marvelous sea—welcome. The boys & I look forward to our walks with you soon. Love always,

Lesley

[Written in a card that features a cat and tulips]

Dear Lesley,

The cat says "Take it easy on your birthday!" I agree.
Happy Birthday!
Much love, Charlea

June 5, 1989

Happy Birthday Lesley!

Dear Lesley & Jerry,

Welcome home! I hope that you had a marvelous vacation together. I have not yet visited Yellowstone or the Tetons & look forward to a full report from you two.

Enclosed are several photos of the MOM (mutts on the move) and the start of the bike race on the Square.

I am enjoying my obstetrics training very much—and even more, enjoying being in California again!

Thanks for taking such good care of me during my visit to Arcata.
I love you both!
Charlea

8 June 89   Yellowstone, WY

Dearest C: We made it to Yellowstone & spent our first full day here hiking (yesterday). Had good weather (it keeps changing sun—rain—wind—clouds). Big skies here with clouds constantly changing color, size & position. We spent most of our day out & around Yellowstone Lake. Not many people yet, (too cool & Calif. schools not out) so the animals are still around: bison, elk, deer. There are also bears in the area so we're wearing "bear bells," but no sign of them. One hike we took was to a place called Stormy Point, a rocky place overlooking Yellowstone Lake—it was awe inspiring there. Winds up, water lapping at the rocks, small waves in the lake & huge skies above—a place I won't forget. It is so fine to be in such beautiful country away from the usual concerns & be worried about sunburns & bears for a change. I love being caught up in the high mountain energy & watching for birds—there are many here already sighted more than I ever expected to. I also loved walking through a herd of bison (two with young) as they grazed in a meadow. They can be dangerous if disturbed, but seemed peaceful enough yesterday. The air is clean & fresh (& thin) & on warm days filled with the sweet scent of pine—delicious. Lots of Canada geese & their young, also saw a trumpeter swan & some white pelicans—very exciting stuff! I'm reading a book called Idaho Poetry (poetry from the Indians and pioneers up to 1980—an anthology). Also reading a book called Mountain Time by Paul Schollery—a ranger writing about his life here & I'm reading A Lady's Life in the Rocky Mountains by Isabella Bird & written by an English woman on a trip in 1873—this book is great—such a contrast to the way we do things today & the way things are. We've been reading at night (9-11) & it's so nice to relax & explore things mentally after a day of physical stimulation. I've been taking pictures, but really need a telephoto—will get one later this year as I want one when we go to Alaska—hopefully next summer—& want to know how to use it. I've been keeping a travel journal though—a written record of what we've seen.

Our trip over was long & uncomfortable but not as bad as I feared. I drove about 1 - 1 1/2 hrs or so each day—J drove 4 or so. We went to Burney Falls to celebrate our anniversary—J. "forgot" to get a card—so we had a bottle of champagne & a picnic dinner at the falls—a lovely way to celebrate I thought. Then came my birthday—he gave me a bear totum & a deck of "Angel cards"— small cards with pictures of angels on them & inspirational words to focus on. The first one I chose (at random) was "healing." Appropriate for me. I do feel being here is healing & I love waking up knowing I have all day to explore this place. Lots of spring flowers in bloom still (snow's still on the ground and it's not really summer here yet). J. "forgot" to bring your gift so I still have it to look forward to. I did fine on my B.D. as I didn't expect much & therefore wasn't disappointed. Gifts and holidays are just not J.'s strong point.

How are you doing at your new job? I hope you are enjoying all that experience. What are you doing during your leisure time? How's Pooka & Aikiko? Soon you'll be a family again. It was so good to spend time with you Charlea. I really appreciate you coming up. I've missed you & am so pleased you're back in California.

I think of you often in this wild, wonderful place & hope you are well & in good spirits.

Love, Lesley

21 June 89   Arcata, CA   Warm & sunny on the longest day—really lovely

Dearest C: Well, we're back—in full swing. It is 6:30 & the "boys" [dogs] & I are out in the back yard enjoying the sunshine. It is finally quiet—after a day of much activity.

We returned Monday afternoon—reluctantly, at least for me. I really dreaded P.'s sentencing hearing the following morning. But as it turned out he received a relatively light sentence—500 community service hours, 5 days in jail (to be served in the roadside cleaning crew on weekends), a fine (I don't know how much yet but a lot for him) or he's subject to the rules of his probation agreement. The judge ruled it a misdemeanor & that was a tremendous relief. Currently P. seems to be doing well. He is working with Michael on our massive yard project—you won't believe the changes. It is a bit overwhelming at times around here! The remodel project continues. It's hectic, but will be really wonderful to have done. But after all our traveling—almost 3,000 miles, I am quite contented to hang around here a while—especially with warm weather.

I opened your wonderful B.D. present on Monday after we settled in. It's really wonderful, Charie, I love it. It "feels" so good—the "texture," weight & size. Thank you so much, it's perfect for me.

Today, the first day I intended (the road to hell is paved with good intentions) to work in my home study, the waterbed heater quit—so I spent most of the day draining the H_2O bed, buying a new heater, etc. It's all set now, but what a lot of work. I did work some in my study, but have a long way to go. I'm still enthusiastic about it though & that seems to be 1/2 the battle. Hopefully, tomorrow will see me diligently applying my talents to the project.

Dan [doctor in office] isn't going to Colorado. They offered him the job but he had to pay his own malpractice insurance—seems odd in a teaching institution—considering the liability—so he's still with us. I think that's good news.

I'm glad you're faring well so far. How do you like your living situation in San Jose? How do you "feel" being back in the OB situation?

I had a NDL profile done today. I was off my diet for the time I was traveling & I'm curious to see what effect it has. Did a lot of walking—my neck bothered me after about 6 miles. I didn't wear the brace but I felt like I did (my neck) when I was on old rickety trains in England. It is odd, but definitely a problem—I took Anaprox twice a day the whole trip—& I did OK, not great, but I was able to do most of what I wanted & I was able to drive quite a bit.

I really enjoyed being away. The hiking was the best part for me I think—&
also the wonderful wild flowers—& wild animals. I least enjoyed the eating
scene. Jerry & I got along pretty well—a few times of tension—esp. for him.
If I can relax it passes & I was even able to discuss it with him while he was
grouchy a few times. I'm not perfect either so I also had to talk to myself—I
mostly wanted time alone some of the time & that was difficult to come by.
I learned earlier in the relationship not to "browse" with Jerry—either in shops
or art galleries. He is bored & makes me nervous. This time we went our
separate ways (he bought a newspaper & drank coffee—I look at art). We're
learning but still have a ways to go.

I look forward to hearing the details of your present life. How did you feel
being close to family again? About Santa Cruz? & so on.

I talked with my sister. She saw a pain dr. for her chronic back pain—he
put her on Motrin three times a day and Elavil nightly at bedtime—she's much
better. Interesting huh?

Take care dear friend & thank you so much for remembering my BD in
such a special way. It makes me feel well loved—a good feeling.

Write soon—I miss you.

Love Lesley

P.S. Jen [cat] wants you to know she's been getting a daily brushing since we've
been back.

Sunday, July 2, 1989
Kiva House/Santa Fe

Dearest Lesley—Sunday morning at Kiva House, (the S.C. equivalent of "our"
hot tub place in Arcata) is for women only. I had a massage and then a hot
tub—wonderful except the massage room was a little too chill for me to relax
completely. This would be a good place for you, Carolyn & I to visit during
your Los Gatos expedition.

Thank you for your marvelous letters and for the one you wrote during
traveling! I want to hear more about your travels and see photos too! I also
am glad that P.'s courtroom day is over—hopefully forever . . . . What are
his plans re the rehab program and college?

I am happy you like your birthday journal book. I got it at a Santa Cruz
artisan's cooperative and met the woman who made it—I spent a long time
choosing because she had so many beautiful combinations.

Perhaps if you adopted another attitude toward your study—like a playground
or garden metaphor (sowing the files, planting the books, etc) you might have
a lighter time with it than otherwise . . . plus rewards for the completion of

certain subprojects within the big plan . . .

I am doing very well. I have enjoyed obstetrics very much, have delivered about forty babies from all over the world: Mexico, Salvador, Brazil, East India, East Africa, Iraq, Pakistan, Cambodia, Vietnam, China, Japan, Indonesia—San Jose has such a cosmopolitan population.

I have two more weeks there, finishing July 14. I am somewhat weary of commuting and not having my own home; but I have had a difficult time starting my search for a place of my own. I don't quite know why yet—? reluctant to live alone again.

I am getting lots of help in arranging to start my practice—I feel very different than when I was in Houston. I have hired a nurse—an R.N. who went to Stanford Nursing School, about 2-3 years older than I am, a developed feminist, lots of varied experience (medical and life)—she has moved more than I have! I'll start in Aptos on Tuesday August 8th.

I am planning to go to Seattle to visit Susan and perhaps Brian in late July— around 7/20 - 7/30. Also, I am hoping to come to Arcata around August 3rd or 4th for 2-3 days. My parents will be visiting Trina & Company. May I stay with you & Jerry again?

So dear sister let's talk soon. I love you and am delighted to be geographically closer to you! Much love, Charlea

P.S. I also appreciate that we are continuing to write to each other despite the more frequent phone & visit time we have living in CA together!

12 July 89   Arcata, CA   More nice weather!   9:15 pm WED.

Dearest C: Happily received 2 July letter & contents. Glad to hear all is well with you. We are listening to a "Mostly Mozart" concert on the T.V. . . . such lovely music.

Kiva House sounds good—but will there ever be a replacement for 10,000 waves—? Sounds especially good since hot tub @ the pool hasn't been on & water in pool so cold it gives me bursitis—but is good for my lap swimming sons. Sorry to hear of cool massage, not the best for relaxing.

Your photos (last letter) were—er—interesting—would you like a few lessons? Smile. Maxx [dog] profile in shadow came out good though. Maxx is quite pleased with himself—He & Holmes [dog] were included in the invitation to Carolyn's 40th B.D. bash on the beach @ the end of the month. Could be wild.

Hopefully, by your Arcata ETA [estimated time of arrival] I'll have my trip scrapbook in order. I did take pictures, but it is really hard to show a lot of the things we saw that were spectacular in real life.

P. plans on working (500 hrs of community service + large fine). He'll postpone school a year. He seems depressed. He is doing some work, but as yet doesn't have a "real" job. I'll keep you posted. I'm still working on backing off while being available—confusing—yes. I'll describe my visit with Theresa (psychic) this afternoon later in the letter. We discussed P.

I like your hints about dealing with my study. Now I'd like to add a "reward" that includes you if I have it in order upon your arrival. Give me about* 5 weeks or so—I should be able to do it, esp. if I think of it as a garden! Smile. *Sorry, misread date. Must get my act together in 3 weeks!

Your OB stuff sounds good. I assume you do a lot on nonverbal communication—do you also have translators? Such a group of home countries—there must be a lot of interesting food available in your area. You'll be done in 2 days: How fast time goes.

I can understand your reluctance in finding a home on your own. A tough task—but Pooka wants me to remind you that you are definitely not "alone." I hold a good thought for the future/when you'll be a bigger family.

Your new nurse sounds good—a nurse can make all the difference (I should know). August 7th will be here soon—so enjoy (or hopefully you are enjoying) your time off.

Will be interesting to see how things are in Seattle re: Brian especially & Susan.

Of course, stay with us Aug 3-4/2-3 days or whenever. We'd love to have you. If you could let me know your schedule here ASAP & I'll schedule myself light.

Well dear one, I'm tired & so I'm off to bed, waves of Mozart fill my head. I'll write more in the morrow. Love Lesley

9 AM 13 July 89 high clouds @ the Wildflower for lunch wheat pancakes. The "boys" & I just did a woods walk. Lovely & quiet, only saw one runner; an Oriental man dressed in all white—he looked wonderful running along through the forest. I have an eye exam at 10:30 & then will meet with Steve Littlejohn at Ira's office. Steve & I are going to use Ira's office (the library) for our new business address. "Meriwether Communication Resources" is what we'll call it, I think. I've gotten forms for use of a fictitious name & a business license—we hope to advertise our services as communication consultants in the fall after the new phone book comes out.

Later—the eye Dr's. I'll fill you in later.

My life feels overfull right now—today lots to do. Makes it easier though since we've had mostly nice weather. The "project," hopefully, will be done in 4 weeks—right about the time HSU starts. It seems to be progressing, but slowly. J. doesn't seem to be into his book—at least not like he was during the school year. He seems adrift. His new computer is all set up & he's still learning to deal with the programs, but I'm beginning to think that he's avoiding his book—I'm not sure how to approach the topic. He seems to be going out to a lot of "lunches" where he has a few beers & then seems a bit out of it to me when I get home—needless to say, an unwelcome sight.

I know I told you before about the great goggles I found—well, I've found an even better one—actually comfortable! "Barracuda" standard (by Skyline Northwest). I'm enclosing rap sheet. Cost 208+ but worth it.

I had read article on "Mapping the Moral Domain"—interesting & valid I think—how valid remains to be seen. It is so difficult to separate the male influences over the ages. Recently there was a panel here to hear the community's reaction to "off-shore drilling" 5 people on it (governor appointed) and no women, no feminine influence at all! And yet more women than men spoke out against the drilling & many did so eloquently—& some a bit comically, but you know what I mean—e.g. woman waving seaweed. I appreciated it but I wondered if some people would write her off? Maybe I've sold out a bit?

I will close & get this off to you. I'll tell you about my psychic visit & my ICU patient next letter.
I love you & miss you—
see you soon
Lesley

You know that book—called something like Living with Gremlins (not the title). Well, I couldn't find it. Could you find out the title or author?

Footnote Bookworks
Aptos, California!
July 18, 1989

Dearest Lesley,

I am sitting at a wonderful bookstore across the street from my office to be—Footnote is an 8-yr. old longhaired, gorgeous black cat with six toes on each of her paws. Last Sunday was her birthday and the shop owners had a party with cake, balloons, etc.—we can visit her while you are here.

I found a house! Yesterday I signed the lease; I'll be able to move in Aug. 1 or 2. The house is a 2 story duplex with cedar shingles. Your guest room is downstairs with a private bath. Upstairs is a living room with a stone fireplace and skylights, a long narrow kitchen and dining area, another full BR and my bedroom. There is a front deck big enough for a table & reading chair. The backyard is large enough for a small garden & the cats to sunbathe. The "cat" is there by special permission. The owner's the wife of a vet and she normally allows no pets!

Enclosed is my probable airline schedule—arriving Wed. 8/2 at 7 pm and leaving Saturday 8/5 evening. I need to check with my parents about their plans & with Trina about hers—we are scheduled to have a birthday party for the Leos (my dad Chic Tai & me) at some point.

8/2   8/4   8/6

Would you & Jerry like to attend?

So—my practice opening plans are going well. I moved most of the furniture to the office today. I have more errands tomorrow. Then to Seattle 7/20—return 7/30. Yes, I'm looking forward to seeing Susan—that will be easy & fun—and Brian has been intermittently enthusiastic & elusive. I have let go of any anticipated outcome—I have been "loved up" a lot recently (more on that in person—the man is someone I was lovers with initially in 1973!) Did you send me bachelors buttons so I could attract single men with all the buttons missing on their shirts?

Thanks for the Barracuda goggles info—I'll look for them. I'm cursing my current pair of goggles.

I'm looking forward to your trip scrapbook. You'll have time for that as your study gardening projects are accomplished more easily and quickly each day. I will also be bringing you a reward for your excellent achievement in organization of the many marvelous areas within your study garden.

Meriwether Communication Resources (MCR) sounds terrific. I want to hear your plans for its growth & development. Did you have fun applying for a fictitious name?

The book: Taming Your Gremlin—I don't remember the author.

Well, dear one, I am thrilled that we will be able to visit again so soon! I'll call again when I return from Seattle.

Take care!

Much love,

Charlie

28 July 89   a foggy summer day in Arcata. not even warm

Dearest Charlea: Thanks for the great letter and enclosures. I can hardly wait to visit the Footnote Bookworks, not to mention your new abode work-wise. At long last a welcome environment.

The house sounds good. It will feel good to move in and get settled. What is your rent? I like the idea of "my room." Of course, I'm more than willing to share it with you know who, reassure her for me. A stone fireplace and skylights . . . great. A small garden, at this stage in your career might be just right. It is all too easy to become a slave to the garden, delightful as most aspects of gardening are, the ensuing guilt from over commitment is often a problem. At least for me. It's a darn good thing you've got room for a cat sunbathing area.

You said you'd call and we can talk about the details of your visit. We would like to attend the Leos' birthday party.

Charie, I really liked the practice announcement. It is so much better than the formal ones I've done. The picture is good too.

Right now you are in Seattle, and hopefully having a good time. I'll be interested in the details, esp. with Brian. Also in "the old lover" details (of a sort).

I am working successfully in my office. I expect August to be a lighter month work wise and am going to spend any loose time on my "files." Many contain outdated material or irrelevant junk. It is such a relief to finally get to these things as I had hoped to do it before I returned to work last year . . . over a year has passed! Time passes quickly when you're having fun?

We will discuss the problems I see Jerry having, and the ones I have, when you are here. You may be right about it being time to return to counseling . . . or at least bring it up as a possibility. This (the possibility) may be a sufficient motivator to force us to deal with our differences. I did hire Sandy, John's [son] girlfriend, to help with the housework, and that feels like a step in the right direction.

I'd also like you to hear my last psychic reading tape. Mostly, I have to let go, and have the trust/faith that it will all work out re: P. I really feel better in a general sense, however, and feel I have more energy since I went to my first psychic reading, and even more since my second. But at the same time P. has also made strides which has helped me psychologically.

I'm looking forward to your Aug. b.d. visit. It is so wonderful to be able to see you often. Lucky me.

Lots of love to you dear one.

Lesley

[Pasted at top of letter is a fortune from a fortune cookie]: "The only rose without a thorn is friendship."

July 28, 1989 Friday
Seattle.

Dearest Lesley — A sunny morning in the Pacific Northwest. Susan has just started a five-day vacation after a stretch of hectic midwifery work. She is pulling weeds in her garden and cut many branches from a shrub-sized oregano — the house is scented with those tiny purple herb flowers.

I have had a very good vacation here. Last Friday Brian & I climbed Mt. Dickerman — 4 miles and 4400 feet to the summit — two hawks sailed through the mist, crying into the mountain clouds. Then, as I wrote in postcard, Susan & I went to Orcas Island over the weekend—taking the inter-island ferry from Anacortes. Eagles catching salmon; seals sunning on the rocks like cats, transparent jelly fish gliding through the green salt water—I think kayaking is as marvelous as snorkeling. I hope to take a kayaking course this fall in Santa Cruz.

The last few days I have been running in the park, reading Michael Odent's "Birth Reborn," visiting the museum, writing. I saw Jean Renoir's Rules of the Game—a remarkable film.

So Brian and I are closer. I am more relaxed and he is also—yet he hesitates and then I retreat. I am willing to let go and see what happens. He leaves for his family cabin on Lake Penage tomorrow morning and I return to Santa Cruz Sunday. He leaves for a six week rock climbing trip in France, Italy and Czechoslovakia and I begin seeing patients in Aptos on August 8th. He has decided not to continue his PhD research, and after his August-October leave of absence from the University of WA, will probably work for private practice orthodontist working in Seattle. I'll talk more about all this when I see you—next week.

Take care, my sweet friend. A hug to Jerry and many pets to the pets. Much love,
Charlea
[Card contains newspaper article and two photographs]

19 August   89 Saturday night 8 pm   Another nice day

Dearest C: It was great to hear from you so soon after your departure. I especially enjoyed the theme: bloom where you are planted. I like the idea of all those coffee houses: the Pacific Roasting Company is on my list. Can you get Peets coffee in your area . . . it is from the Berkeley area and really tasty.

Glad you enjoyed your b.d. am looking forward to seeing New Brighton Beach, but I'll have to pass on the roller skating. I liked the aquarium a lot when I saw it a few years ago. Seems like you must have some psychic connection with poppy seed cakes, at least in the eyes of your family.

That t-shirt reminded me of you so I'm glad you like it.

Well, the project did not pass the final inspection on Friday (not a complete surprise, but a disappointment). So the sons still are unable to move in. Frustrating for them, but hopefully they will be in when school starts. Peter [son] has a real job! Working right across the street at Angelo's Pizza Parlor . . . no transportation problems. He has a second temporary job as a picket at a HSU construction site . . . 40$ day + lunch, and is also doing his community service at the recycling center. Keeps the kid busy. "I'm working nine days in a row," says he to his unsympathetic mother. Secret smiles fill my face.

Michael is working at a job building houses and will probably work til Nov. and take an English class at night. Next semester he'll take his last three classes at the JC: logic, calculus, and speech communication. He is now unsure of his future goals.

John will return to college full-time and work part-time. So all seems to be going in the right direction.

My "Group" finally got going . . . in my book. Some shouting, some crying, finally some real feelings and issues. It was our 4th meeting and everyone was there. I felt I had done enough group building and was ready for the action. Now we have scheduled a mini-retreat to take place early next month. Now that they are beginning to face how much tension is really there, they seem ready to begin to deal with it and were frustrated with the short amount of time we had set aside. Smile. So far so good. Of course, the proof is in the pudding . . . I'll keep you posted.

Meanwhile, my health: On the fourth day of my period for the second month in a row I developed a migraine. Both times it lasted three days (almost) . . . I couldn't read and was nauseated along with having a painful headache, etc. So I am off the hormone replacement therapy. The headaches occurred on the first day of lighter bleeding following three days of mod/heavy bleeding and when I'd only been off the estrogen three days. So I don't know. I've decided to go back to an intensive exercise program so I can go back to sleep more easily after my night sweats. Again, I'll keep you posted.

My patient continues to progress towards independence. My last time with her was spent going to town and into a restaurant. This week we will walk at the marsh. She is doing well in all areas except with her vision.

I am busily planning my retreat at home. I have taken a week off work (Labor Day week) and will spend from Tuesday-Sat on my own mostly and at home or somewhere out in nature. I want to meditate, write, and paint. My office is in even better shape than when you were here and will be remarkedly improved as soon as I can move my "boxes" into Michael's attic. So I am anticipating a fairly orderly office by that time. I will read art related material: Dear Theo (Letters of Vincent Van Gogh to his brother) and Letters on Cezanne by Rainer Maria Rilke. I'm looking forward to it. Am just beginning Alice Walker's The Temple of My Familiar.

It feels like I've run out of steam so I will close with the thought of you happily settling in your new home and job. Take care and write soon.

Love
Lesley

[Postcard]
27 Aug 89

Dearest C: Just a note to say thanks for the great conversation Sat am. I really enjoyed it & you continue to inspire me re: my study/art.

I would appreciate it if you'd send my address to your Dad. He has a magazine (maybe) I'd like: "Outdoor Photographer" Jun. 89. (on wolves). He said he'd send it along if he has it.

Meanwhile, it's Sunday & I am actually working on my study & listening to Prairie Home Companion . . . it's foggy & dull outside so it's easier to stay indoors (at the moment).

Lots of love dear heart. L

[Pasted at top of letter is a quote from a box of Celestial Seasonings Tea]: "A friend is one before whom I may think aloud." Ralph Waldo Emerson

Round Midnight
September 3-4, 1989

Dearest Lesley,

I remember you once told me in Arcata "Nobody should marry a doctor." I think about that — and I quote that observation at times; and I thought about that as I drove home from Dominican Hospital at midnight. This is my first weekend on call — an easy street of phone calls with one intensive care unit admission — a 59 yr. woman who woke with chest pain after a nightmare about the husband and a 6 yr grandson.

This afternoon I "birthed" a worm bed — I have wanted to have worms eat my garbage for years; I am tired of burying the garbage to slowly rot in the ground. So I built a 2' x 2' box, got the red worms, prepared the bedding (shredded newsprint and brown bags) and today mixed all these elements with the past few days' account of melon rinds, coffee grounds, peels & lettuce, etc. Now that is purported to be transformed into rich "worm diet." We'll see.

This afternoon I also was debriding my study of clutter. Actually doing basic unpacking — and after three hours I felt exhausted & discouraged . . . Thought about your "three hours on the list" behavior so at least I just rested on the living room floor rather than totally expending my remaining energy.

So, I am thinking of you and your week — seems like a gentle rehearsal of retirement — like the stages created of separating from the boys (ongoing).

Send you love & energy, sweet friend!
Charlea

10 Sept 89   Arcata 9:30   High fog, coolish, waiting for the sun to break
through so I can garden and be warm at the same time . . . It is the last day
of my retreat & I've been at my desk since 7 AM doing odds & ends. Last
night was the 5 hour group meeting. I think it turned out as well as possible.
To begin I asked them to visualize themselves @ the end of the 5 hrs. & how
they wanted to be. Then I asked them to visualize the "group's energy." Then
we did the communication handout & worked our way into the problems. We
went for 2 quick hrs & took a one hr. break for dinner & back for 2 hours
8-10. Our last 1/2 hour was "brainstorming" just ideas in general for morale
boosting & anything else anyone thought of. We concluded in a circle holding
hands & sensing energy. I am really pleased & can look forward to the next
2 hr. meeting Friday 13 Oct. So I ended up doing 11 contact hrs. on my week
off but they seemed much more leisurely than my 15-18 I usually do.

I loved the rose/wave card & it came at a perfect time on Wednesday. I'd
really felt like I had taken a break with you. I also loved talking to you Thursday
AM. I enjoy staying in touch & having frequent contact.

I thought of you & I when I saw this card . . . having tea/coffee/lemonade
in some warm exotic place. I really feel close to you when I'm at our table
@ the Walrus & The Carpenter. I had a coffee there as a break this afternoon,
but felt like writing to you now.

I'll give Karen the booklist. I found a $3.98 copy of Touchstones while looking
for Anne Dillard's book for you. Mark said there were no more hardbacks
available but that it is now out in a paperback. Do you want to borrow mine?

Yesterday my patient moved (with mixed emotions) & she actually drove
with her bro. over the road where her car accident occurred. She will call
me next weekend.

I'll send a note to your father.

A new patient of mine has developed a severe depression. She is a talented
& very bright woman. She loaned me two books she recently purchased in
New York: On Not Being Able to Paint & A Life of One's Own by Joanna
Field. The synchronicity doesn't scare me. She may call you for a bit of moral
support re: depression. She needs to know she'll get better.

I am enclosing notes on the consult. I'll be interested to know how that goes.
I called Deborah re the gestalt workshop and she said it was not very full
and there is a possibility that if there are not enough people she won't do it . . . a
disappointing thought.

Am enclosing newspaper article that made me laugh out loud in the last
paragraph — good reading for the bathroom. I love the "Sylvia" cartoons, but
we don't have them in the papers we read. I think I have firbromylsia (you
once thought I might). I read an article in NYT by Jane Brody on it and I
have the symptoms, the history, and the treatment I use is the one suggested
(aerobic exercise). I hope Mother Theresa does well with her new pacemaker.

She is such an incredible woman and the closest thing I can imagine to a saint.

I liked the Celestial Seasoning thought on friendship. How's the worm thing coming? We still have reminders of Michael's worm project long ago. Just remember to water them enough. Lots of love to you dear friend. I think of you every day and am so pleased at how well you feel and how happy you are.

Love,
L.

[Postcard from Yosemite]

9-10-89

Dear Lesley & Jerry—

Hello from the Ahnaknee Hotel in Yosemite. I'm here with my friends Robbie & Lebeth from Houston. This is my first trip here—arrived in the full moon floodlights last night; a coyote crossed the road—that's my kind of Park Ranger! Love, Charlea

19

MOTHER-CHILD INTERACTION

Cindy L. Griffin

"Our culture tends to devalue children as people who are able to sort out their world and make choices about how to act in it," believes Cindy Griffin. In her talk with her two-year-old son, Joseph Sunden Griffin-Harte, she is guided by the desire to accord value to Joseph's perceptions, reasoning processes, and choices. She tries to talk with him and treat him as a "little person."

Griffin is juggling the raising of her son with her doctoral studies in speech communication at Indiana University. Her skills in this area are well developed; Joseph was born while Cindy was working on her master's degree in speech at the University of Oregon. Although balancing her many roles is difficult, Griffin sees positive consequences, too: "Being a parent and a student and having a relationship forces me to define who I am because if I don't, I'll just disappear. So I have to think about where's the Cindy who's the mother, where's the Cindy who's the student, where's the Cindy who's in this relationship, and do I feel good about that?"

Joseph is cared for weekday mornings—about 30 hours a week—by a neighbor who cares for children in her home. When her responsibilities at school are over, Griffin picks Joseph up, usually at 2:00 or 2:30. From then until Joseph goes to bed at 7:00, she talks with him, plays with him, and focuses her attention on him. Cindy's husband joins in when he returns from work and on weekends.

Griffin's interaction with Joseph is guided by several principles, but gentleness is primary. She strives to be gentle in her interaction with Joseph and to teach

205

him to be the same; she feels this quality is particularly important for him to develop because he is a boy. She fosters gentleness by trying to model it in her own talk and actions; she uses "please" and "thank you" in talking to Joseph, for example, and asks him to use those words when talking with her. She doesn't use physical force to get him to do what she wants, and she doesn't "growl at Joseph the way many parents do. They verbally assault their kids, like 'Get over here!' I never say that to Joseph, and I feel terrible if I hear myself ordering him around." Cindy explains to Joseph why gentleness is important and teaches him alternatives to pushing, shoving, and hitting. In addition, she teaches him to take care of things—his own toys, other people, and other objects in the world, and she takes the violence out of stories she reads to him, "which pops up in the most unsuspecting places," she states.

Griffin's handling of Joseph's tantrums or potential tantrums enacts her belief in gentleness as a primary value in interaction with him. She encourages Joseph to use words in place of the usual tantrums in which two-year-old children are likely to engage in order to achieve their goals or express their feelings. "I think children have tantrums because they aren't able to ask for what they need and want," Cindy explains, and she works to provide Joseph with verbal options when he is on the verge of a tantrum.

Griffin's interaction with Joseph also is based on her desire to provide him with choices. Instead of telling him what to do, she tries to give him choices—which socks he would like to wear or what he would like to eat for lunch. She controls his choices, to some degree, by picking the alternatives from which Joseph can select, but he has real options within the framework she provides. She does not want Joseph to feel acted on but rather empowered, acting as a human being in the world, with freedom and knowledge of the consequences of his choices.

Yet another principle that underlies Cindy's interaction with Joseph is her desire that he develop both masculine and feminine traits. She feels the "cards are stacked against him" because of the masculine socialization that is applied to boys in our culture, much of which limits and restricts boys and men in undesirable ways. She encourages the development of a whole spectrum of behaviors—both typically masculine and feminine behaviors—by asking Joseph to help her do laundry, clean house, and cook meals. She gives him both trucks and dolls with which to play, and she switches the sex of characters in books she reads and stories she invents to expand the options for masculine and feminine behavior. Because Griffin and her husband do not have a television, Joseph has not yet been exposed to the sex-stereotyped behaviors shown through that medium, for which they are grateful.

The effort to normalize differences is another principle that informs Cindy's interaction with her son. She realizes that "Joseph isn't going to be quite the same as everyone else. We don't have a TV, we don't eat meat, we recycle, his mom is in a Ph.D. program, his dad is quite radical in his beliefs." What she wants is for him "to learn how to live within those differences happily." Her initial response to different kinds of interactions with Joseph by his day-care provider, for example, was to consider moving him to another provider whose style of interaction might be more consistent with Griffin's. But she has come to see these experiences as inevitable and necessary for Joseph because they allow him to "live differences as normal from a young age"; she hopes he won't be shocked and embarrassed when he discovers how different he is from others as he grows older.

Cindy sees differences between Joseph and other children, and she suspects they may be a result of her parenting style. He "has a sweeter personality" than many other children, and "he's such an enthusiastic child. When the little girl across the street comes over, for example, he gets so excited and wants to show her things." Griffin observes other children who are loud and boisterous, "but Joseph's is a different kind of excitement, a zest, a sort of a thrill with whatever the thing is, and theirs is a kind of energy that seems more harsh and powerful."

Cindy recounts an episode that occurred when she and Joseph were playing in the back yard to suggest differences in behavior she has noticed between Joseph and other children. Joseph was running down a small hill, calling out, "You do it, Mom; you do it, Mom" and "Here comes Joseph; here comes Joseph." Griffin finishes the story: "There were some kids next door—two little boys—and they were flying a kite, and we were talking about the kite. Joseph found some sticks on the ground, and he began 'flying' the sticks up to the clouds, pretending they were a kite. The two boys saw Joseph and thought this was a pretty good deal, so they came over to play. They started running down the hill quite boisterously and energetically, playing Superman. Well, my kid doesn't have a clue as to who Superman is, and as they're running up and down the hill, Joseph stood back and watched, as in 'What is this?' He had been 'Here comes Joseph' and 'You do it, Mom,' and we were flying sticks to the clouds, and here come these rrrrrrrrrrrRRRRRR Superman kids. . . . And as we walked away, I thought, my kid flies sticks to the clouds, and these kids are screaming up and down the hill playing Superman. We went to pick daffodils, and they went inside to watch whatever was on TV."

What follows is a transcript of a one-hour time period in which Cindy and Joseph interacted in their home in Ellettsville, Indiana. "The time when a mother interacts with her child is very personal and private," admits Griffin. "Mothers usually want to hide this talk from others because others tend to evaluate it and to make judgments about your fitness as a mother as a result. Revealing my talk with Joseph makes me feel very vulnerable."

Interaction

August, 1989

J: Ball, Mom. Were is a ball, Mom?
C: Where is the ball?
J: Where is at ball?
C: I don't know. You find it, OK?
J: I find it.
C: Is that gonna work?
J: Where's a ball, Mom?
C: Here's more blocks. Here's a small ball; how about that ball? There's a ball for you. It bounces kinda funny.
J: Kitty, kitty ball?
C: Does the kitty want the ball?
J: (Screams)
C: What is that all about?
J: That's ball. Kitty, Mom? Ball, Mom. Ball, Mom.
C: More, more what?
J: More?
C: Oh, honey, I can't get those if you put them [paper bags] back there [behind the stove]. No. No, Joseph, no.
J: See, Mom?
C: This is Momma's paper bag. Watch what I do. I'll show you. I'll show you, OK? Yeah, I'll show you.
J: Show ya. OK.
C: You're putting them behind the stove. How am I supposed to get those?
J: You get?
C: How am I supposed to get those?
J: Kitty, Mommy?
C: Hmm? OK, Momma will be right back.
J: Mommy.
C: Hmm hmm. I'm coming right back.
J: Be right back? Come Mommy? Can I coming, Mommy? Kitty, Mommy? Hear hear water, Mom? [water is running in the sink]
C: Do you hear the water? Yeah, I heard the water, too. Joseph, no. No, Joseph, come out. [Joseph goes into the bathroom] I appreciate your help, but no.
J: Is that? Diaper pail.
C: No playing with the diaper pail. Do you want some more breakfast?
J: Mo breakfast.

C: More puffs? [puffed-corn breakfast cereal]
J: All done? Doin, Mommy?
C: Mommy's having breakfast.
J: I wan dis, Mom? Dis, Mom.
C: You want some bites of mine?
J: I wanna bites a mine.
C: OK. Thank you.
J: I bites a mine.
C: Bites of mine.
J: I bites a mine, I bites a mine. Is at, Mommy? Is at, Mommy?
C: Those are bowls. You gonna make some breakfast? You gonna cook something? What are you going to cook? Can you make me some breakfast?
J: I wan, Mom
C: Wow, look at those. What are you going to make?
J: Is at, Mom?
C: Bowls.
J: Bowls.
C: Umm hmm.
J: (Sings a few notes) Where's bowls, Mom?
C: Umm hmm.
J: Puffs. I get a bowl.
C: Are you going to get a bowl? Another one?
J: Nother one. I wan, I wan, I wan a a.
C: Wow, those are big. Are you going to have some from last time, huh? It probably doesn't taste very good.
J: (Bangs bowls) Umm mm, Mom, more soap, Mom. Wan mo soap.
C: More soap. How about a few puffs?
J: More puffs, Mom.
C: Here you go.
J: Puffs.
C: You need a spoon, too. Let me get you another one. Here's a spoon. There. That's quite a big bowl for those puffs. Is that what you made for breakfast?
J: Don know. I no know.
C: Don't know? What's going to be in that bowl?
J: I'm ana ba.
C: You wanna ball?
J: I wanna baska ball.
C: Well, I have to blow the basketball up.
J: Ahh, ahh, ahh. Umm ma? More ba, Mom?
C: Go find the ball. Oh, more bowls, OK.

J: (Whining) [attempts to get glass bowls from cupboard]
C: No, honey, those are glass ones.
J: Gass ones? All done. All done, Mom.
C: OK, thanks. I'll take this.
J: I all done. I wan, I wan take it.
C: Can you find one of the bowls that that goes in?
J: I wan that bo goes.
C: You gonna make tacos?
J: Make tacos.
C: Millet tacos. I know, that was good wasn't it? Which bowl do you need for millet tacos?
J: I wan, I wan.
C: There's no more [millet tacos] in the refrigerater, Hon. Daddy took it for lunch.
J: Daddy ate it?
C: Daddy ate it.
J: Is at, Mom?
C: Let's see.
J: That?
C: What is what?
J: That.
C: That's a blender.
J: Da bender?
C: Umm hmm.
J: Da bender.
C: That's the blender. Daddy uses that to cook with—to mix things up. It makes a loud noise. Remember? Remember noise?
J: Remema noise?
C: Makes a loud noise.
J: That, Mom?
C: When Daddy uses it. Blender.
J: Da bender.
C: Umm hmm.
J: Kitty the blender?
C: Does the kitty want the blender? I don't know. Let's ask. Doesn't look like it, does it?
J: No pens. [cat is playing with pens]
C: He seems to be busy with the pen. It's all right.
J: Uh oh, pens, Mom.
C: It's OK to play with pens.
J: Daddy, Mom. Is at Mommy?
C: That's the blender.

J: Das blender, Mom?

C: No, it's not a toy.

J: Das blender. Kitty, Mom?

C: Umm hmm. No blender.

J: (Singing) I nooo bender, bender. Kitty, Mom?

C: He says, "I think I'll cook something, too."

J: (Garbled response)

C: Which bowl should I use?

J: I wanna bite.

C: Please? I want a bite, please?

J: That, Mom?

C: That's a lid to a bowl.

J: Tha a li to bowl?

C: A lid to a bowl. Keeps things fresh. What's that? What's that?

J: (Banging) Mommy! Kitty, Mommy.

C: I think, you know what I think? I think the kitty would like this
     milk. Shall we give the kitty the milk?

J: No milk.

C: How about this milk? Here we go.

J: How bout this milk? I wan milk, Mommy.

C: Let's wait 'til he's done, OK?

J: I wan this milk, Mommy.

C: No.

J: I wan this milk, Mommy.

C: That's for Copperfield [cat], Honey.

J: Wan dis mil.

C: No, we're going to let him finish. Here, you come here and watch.
     Drink some. See how he drinks that?

J: What, Mom? Coffee, Mom?

C: No coffee for you.

J: Want the pencil, Mom.

C: OK.

J: All done.

C: All done with the spoon?

J: Paper, Mom?

C: The paper's on the floor. You want to draw on the paper?

J: I'n done, donc. I anna draw on paper. I anna draw on it.

C: Draw on the paper.

J: Done? A done?

C: Umm hmm. That makes good marks doesn't it?
     [paper on which Joseph is drawing moves]

J: (Crying) My pencil move!

C: The paper moves, doesn't it? It's [the paper] stuck on your finger. Goodness sakes. [both laugh because paper sticks to Joseph's hand]

J: Kitty, Mom?

C: Having milk? Oops, oops, let's don't draw on you. Let's don't write on your face.

J: I wanna go outside, Mom.

C: It's raining pretty hard out there.

J: Raining hard?

C: Yeah. Thunder and lightning out there last night.

J: Fun light. I'm gonna go, Mom. Hey—pencil out.

C: The pencil was out, and now it's back in.

J: Now's back in, now's all gone.

C: Back in? Did you stick it in? Is it stuck in? There, that takes good coordination, Joe. Sounds like a music box here.

J: Is meedic box?

C: Umm hmm.

J: Me meedic?

C: Yeah, like your music box.

J: Doin, Mommy?

C: Watching you.

J: All tan annon.

C: It doesn't make music, Honey; it's a pen.

J: Do pen.

C: You just write with it, that's all.

J: That all.

C: Umm hmm.

J: Wan dis more.

C: There, Copperfield says, "Thanks, Joseph, for the milk. Thanks." He says, "Now I have a full tummy."

J: I a shoes or sandles?

C: You want your shoes on?

J: My shoes on, Mom.

C: It's too wet outside, Joe.

J: It too wet side.

C: Umm hmm. Too wet outside.

J: Doin, Mom? Kitty, Mom. Kitty, Mom?

C: Playing with your blocks.

J: Kitty, Mom? Boats [another cat], Mommy?

C: Boats went outside. He says, "I don't care about the rain; I'll go outside."

J: I wan shoes on.

C: That's what you say, too, you say you don't care about the rain.

J: OK! ee shoes on, Mom. I wan shoes on.
C: What are you going to do with those shoes on? Hmm?
J: Outside! Oh, oh. Ah ah ah choo.
C: That's Daddy's game, huh?
J: Daddy, Mom? Daddy, Mom? Daddy, Mom?
C: He's at work. No more job interviews; now he goes to work.
J: Wanna a Becca's. [Rebecca, Joseph's day-care provider]
C: Do you want to go to Rebecca's today?
J: I car.
C: In a car?
J: (Singing) Daddy, Daddy, oh. Blocks, Mom, blocks, Mom. [cat is
     playing with blocks]
C: Yeah. Oh, Joseph, the kitty can play with the blocks.
J: Kitty blocks.
C: You have to be friendly and share.
J: Share?
C: Umm hmm.
J: Kitty, Mommy.
C: He's looking at your bowls.
J: I wan mo milk a, Mom.
C: He's scoping out the possibilities.
J: Mee, Mommy.
C: Umm hmm.
J: De soap, Mom?
C: The soap?
J: Soap.
C: It looks like milk to me. Should we get some water in there?
J: I wan water in there.
C: Please?
J: I wan water in there.
C: Please?
J: A wan mo wader.
C: I want more water, please?
J: I want [Joseph heads for the bathroom to get water]
C: No, stay out of the bathroom, Joe.
J: I wan wader, Mommy.
C: Can you say "please"?
J: Ina see see pese.
C: Yes. Can you hear that rain? More water, please?
J: More wanna, pease.
C: There you go.
J: It's raining, Mom. It stop raining, Mom.

C: It just started raining again. Here's some water.
J: Here wader, Mom. Sank you, Mom.
C: You're welcome, Joe.
J: Sanks.
C: You're welcome.
    (Joseph clangs bowls)
C: Make me some cookies, OK?
J: I'm a mak a de cookies.
C: Can you make me a batch of cookies?
J: I'n a make cookies, Mom?
C: Umm, that sounds good.
J: (Whining) I wan cookie, Mom.
C: No, we have to make them.
J: Make them.
C: You have to help me make them.
J: Make them?
C: Umm hmm. Make them.
J: Make em?
C: Would you like them? Umm hmm, make some cookies.
J: Let's make a dem cookies.
C: Well, we'll get some stuff out so we can make some cookies.
J: Make cookies.
C: Bring your bowl in here.
J: No, Mommy.
C: 'Cause we'll need that for cookies.
J: Nee nee cookies.
C: Umm hmm.
J: I wan shoes on.
C: You want your shoes on? We're not going outside; we're going to
    make cookies, OK?
J: Doin, Mommy?
C: I'm going to make some cookies with you.
J: Mo cookies?
C: Yeah, with you. You want to help me? Yeah.
J: No, Mommy.
C: No? Well, we have to make them.
J: Make em?
C: Umm hmm.
J: Ee, Mommy.
C: Melting margarine.
J: Magarine?
C: Yeah.

J: Magarine.
C: Melt the margarine.
J: Do, Mommy. Do, Mommy see egg.
C: Oh yes, we do need an egg. You're very smart.
J: Mommy.
C: You're very smart because we do need an egg, don't we?
J: Dee, Mom?
C: OK. Should we use one of your bowls? Let's use one of your bowls.
    This looks like a good one.
J: Dis cookies.
C: Can we make them in here?
J: O ma cookies, Mom.
C: We'll use this bowl.
J: Cookies, Mom.
C: You're going to make cookies?
J: Umm, Mommy.
    [Joseph pulls a pan out from the cupboard]
C: Goodness sakes. You're going to use that pan?
J: (Whining)
C: Settle down, it's all right. Here, here. You can ask for help. You can
    say, "Momma, can you help me?" Can you do that?
J: I'm nee. I nee nee a egg.
C: Do you need an egg?
J: See a Mommy.
C: OK, here's your egg. Here's an egg. You can put that in your pan.
    There you go.
J: Kitty, Mom?
C: The kitty is playing with your blocks. There, mix that egg up. Are
    we having egg shells?
J: A egg.
C: Are we having egg shells in your cookies?
J: Mo egg, Mommy. Mo egg a Mommy?
C: More egg? Can you use more eggs? Egg-shell cookies. That sounds
    good.
J: Mo egg. Egg, Mom?
C: Here's an egg. Egg shell.
J: Egg shell?
C: Egg shell. That's an egg shell.
J: Is it Mommy?
    [Joseph tastes the egg shell]
C: Hmm? Does it taste funny?
J: Tase funny.

C: Umm hmm.

J: Mom?

C: We don't usually eat egg shells; we eat what's in them. But they're fun to play with, huh?

J: I egg, Mommy?

C: That's all the egg that we have, so you'll have to make do with that.

J: Kitty, Mommy.

C: Is the kitty helping you?

J: Oh egg. Oh egg.

C: You don't think he should eat those eggs?

J: Was cook.

C: Are they cooked?

J: (Calling/singing) Coppers? Coppers? A Copperfield? Here, Coppers.

C: Are you trying to feed him those eggs? (Both laugh)

J: Copperfield.

C: He doesn't look very interested, does he?

J: Copperfield. [Joseph takes bowl of egg shells into living room]

C: Joseph, bring the eggs back in the kitchen, please.

J: OK.

C: OK. Come on back in.

J: Come back.

C: There you go.

J: Kitty, Mommy.

C: Copperfield was running from you. He said, "No, thanks," to the eggs. "No, thanks, Joseph." He says, "Egg shells aren't my kind of thing."

J: I wan. [Joseph dumps bowl of egg shells on kitchen floor]

C: Well, geez, I've got quite a mess to clean up, Joe.

J: Kitty, Mommy?

C: He is looking at you, saying, "What are you doing?" Let's pick these up before this turns into a real disaster.

J: Nooooo!

C: Are you standing on those?

J: Standin.

C: What does it feel like? Dad would flip if he saw this. Yeah, you know what I'm gonna have to do now?

J: What?

C: Vacuum.

J: Vacuum?

C: Umm hmm.

J: Oh no, Mommy!

C: Well, not for a while. While you have a nap.

J: (Giggles) See, Mommy, see, Mommy?
C: Umm hmm.
J: I got it, Mom.
C: What do you have?
J: A mo mo egg.
C: No more egg. That was very messy.
J: See, Mommy.
C: Putting oats in for the cookies.
J: Can see it, Mom?
C: There.
J: Is at, Mommy?
C: That's a spatula.
J: I wan a pick-you-up, Mom.
C: I have to mix this up first. You wanna see? OK, let's add a little bit
     more; it's kind of runny still.
J: Wanna pick-you-up.
C: You want a pick-you-up. OK, let me mix this up first.
J: Wan a mo mo mo.
C: You wanna help more? Here you go. No, it stays in the bowl. You
     can have a bite as soon as I'm done mixing, OK? Let's get you a
     spoon.
J: I'n get a spoon.
C: Here you go.
J: Here go.
C: Thanks, Mom. Thanks, Mom. Is it good?
     (Joseph humms and eats)
J: Goo goo goooood.
C: It's good, huh?
J: Kitty mo mo?
C: Hmm? You look like you're surfing in that bowl. [Joseph is standing
     in a large mixing bowl]
J: Bake, umm mo cookie, Mama?
C: More cookies, please?
J: Mo cookie.
C: More cookie, please? Here you go. You've got a mouthful, huh? Let's
     pick up these shells. Do you see how they've all cracked into little
     pieces, Joe? You look like you're sleeping in your bowl.
J: Hi, Kitty. [Joseph hits the cat]
C: Be soft, Honey, be soft. Joseph, no, no, let go. What have we said
     about being soft with the kitten? That wasn't very soft, was it?
J: I wan mo mo mo egg.
C: Please.

J: I wan mo mo. I wan mo mo mo cookie, Mom.

C: Where's the please?

J: I wan mo mo mo cook. I wan mo cookie, Mommy!

C: I want more cookie, please, Mama?

J: I wan mo mo cookie, Mom?

C: Please, Momma?

J: Mo cook.

C: Where's the please? Where's that word "please"?

J: I'n a pees a pick-you-up.

C: Well, let me finish putting these cookies on the tray.

J: I wan a pick-you-up. [Cindy picks Joseph up]

C: It's hard to cook with only one hand. That doesn't matter does it, Joseph?

J: Mo bites?

C: Well, you need to ask for please. More bites, please.

J: Mo bites pease?

C: There you go. OK, now I'm going to put you down while you eat that because I don't need to wear cookies. [Cindy puts Joseph down; he grabs cat's tail] Joseph, be gentle. What's that all about?

J: The kitty, Mom.

C: Yeah.

    (Eating and singing noises by Joseph)

J: Doin, Mom?

C: Well, that's one cookie tray, so this is the second one.

J: Mo cookie, Momma?

C: More cookie, please?

J: Mo cookie, Mom?

C: Please? More cookie please, Mom?

J: Mo mo cookie pease, Momma?

C: There you go. Sure.

J: Mo mo Mom?

C: Sure. Thanks, Mom.

J: Tanks, Mom.

C: You're welcome.

    [Joseph grabs the cat's fur]

C: Joseph, no, no. You do not do that. All done with the cookies. Joseph, are you being soft or are you beating on that cat? OK, you could hurt him, you know. That's the way. That's how you do it, you play nice and gently. [cat leaves the room]

J: Kitty, Mommy.

C: He's probably running from you, and I don't blame him.

J: I'n a ride da horsey, Mom. [Joseph climbs on rocking horse]

C: OK. You gonna ride that?

J: I wan mo wan ride da horsie, Mom?

C: Just a minute.

J: Ride the horsie, Mommy?

C: Let me clean up this mess here.

J: Ride a horsie, Mom?

C: You want to ride the horsie, Joe?

J: Ride da horsie, Mom?

C: You want me to ride it with you?

J: Ride a horsie, Mom?

C: OK, just a minute.

J: Dad ride a horsie, Mom.

C: Just a minute.

J: Ri horsie, Mom. Mommy!

C: I'm coming.

J: Ride a horsie, too, Mom?

C: I'm coming.

J: Momma.

C: Let me check the time [for the cookies to bake]. Scoot up, partner. [Cindy joins Joseph on the rocking horse]

J: I'n wow!

C: Whoaaaaa. [Cindy tips horse backwards and both fall off, with Joseph landing on top of Cindy] (Cindy and Joseph laugh) Momma tipped you over. Now what? We're stuck. Wow! [Cindy tips horse back up] Look at him go! Whew!

J: Up?

C: You wanna get back on?

J: Mom? Mo mo, Mom.

C: Should I get on, too?

J: Ge yon.

C: Whoaaaaa. [Cindy tips horse backwards again] (Both Cindy and Joseph laugh) Ohhh, I tipped it over again. (Cindy and Joseph laugh) Did you get bumped?

J: Get bumped. Mom ge yon again.

C: Get on again?

J: Mom gona ge on, too?

C: Umm hmm, I'll get on, too. You'll have to scoot up, though. (Cindy and Joseph giggle)

J: I wanna get off, Mommy.

C: You want to get off?

J: Mom.

C: There you go. That's a wild ride, isn't it? What have you got in your
    mouth, Honey?

J: Yum.

C: Paper. That's not a very good thing to have in your mouth.

J: Is it, Mom?

C: That's a garbage can.

J: Is it?

C: Garbage can. What do you say we clean up these egg shells? Hmm?
    What do you say we clean up these egg shells? There. Want to get
    the vacuum for me?

J: No, Mom.

C: No.

J: (Whining) No, Momma. No, Momma.

C: No vacuum?

J: No vacuum, no vacuum.

C: You don't like it, do you?

J: Don like it.

C: I don't blame you.

J: I don, no, Mommy! No, Momma! No, Mommy! No, Mommy,
    Mommy, Mommy. No, Mommy, no, Mommy. I'n a pick-you-up,
    Mommy. [Joseph goes into his bedroom]

C: I'll pick you up, Joseph.

J: I'n a pick-you-up, Mom.

C: Come and help me.

J: (Crying) I wanna pick-you-up, Mommy.

C: Can you come and help me?

J: Help, Mommy?

C: OK. I will. [Cindy vacuums]

J: Help, Mommy.

C: Yes, but you have to come in the kitchen.

J: Pick-you-up, Mommy. I wan pick-you-up, Mommy.

C: OK, all done.

J: All done.

C: All done.

J: All done.

C: What are you doing back there? (Cindy and Joseph laugh)

J: I'n a pick-you-up.

C: OK, come on in. All done vacuuming. You didn't like that, huh?

J: No like that, Mom.

C: You didn't like that? But it was good to stay in the bedroom. I'm
    done.

J: All done. Doin, Mom?

C: Putting it away. (Joseph cries) What happened?
J: Mommy.
C: Yeah?
J: Mommy?
C: Where are you?
J: Mom. [Joseph stops crying]
C: What are you doing?
J: Mama.
C: What did you find? Let's see. Let me see what it is before you go running around.
J: Mommy.
C: It's a screw. It's not a safe toy to play with.
J: I wan it. Wan a screws, Mom.
C: No, no screws.
J: I wan it.
C: No screws. It's cookies.
J: Cookie, Mom.
C: See the cookies? Can you turn the light on? There.
J: Yeah, cookie.
C: You want to sit and read a little bit?
J: I sit. I wanna cookie, Mommy.
C: Well, it's not done cooking yet.
J: (Whining) It's done, it's done, Mommy. No nap! Mommy.
C: Oh, Honey, I'm not going to put you down for a nap. It's too early for a nap.
J: Put shoes on and go outside?
C: Let's look at the rain, Sweetheart, it's very wet.
J: It's wet.
C: Umm hmm. Hi, Boats. You want Boats to come in? He says he'll stay outside for a while. Oh, it's locked.
J: It locked, Mommy.
C: It's latched now. You wanna cookie now?
J: I wanna go Becca's.
C: You want to go to Rebecca's now?
J: Book, Mom. [Joseph is rubbing his eyes]
C: Book, oh my goodness, someone's so tired. Someone's so tired.
J: I banket, Mommy. I got it. Banket, Mom.
C: You going to get your blanket?
J: Kitty, Mom?
C: Kitty wants to play with the plant. He hasn't learned that no one gets to play with plants in the house.
J: Kitty.

C: He's soft, I know, but you can't squash him.

J: Kitty.

C: Do you know how soft Mommy is with you? That's how soft you want to be with the cat. There you go.

J: I'm a mo.

C: There, nice and soft like that.

J: Hi, kitty.

C: Kitty.

J: Go outside, kitty. Go outside, kitty?

C: Does the kitty want to go outside? Probably. What's that? That's your tummy, huh? That's your tummy on the couch. [Joseph grabs at the cat]

C: OK, Honey, be gentle, you'll squash him. Joseph. Copperfield is a live little animal, Honey, and you can hurt him. You can't pinch it like that.

J: Is that?

C: That's the mail. Yesterday's mail. Want to open it?

J: Wan wan open it.

C: Do you want to open it up?

J: I wan open the mail. Open.

C: There you go. What does it say? Hmm? Should I read it to you? It says, "The all new JC Penney. Now the JC Penney charge card."

J: Penny.

C: Yeah, interesting, huh?

J: Inneresting.

C: You look like a bridge from the table to the couch.

J: (Whining) [He is stuck halfway on the couch and halfway on the table]

C: Are you stuck?

J: (Noises) I stuck, Mommy.

C: What should I do? You need some help? OK, there you go. (Cindy and Joseph laugh) You thought that was funny, huh? No, put your feet on the ground. [Joseph puts his feet on the table] Put your feet on the ground. Joseph. No.

J: (Whines)

C: Oops. You bumped into the chair, huh?

J: (Cries) Boats, Mom? Boats, Mom?

C: I think Boats wants to stay outside.

J: Kitty, Mommy? (Garbled)

C: You want the lawnmower?

J: No lawnmower.

C: The boat, motor boat?

J: A boat.
C: That's a boat, Hon. (Cindy and Joseph make boat sounds) Can you make it go?
J: Make it go, Mom.
C: OK, let's see.
J: I make it go. I make it go, Mom. (Boat noises)
C: This boat only has one wheel. Where do you suppose the other wheels are? Oh, my cookies! [Cindy and Joseph run into the kitchen]
J: See, Mommy?
C: Yeah, the cookies, before they're all burned up.
J: See, Mommy?
C: Whew, Joseph! I almost forgot all about them. There!

20

MOTHERHOOD

Christine Myers

Christine Myers, who has chosen to have children and to stay home with them while they are young, is meeting more and more professional women who also are taking time out to raise families: "But it's scary; by choosing to spend time with our children, we're afraid of turning into our mothers of the '50s." Myers, a resident of Barrington, Illinois, is the mother of two children: Drew Adrian Myers Regulinski, born in 1987, and James Marshall Myers Regulinski, born in 1989.

While she currently is committed to "cherishing my family," she has a continuing interest in working to improve the health conditions of women and their children. When she works outside the home, Myers is a consultant on health education to various national and international organizations, such as the World Bank, that are concerned with health issues in the developing world. Other ongoing interests are "education, getting the facts right, communicating, and learning to be honest." She sees her life as a series of phases; she had an "adventure" phase, when she joined the Navy and traveled throughout Europe. Then she had a "student" phase, when she completed her formal education — a B.A. in communication and a masters in applied communication and research. She next moved into a "consulting" phase and now admits — although somewhat reluctantly — that she's in a "mothering" phase.

Christine's reluctant acceptance of her mothering phase "is about values." As a professional, she had learned to value herself for paid work: "I never placed value on children — and on the amount of energy and work involved in mothering." These feelings are compounded because, while the economic value of work at home was talked about frequently in the early days of the women's movement, "it's not an issue that is of great concern anymore." For Myers, this increases her sense of alienation about her choices. Furthermore, parenting does not offer immediate rewards, "so it's hard to say that what I'm doing is important."

One of the ways Christine reframes her situation in order to focus on the importance of the parenting role is to separate what she does from housewifery: "I don't see the point of saying I'm staying home with my children if I end up doing household chores; I don't hang around just to clean house and do laundry." She hires someone to do those chores so that she does spend her time with her children.

The following essay begins with excerpts from Myers' journal about the birth of her second child, James. These are followed by reflections on the process of having and raising children.

Motherhood

A sense of impending disaster. The pregnancy weighs on my pelvis; my back aches. I don't want Stephan [husband] to travel tonight, next week, ever. I'm waiting for a Sign—mucus plug unplugged, broken water, spilled blood. The body ejects other burdens before ejecting the baby. Hovering rain clouds, dread. Maybe only lack of sleep—the baby is busier these days—our night movements mimic one another—rolling over, kicking, stretching, looking for a comfortable position. Muscles burn. Rising panic. On the examining table I feel small again, not so pregnant, the way I feel light in the water now.

Clunks in the pelvis. All experience only relative to my body. October 18. Snow last night. I awoke to the waves of contractions. Eighty minutes of timing, watching clocks, reading, breathing, counting seconds. More snow. Tomato soup. Anxiety. Urge to do nails, not write. Another clunk, a thud as baby moves closer to its goal. Is part of its brain saying "no, no I don't want to go you can't make me what's the world like out there anyway?"

Weightiness largeness gingerly lowering myself into the hot tub—now a lukewarm tub in deference to the baby's mental growth.

I leave the tub, lumber to the bedroom to give birth. The music drifts through. They set up the equipment. I breathe. We talk. Later they want to break my water. The baby still hasn't dropped. I just am. Breathing. No expectations. So is everyone else. Just there. Presences.

James at two months. He came into our lives gently, but the family, though only nudged, transformed. Those more volatile of us feel at the stronger ends of scales anger and joy. Stupefied by his beauty and demands, constant awareness of his presence, anticipation of his needs, fatigue from caring for him and the privilege of feeling hot breath and murmurs on the back of the neck. A few weeks ago I woke to his sucking on the back of my nightgown. We conform to him not willing to disrupt his patterns. This is a physical time, sensual. We touch and feel, nurse, watch, wonder at a level apart from intellect, like new lovers revelling in each others' bodies. I long for him, need to touch him, force myself out of his sight in order to work. His smile now is sheer joy. Only conscious an hour at a time, then back to the business of getting comfortable enough to sleep again.

I am writing this on an island off the coast of southern Thailand. As I'm writing, the bartender puts on a tape of "We Are the World." I'd like to say that the decision to have children is about hope for the future and very symbolic, but it's not true for me. I needed to have children. It wasn't a rational process—it was a drive even stronger than the need to write. It's impossible to know what you're getting into at least emotionally and probably in terms of time, energy, work, money, loss of self, growth, stress on marriage. Children are gifts in terms of the joy they bring and the maturity that comes with the responsibility, but I didn't responsibly make the decision—not many of my decisions are made rationally or responsibly. I wanted to have children so that I would stop being afraid of my own mortality, so I wouldn't have so much time on my hands, so I could teach someone else what I have learned about the world— the same reasons I write. I don't know before I write what I will write; I don't know what I will learn from/teach children before it happens. Much of it is experienced whole, through total immersion, so that later it can be looked at twenty ways in mosaic pieces.

The decision to have children took less courage than the decision to write. They were both decisions of the heart, longings that had a spiritual voice, not a practical one. The spirits of my babies hovered near and powerfully, waiting for life. They had either found a sucker or a potential loving mother. I sensed them, and that awareness created powerful baby lust, a resonating desire for them to take form. I felt that if they did not come into my life, I would be without a certain kind of understanding—not less a person, but without a dimension that I needed to continue to grow. It was far easier to explain an overwhelming need to have children than an overwhelming need to write. But I need to write in much the same way. I am a fuller, happier person when I'm writing. The experience is channeled, the writing teaches, enriches. There is so much less time, though. My head is full of voices—as I spend hour after hour in playdoh embraces—with no time to write them as a jealous toddler insists on attention. Now I find a dozen other mothers to support the work I do with my children, but who is there to support trying to write with children?

Many conversations about mothering with those who have young children include rationalization/reorganization of values in order to accept motherhood, especially among those who are at home with their children. In order to accept that we had not valued this work before and need to value it or lose all self-esteem, some say that this is their work. Many can say it honestly; I cannot. This is what I am doing. This is my current contribution to society. This is where almost every bit of my energy goes. But it is not my work my bliss my cherished moments my satisfaction my way of knowing or of understanding.

Ursula Le Guin wrote an article calling for more mothers to write about their realities in order to break the silence that invalidates experience. Mothers of young children don't have time to do both. Fleeting records of a day every couple of months passes for a baby book.

I tried to write an article about parenting. It was written in 20-minute snippets during time snatched while Drew built towers or napped. There were maybe a dozen pieces and I had in mind to fit them into a single, coherent paper. When I got them all organized on the computer (while she made a meal of blue playdoh), I realized that they were in twelve different voices. I couldn't find a single clear, cohesive voice. Each of my paragraphs was colored by the most recent childtime experience, reflecting the emotional volatility of the parent state. But it's also an accurate reflection of the many sides of parenting.

When James begins to coo and rustle in his sleep, I feel dread and anticipation. Once he is awake I only want to hold him, have him with me—at the same time it means the end of sleep or finished thoughts or writing. Drew wakes switched on. On a good day, I am rested and welcome her intensity, her questions, her hunger for attention. She can't be escaped, though, and I resent the extent to which she forces the focus on herself. If I try to control or battle with Drew as we spend time together, much of the value is lost. My temper gets in the way part of the time and hers much of the time. I am astounded by her intelligence, ferocity, sensitivity, curiosity—I am exhausted by the same qualities. I am refreshed by her affection-washed hugs. When she goes to sleep, I feel only relief. I never know what she will absorb and what will take a hundred repetitions. The joy and wonder re-emerge, even masked by fatigue. Time is always an issue—my life is rushing past in days that are always too long, too boring, too lonely, time with Stephan too short—then a week is gone in an instant.

Some mechanism of survival is out-of-kilter, always putting the wrong priority on the balance of Stephan, the children, myself, so that I am overwhelmed by the feeling of shortchanging all of them/us. None of us gets my full attention though the goal is that but sequentially.

I am with my friend, Nan. We have four children between us, aged four months to three years. We are tired, harried, tormented by our children's whining. We talk about having too much in our heads to do much outside work, about not having enough sleep and psychological warfare; siblings and toddlers. Cut to five years later—how will we see mothering differently? I want perspective, want reassurance that this phase of parenting will pass and I will wistfully look back on the days when the babies were babies. No aching backs, few uninterrupted nights. They will run and play on their own, won't need us. No more humming songs from Sesame Street or discussions of diapering options at dinner parties.

Adrienne Rich said that mothers of young children never get to finish their dreams, so that psychically we are damaged. Perhaps she meant chronically stalled or unable to analyze. It's not just the dreams, though, it's the thoughts, the sentences. We develop shorthand for caring. Mothers have a tenaciousness about their communication—we come back to our thoughts time and time again, so that a conversation may take hours instead of minutes.

I think the ideal way of coping with a two-year-old is to remove oneself from the constant ups and downs of the emotions they express. The reason it's difficult to analyze or describe how parenting changes/defines/announces me is that it's all done on my feet. The snippets of truth that come to me aren't often examined and, in the interest of time, they are embraced without examination or (when they are *really* profound) tested against the realities of friends in five-minute phone conversations while the children are napping. The social scientist in me tries to watch the culture of women who are rearing young children. This is often a diversion and just as often a denial of what my life is these years. The issues that come up with friends who have recently become mothers are often around the reality that we who choose to stay home with our children are doing work that we (and usually the children's fathers) don't really respect. So we begin to despise a part of ourselves, despise the work that we do. I do, anyway.

Raising the children is often how I fantasize what writing a novel must be. You can start with some vague notions of what will happen, but the characters and plots really shape themselves. Events and genes and histories determine the mother-child dance, with each response calling for another and creating what our relationship will be. A young woman asked me whether it was true that when you have children you become your mother. I said no, but you do become someone else who is *a* mother, if not your own. It's enforced growth— dumping the parts of ourselves that don't fit with a constantly evolving philosophy of parenting, embracing the qualities of my own mother that I most loved. That process creates and perpetuates traditions. Drew will carry on whichever she chooses. Being the mother of a daughter is, I think, different than being the mother of a son. With Drew, the psychological warfare is already terrific, and she's not yet three. My fears for the future are that she will be so much like me that we won't be able to talk, and the battles with my own mother that I thought I had put behind me will beg resolution. I know this, and I'm still not in therapy.

Mother love is self-killing love. We are women who love too much, but we can't just break off the relationship with our children. Instead, the attention comes in bursts, then withdrawal, then worry that the withdrawal will feel like rejection to her. But she will absorb more than all I can give her. I think that this is two-year-old love, but child-energy cannot be reduced or increased, it only changes its form as they grow older. It's their needs that determine the form, not mine. Having children has weakened the I, and when I am depressed, I think that it has diminished who I am.

There is too much in my life now that follows a traditional path, making for stress and struggle against slipping into my mother's life. This condition didn't come with the children so much as the move to Chicago. We decided before we had children that one of us would always have primary responsibility for childcare. I just didn't ever imagine that it would be me for both of them, for so many years, in such a way that I am not distinguishable from those without options.

I am a different parent than Stephan. I do not know how the children would be different—not much probably—if he were the one they spent the most time with. He is creative, patient, careful, affectionate, loving. I am dutiful, resentful, sullen, cranky. He is forgetful, disorganized, preoccupied, shortsighted. I am resourceful, social, thoughtful. We don't harbor illusions about the innate ability of either to parent. Our roles are a result of economics. When Stephan works at his occupation, we are tired and rich. When I alone work at mine, we are tired and struggling. What does this teach Drew? As long as I interpret it, as long as it's temporary, as long as she sees other options, it's probably not damaging.

Having children means rethinking ambitions, creating new opportunities, defining new paths that are richer, more spiritually fulfilling than the traditional paths of male or female careers. I feel tremendous frustration and guilt when I try to follow either model. Children have made me less interested in trends and more in understanding what really makes me happy. It has let me remove extraneous pasttimes, shed an occupation that no longer fits, let lapse friendships that do not nurture or inspire and seek out other mothers. I have become more needful of my friends and supporters, more appreciative of neighbors; I define myself more as a member of society than as an observer. Practically, I am far more organized than before. I am less single minded, better able to see wholes—whole time, larger chunks of future imposed on each now. Streamlined motherhood life. I am a better observer of humans for being a mother, and more tolerant of others—especially other mothers. I am also more critical of those who I think are doing the job badly, sloppily, selfishly.

21

NEEDLEWORK

Judy Chicago and Needleworkers

"I am still trying to change women's circumstances, to introduce a female point of view, to create art that affirms our womanhood and to make art relevant to people's lives."[1] This statement, made in 1976, continues to be an appropriate summary of Judy Chicago's goals as a visual artist. Her efforts to introduce a female point of view into art began with her art studies at the University of California at Los Angeles. There, the sexually feminine images she employed in her work were ridiculed by her male professors: "When I showed these paintings to the two painting instructors on my thesis committee, they became irate and began to make irrational objections to the work. I didn't understand why they were upset, and obviously neither did they. . . . However, I was getting one message loud and clear. I was putting something into my work that wasn't supposed to be there."[2]

After some efforts to abandon her female-centered images and to create "male" art, Chicago realized that she could not create art that so totally denied who she was and that images produced by women artists would be different from those produced by men: "I could no longer pretend in my art that being a woman had no meaning in my life; my entire experience was being shaped by it. I decided to try and deal with it in my work, to symbolize my sense of myself."[3] She communicated her commitment to working as a feminist artist

[1] Judy Chicago, *Through the Flower: My Struggle as a Woman Artist* (Garden City, NY: Anchor/Doubleday, 1977), p. ix.
[2] Chicago, *Through the Flower*, p. 34.
[3] Chicago, *Through the Flower*, p. 51.

in 1969, when she renounced "all names imposed upon her through male social dominance" and chose her own name, Judy Chicago, after the city of her birth.[4]

Judy's work as an artist always has been interspersed with her desire to provide support for women artists. While teaching at Fresno State University, she organized an art class for women; together, they founded Womanspace, an exhibition space for women housed in an old mansion in Los Angeles. She also developed the Feminist Art Program at the California Institute of the Arts in Valencia and the Feminist Studio Workshop, which attracted thirty women from around the country who shared a desire to work in a feminist context. In 1973, Womanspace, the Feminist Studio Workshop, a feminist bookstore, women's performing groups, feminist galleries, and feminist organizations were incorporated into the Woman's Building in Los Angeles, which was designed to provide a feminist context for women artists.

Chicago's own feminist work attracted widespread national attention with the opening of *The Dinner Party* at the San Francisco Museum of Modern Art in 1979. A room-sized installation piece, it features an open-centered, triangular table on which rest 39 sculptured plates, each representing a woman from history. Each place setting includes a ceramic plate and an elaborate needlework runner that contains the name of the woman represented. *The Dinner Party* was a cooperative work of art in that Judy had the assistance of approximately 500 individuals in the execution of her designs for the plates and runners.

Chicago's second cooperative art work, *The Birth Project*, evolved out of a number of discoveries she made during her work on *The Dinner Party*: "The first was my realization that I had a natural ability to design for—and an intense interest in—needlework. The second was an awareness that, after years of exploring female subject matter, I still had more to say as an artist about the nature of women's lives and experiences. The third discovery had to do with the huge audience response to *The Dinner Party* (as well as some of my earlier work) and to the possibility of participating in my ongoing art-making process."[5] She decided to focus in her next work on birth as a result of her discovery that there "are no birth images in the history of art."[6] Although birth is "a universal human experience and one that is central to women's lives,"[7] it "is virtually a 'taboo' area for open human expression. Little attests to or explains or symbolizes or honors or renders this primary experience, . . ."[8]

The result was a work of art, completed in 1984, that includes 80 works designed by Judy and executed by close to 150 needleworkers. Its purpose best

[4] Chicago, *Through the Flower*, p. 63.
[5] Judy Chicago, *The Birth Project* (Garden City, NY: Doubleday, 1985), p. 4.
[6] Chicago, *The Birth Project*, p. 17.
[7] Chicago, *The Birth Project*, p. 6.
[8] Chicago, *The Birth Project*, p. 19.

is explained by Chicago herself: "I have approached the subject of birth with awe, terror, and fascination, and I have tried to present different aspects of this universal experience—the mythical, the celebratory, and the painful—through *The Birth Project*."[9] *The Birth Project* was a collaboration between the different knowledge and skills of Judy and the needleworkers: "Even though I had painted the image and controlled the color and thread range," I did not want to predetermine the final form of the piece."[10]

Since there was no "art-historical context for creating birth images," Chicago was required "to work out of raw experience and build a whole iconography"[11] for the images of *The Birth Project*. She set out to discover women's experiences of birth and to develop the visual vocabulary to give form to those experiences. She asked women to tell her about their birth experiences and witnessed a birth, recording with sketches and photographs the vivid visual images of the process.

Using brochures and newspaper coverage, Judy recruited needleworkers to execute the images of birth she created. To select the needleworkers for the project, Chicago and the technical supervisor for *The Birth Project*, Sally Babson, developed an application procedure. Each applicant was given a sample pattern of one of Judy's designs and asked to stitch it in any technique and color she wanted. The information the sample provided about the applicant's needle skills, visual acuity, and color abilities allowed Chicago either to reject her application for participation in the project or to assign her to execute a piece consistent with her abilities.

Throughout the work on their pieces, Judy regularly reviewed the needleworkers' progress. She held a review for each needleworker or group of needleworkers every two or three months in Benicia, California, the headquarters for the project; in the needleworkers' homes; or in cities near where they lived. If the work done on samples or the actual pieces satisfied Chicago, the needleworkers would finish that section of the piece; if it did not, they would "reverse-stitch" the section, the euphemism that developed for taking work out.

The process of the collaborative execution of the works was not always an easy one for Judy or the needleworkers. For Chicago, the sharing of her images felt "terrific," but it required that she give away "the activity I like the best: the day-to-day work in the studio, making the images come alive."[12] She also was concerned that the needleworkers would not produce works as she envisioned them: "I'm so scared they won't come through," Judy admitted

[9] Chicago, *The Birth Project*, back cover.
[10] Chicago, *The Birth Project*, p. 21.
[11] Chicago, *The Birth Project*, p. 143.
[12] Chicago, *The Birth Project*, pp. 224-25.

at the beginning of the work on *The Birth Project*.[13] "Do I trust women?"
Chicago wondered. "At what level? With my person? With my art? With my
life and ideas? I don't know."[14] By the end of the project, she had seen her
trust in her co-workers confirmed: "I gloried in seeing my designs come alive
as a result of the deft manipulation of needle and thread," she could say.[15]

The three works from *The Birth Project* included here suggest the range
of works in the project. The first, *Birth Trinity Quilt*, depicts the upheaval
in the body and the earth that is necessary for life to begin. The piece, 47
3/4 by 128 inches, was executed in reverse appliqué and quilting. Barbara
Velazquez of Walnut Creek, California, did the initial reverse appliqué, which
involves basting together different pieces of fabric and cutting through and
turning under all the layers. When Velazquez moved to the East and could
not continue working on the piece, Ann Raschke, a quilter from Nebraska,
worked all the edges of the forms in tiny, regular, almost invisible stitches.
Jacquelyn Moore then quilted the body shapes in regular stitches that flowed
with the forms.

The second piece, *Guided by the Goddess*, a rectangle 54 by 107 inches,
shows the goddess giving birth to and providing nourishment for the human
race. The creatures being born have emerged from both the body of the goddess
and the body of the female Earth. Judy spray painted the image and hand
outlined the forms. Marjorie Smith of Solon, Ohio, then used pulled-thread
and satin-stitch embroidery techniques to execute the images.

In *Earth Birth*, Chicago wanted to portray the landscape as female in form.
She spray painted the 5-by-12-foot fabric, and Jacquelyn Moore of Massachusetts
then quilted it to a batting with tiny stitches that followed the forms. As she
quilted, she changed the color of the quilting thread to blend with the tones
of Judy's sprayed painting.

[13] Chicago, *The Birth Project*, p. 33.
[14] Chicago, *The Birth Project*, p. 62.
[15] Chicago, *The Birth Project*, p. 227.

Judy Chicago with Barbara Velasquez, Ann Raschke, Jacquelyn Moore, **Birth Trinity Quilt**
@ Judy Chicago 1983
Photograph: Michele Maier

Judy Chicago with Marjorie Smith, Guided by the Goddess
@ Judy Chicago 1983
Photograph: Michele Maier

Judy Chicago with Jacquelyn Moore, **Earth Birth**
@ Judy Chicago 1983
Photograph: Michele Maier

22

NEWSLETTERS
The L-Word

Dear Lucy:

Help! My new lover's ex-lover is coming to dinner! What should I wear? What should I do? What should I say? Do you think it would be OK if I asked her if she still can't stand to have her toes kissed? I'm dying of curiosity and my lover refuses to ask.

Nervous Nancy[1]

This letter is addressed to Lucy L.'s advice column, "Ask Lucy L.," one of the standard features in *The L-Word*, an eight-page newsletter produced monthly by and for the lesbian community in Humboldt County, California. The idea of producing a newsletter was the brainchild of seven women at one of the monthly "dyke hikes" for the lesbian community in the summer of 1988; the women discussed the need for some kind of formal means of communication within the local lesbian community. A newsletter seemed to be a natural format, and the first issue, which was two pages long, appeared in August of 1988.

The women who have been consistently involved in the publication of *The L-Word* are Emily, Sue, Lynda, Ruth, Susan, and Wendy.[2] Layout is done on the last Sunday of every month, and anyone is welcome to help. A staff member, reminiscing about the process of producing *The L-Word*, speaks especially fondly about layout in the September, 1989, issue: "My favorite part is layout. It starts

[1] "Ask Lucy L.," *The L-Word*, 2 (September 1, 1989), 3.
[2] Only first names are used in the newsletter, so we are conforming to that practice, as well.

238

with lots of articles, some not even done or typed up, and a feeling of how-will-it-all-come together. Then things settle down, pages start to develop. In only a few hours it's done, along with lots of chatting, joking and general fun and silliness. It's a social event I hate to miss." [3]

The L-Word is supported by funds from various sources. Copies of *The L-Word* sell for 25¢, and T-shirts with *The L-Word* logo are sold to support the cost of the newsletter. The bulk of the funding, however, comes from advertisements placed in the newsletter by local businesses. Camera-ready, business-card-size ads sell for $5.00 each. The Humboldt Access Project also contributes to the funding; it donates the use of its copy machine for copying the newsletter. *The L-Word* is distributed at three local bookstores and at the campus Women's Center; approximately 175 copies are sold monthly.

The format of *The L-Word* remains consistent across issues. A feature article appears on the front page—one related to the time of year, a local issue of importance to the lesbian community, or simply reflections on topics of particular interest to women. "Lizard Louise Reviews" typically follows; this is a section of commentaries about books of special interest to lesbians. The advice column, "Ask Lucy L," appears next; it deals with issues from readers and alleged readers. While the questions and answers in this column are sometimes serious, more often than not, they are humorous and tongue in cheek. A calendar of events also is included that acquaints readers with events of special interest to lesbians in Humboldt County and in surrounding areas. "Connections" and "Resources" are the sections that end the newsletter. "Connections" is a classified ad section. For $2.00, readers can advertise items to sell or give away, jobs wanted or available, vacation trips and lodging, and housing needs. Personals also can be sent to *The L-Word* at a cost of $5.00 for thirty words. "Resources" is a list of services of special interest to lesbians, including rap groups, information about shelters for battered women, radio programs of interest to women, and Alcoholics Anonymous meetings for women. Crossword puzzles, horoscopes, interviews, and other topical essays appear throughout *The L-Word*, although not always on a regular basis.

The December 1, 1988 issue of *The L-Word* is included here and reflects its typical content and form. In her response to "Nervous Nancy," who wrote asking about how to handle the dinner with her lover's ex-lover, Lucy's reply contains the combination of common sense, playfulness, and caring that characterizes *The L-Word*: "No. The general rule of etiquette in these situations seems to be to not acknowledge what all of the people present know to be true. This means you and your lover do not engage in public displays of affection, nor do you wear your matching sweatsuits, and you certainly do not discuss your lover's ex's personal sexual idiosyncracies. You can discuss

---

[3] "Happy Birthday," *The L-Word*, 2 (September 1, 1989), 5.

the personal idiosyncracies of the person that everyone present knows, that is, your lover, and it has been my personal observation that in fact that is a very common activity at these sorts of events. Which tends to be great fun for everyone but the person being discussed, but after all, she asked for it. Have fun." [4]

[4] "Ask Lucy L.," *The L-Word*, 2 (September 1, 1989), 3.

THE "L" WORD

December 1, 1988   Vol. 1, No. 4   P.O. Box 272, Bayside, Ca. 95524

Xmas: stolen from the Goddess

The house is decorated with holly, mistletoe, and wreaths of pine. Laughing people are singing carols and drinking wassail around a blazing Yule log, waiting for dinner of roast suckling pig. Gifts will be exchanged later.

Sound like a traditional Christmas? Actually this ancient scene could be a pagan Norse winter solstice gathering. The winter solstice (Dec. 21) is the shortest day of the year, the end of the sun's long decline and the beginning of a new cycle.

All over Europe and the Near East, festivals celebrated the birth of a god in late December. He had many names (Attis, Dionysus, Osiris, Baal, Frey) and many functions. Typically he was a savior-god who lead newly dead souls into heaven, and the consort of the Goddess, sacrificed and reborn each year in a vital fertility cycle.

The actual birthdate of Jesus has never been known. The Romans usually held their census and tax collection (occasion of the hectic trip to Bethlehem) in spring. The date December 25 was selected by church leaders centuries later. At that time the church was aggressively seeking converts and adapting to local conditions by coopting existing faiths--so a date that already honored the birth of a god made perfect sense.

Most of the symbols we associate with Christmas come not from the Mediterranean roots of Christianity, but from Northern Europe and ancient Goddess religion.

Mistletoe is a parasite of the oak, a tree sacred to the Druids. Mistletoe with its white berries was a male symbol, and red-berried holly female, in this celebration of returning fecundity. A pine tree was cut from the sacred groves of the Great Mother, decorated, and brought into the temple.

Regeneration was symbolized by the roast suckling pig, the apple in its mouth a resurrection charm. Pigs were associated both with the Goddess and her cyclicly sacrified consort-gods. Carolling was a common activity at solstice gatherings.

So whatever holiday you celebrate this season (Hanukkah also has ties to the winter solstice), you can enjoy the connection to women's roots.

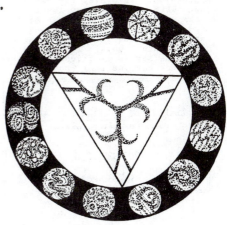

Back into the closet

Lesbians often talk about coming out of the closet, and all the many ways that can happen. Lately, however, I've had to look at the issue of going back into the closet. It's been a very different perspective.

I've gone into a different kind of work, education. As we all know, the world has some weird misinformation about gays and children. I decided I wouldn't come out to anyone connected with education. But then there's guilt about not being out and educating people just by being an out lesbian. Although I wasn't out to everyone at work, there were always at least a few people who knew. I also didn't feel particularly worried about being out in the rest of my life. I started only coming out to other gays and to people I was close friends with. I started being careful.

It hasn't been easy trying to be so much more careful than I've ever been before. I don't like being nervous about who knows I'm a dyke. And I wonder how much it feeds into any other feelings of insecurity I have. Am I buying into my own oppression? It's also been an issue with my lover. My lover looks very dykey, and it can be hard if we're out someplace and I run into someone I know from the school where I work. I just introduce her as my friend, but she knows how nervous I am about it.

What helps me is deciding to be an great "ally" of gays, no matter how much I have to pretend to be straight. I remind myself that it's really possible to be straight and have lesbian friends. I can say, "Some of my best friends are lesbians" (like my lover, ha!). I can model that for the world. I can also talk about gay rights issues and challenge homophobia whenever it comes up. It does feel scarey, but it is also exciting. Sometimes I get into conversations that might never have happened if they knew they were talking to a lesbian.

If I take pride in my disguise of "ally" of gay people, I can feel good about my decsion to partly go back into the closet. --"Hannah Senesch" (A Jewish resistance fighter who died in a Nazi concentration camp. Her diaries indicate she may have been a lesbian.)

Advice for women in 1850 included the following: "True feminine genis is ever timid, doubtful, and clingingly dependent; a perpetual childhood."

Lizard Louise Reviews

Double Daughters, by Vicki P. McConnell (Naiad).
The third Nyla Wade mystery is finally out! This time she's separated from her true love Lucy and back in Denver, Colorado, pursuing the perpetrators of violence against gay and lesbian professors at her alma mater. Light-hearted entertainment.

Diamonds are a Dyke's Best Friend, by Yvonne Zipter (Firebrand).
An overview of lesbians and softball, a subject about which I was fairly ignorant, by a woman who is a cross-over between the two basic groups of lesbians: jocks and political/intellectuals. Educational and entertaining, it added to my knowledge of lesbian culture and challenged some of my own attitudes towards sports. Much of the text is quotes from women interviewed for this book, and I especially enjoyed Pat Parker's comments. My favorite chapter was on how the "feminists" and the "jocks" perceive and mis-perceive each other. Including photos, cartoons, song lyrics, 2 appendices and a bibliography, Yvonne Zipter covers all the bases and pays loving tribute to the "lesbian national pastime".

The Prosperine Papers, by Jan Clausen (Crossing Press), for those hungering for a truly literate voice in a lesbian novel. About lesbian feminist academic Dale McNab and her grand-mother Rose, whose diaries and letters reveal a lover who was a lesbian radi-cal in the days of the IWW miner's strikes in Minnesota. About families, relationships, workers' rights, and our lesbian foremothers, Jan Clausen writes well and touches deeply.
This book engrossed me thoroughly and left a good aftertaste. The portrayal of Dale's midwestern rela-tives was extremely well done. My only complaint is that she covered so many subjects there wasn't as much focussed attention on any one area (relationship, career, family, grandmother's early life) as I would have liked--and Jan Clausen does refuse to tie up ends neatly. But her integrity and her fine writing provide the pleasure only a really good novel can give.

Crush, by Jane Futcher (Alyson).
An excellent portrayal of awakening love and sexual feeling in an Eastern girls' boarding school. Jinx is a hockey player and artist who finds herself powerfully drawn to Lexie, a beautiful manipulator. Besides the intensity of adolescent feeling which Jane Futcher so vivid-ly conveys, I particularly appreciated Jinx's self-respect, her loyalty to her own values and goals side by side with her recognition of her powerful attraction to Lexie. I found out later this is a "young adult" lesbian novel--best one I've read since Annie on My Mind, by Nancy Garden. Jane Futcher is a gifted writer, and the cover is exquisite.

The Amazon Trail, by Lee Lynch (Naiad). Those who've enjoyed Lee Lynch's novels and short stories will appreciate the view of her own life, loves and writing shown through this collection of her syndicated column by the same name.

Lesbian rap open to all

Following is an interview with Lynda,
facilitator of the Lesbian Rap at the
Women's Center.

LW: Is the rap just for HSU students?
L: No, it's open to everyone--students,
community and everyone. This year we have
a really good range, from about 18 to mid
40's, and a fairly even mix of students
and community.

LW: What do you talk about?
L: Subjects that people in rap themselves
have brought up, ranging from political to
funny and everywhere in between. A lot of
support for people having problems with
family. Beginnings and endings of relationships seem to be a real big topic.
Being gay at work. Whether to be out and
how out to be.

LW: What if you want to come, but don't
feel like talking?
L: That's fine. No one has to talk. You
can talk if you feel like it and if you
don't that's okay. Everyone is really
friendly and usually tries to make a new
person comfortable. After a few minutes
new people often warm up and join in. But
if you just want to be in a woman-oriented
environment, that's okay.

LW: What happens at rap?
L: It's rather informal. We have check in
where we give a first name, then tell something about ourselves or our week. Then we
have announcements, a discussion of what the
topic will be, and then we usually have an
hour and a half to talk about the topic.

LW: How do you decide what to talk about?
L: At the first of the year we all wrote
topics down, and before rap starts I choose
four out of a hat, and then we vote on
which to talk about. Or anyone can bring
up a topic at any time that they really
want to talk about. They can let us know
at the Women's Center. We even had a
guest speaker in the recent past.

LW: What about childcare?
L: We have childcare available if people
will let us know a day ahead of time. Call
the Women's Center, 826-4216, and leave a
message that you need childcare for the rap.

LW: What other things do you do?
L: There was interest expressed in learning
more about the connection between lesbians
and AIDS, so we had a speaker from the
County Health Department come out and give
us a 45 minute talk, and had some brochures
from the San Francisco AIDS Project which
were very informative. We could do other
lesbian health issues. We're also going to
have some fun nights this year. We have the
use of the Women's Center some Friday evenings, and are planning to show videos:
Desert Hearts, Liana, Waiting for the Moon,
and anything else people want to see.

Lesbian Rap meets every Tuesday evening
at 7 in the Women's Center at HSU.

-4-

ask Lucy L.

Dear Lucy:
    Lover relationships are just too complicated and painful for me. Is it possible to find happiness in celibacy?
                                        Torn

Dear Torn:
    Of course it's possible, and I think celibacy is a great idea. (I also think that monagamy, and non-monagamy, and all the different way we chose to relate to each other are great ideas). You do realize that being celibate won't necessarily keep you from having complicated and painful relationships, don't you? In my experience, happiness isn't something you can go looking for. Do what you think is the best thing for you and maybe happiness will find you.
                                        LL

Dear Lucy L:
    Are you sure you're not Lucille Ball in disguise?   Love, Ethyl L.
Dear Ethyl:
    My publishers tell me that their lawyer told them that I shouldn't discuss my identity in print. But if you'll send me your phone number maybe we could make a private date to talk about it.
                                Love, Lucy

Dear Lucy L:
    My friend and I think we know what your last name is, but were you born that way or did you change it? Do you have trouble cashing checks? My lover and I were thinking of combining our names to honor our realtionship. Is this politically correct or politically incorrect in the 80's? Reactionary politics are so hard to figure out. Dear Lucy, I hope you can help us.
    Olive Y. Curls
    Hope U. Geweer
            (soon to be the Geweer-Curls)
Dear Geweer Curls:
    The only thing I can figure out about P.C. and P.I. in the 80's is that it's P.I. to try to decide what's P.C. So you're probably ok whatever you do. As for my name, isn't the question of whether we were born that way one of those religious-type questions? What do you think? Congratulations,   Lucy

Thomas Jefferson, author of the famous phrase "all men are created equal", underscored the word men with his comment that American women "would be too wise to wrinkle their foreheads with politics."   -5-

lavender blooms
flowers
Wed-Fri, 11-5:30
7th & F, Arcata

calendar

Dec. 2--Film "Miss or Myth?" on
          Nikki Craft & the Miss
          California Pageant, 7 pm,,
          HSU Women's Center (House 55
          behind library)

Dec. 3--GAY DANCE! Black & White Ball
          sponsored by Gay & Lesbian
          Student Union. Arcata Veteran's
          Memorial Bldg., 14th & J, $3.50,
          must be 18.

Dec. 4--Women's Brunch in Arcata, 11am,
          call 822-6992 for directions.

Dec. 6--Lesbian Rap, 7 pm, HSU Women's
          Center.

Dec. 11--Dyke Hike meets at HSU Women's
          Center 10:30 am, cancelled in
          case of heavy rain.

Dec. 11--Ruth Mountaingrove, Performance
          & Poetry, Humboldt Cultural
          Center, 1st & E Sts, Eureka,
          1:30 pm.

Dec. 13--Lesbian Rap

Dec. 18--"Lesbian Concentrate" Show
          on KHSU 90.5 FM, 3:30-5 pm.

Dec. 20--Lesbian Rap takes a break

Dec. 21--Winter Solstice

Dec. 27--Lesbian Rap takes a break

Dec. 30--Lesbian Night at the
          Movies, "Gorillas in
          the Mist" 7:45, Arcata
          Theater.

Jan. 13--Robin Flower & Libby
          McClaren performing in
          Mendocino, 8 pm, sliding
          scale $6-3.

Feb. 11--All Women Valentine Day
          Dance with Moo Moo & the
          Creamers, R&R direct from
          Garberville, performance
          in Mendocino, sliding scale.

HELLO AGAIN!

Solstice Greetings to the Lesbian
Community from all of us here at
the "L" Word. That includes cele-
brators of any and all holidays
and all you Bah-Humbuggers too.

Check our advertisers for gift
ideas: Booklegger has many lesbian
books in stock as well as the
lesbian Trivia cards D.Y.K.E. (Do
You Know Enough?), Northtown has
a full shelf of new lesbian books,
Lavender Blooms has beautiful
flowers.

We love our readers and appreciate
so much your support--we never expected to expand so quickly, main-
taining our 8-page size, and selling almost 175 copies each month.
Ads are coming in, and t-shirts are
next (see p. 4).

Another nice offshoot has been
Lesbian Night at the Movies once
a month. This month we've picked
"Gorillas in the Mist" Friday
Dec. 30, 7:45 at the Arcata Theater.
See you on the left side, towards
the back!

We still need articles, graphics,
and letters (sorry, no poetry).
-6- Happy New Year, and see you some
time around the first!

Kitchen Table: Women of Color Press,
The Third Wave; Feminist Perspectives
on Racism. Send contributions (5
copies) to Sharon Day, 444 Lafayette
Rd., St. Paul, MN 55155.   Deadline
January 1, 1989. Max. 30 pp, double-sp.

Cleis Press, Different Kids, ed.
by Louise Rafkin. Writings and
interviews with children of lesbians.
Interested parents or children (including adult children) write her
at Cleis Press, P.O. Box 14684, San
Francisco, CA 94114. (415) 420-
0592. If possible, include information
about your situation & background.

In Our Own Voices: Fat Dykes Break
the Silence. Previous writing experience is not important. All accepted
pieces will be published in the
language in which they are written.
Send contributions with SASE by Jan. 1,
1989 to: Toni L. Cassita, P.O. Box
2968, Santa Cruz, CA 95063. (408)
423-4734.

IF YOU HAVE EXPERIENCED DISCRIMINATION
BASED SOLELY ON YOUR WEIGHT, PLEASE
DOCUMENT, DATE DISCRIMINATION HAPPENED,
AND AS ACCURATE AS POSSIBLE THE DETAILS
OF WHAT HAPPENED, PLUS ANY RELEVANT
INFORMATION.

DOCUMENTATION IS NEEDED TO AMEND
CURRENT STATE CIVIL RIGHTS LAWS TO
INCLUDE WEIGHT, WHICH WOULD PROHIBIT
FURTHER DISCRIMINATION BASED ON A
PERSON'S BODY SIZE.

SEND RESPONSES TO:
    "WEIGHT" PUT IT ON!
    P.O. BOX 2968
    SANTA CRUZ, CA 95063
    (408) 423-4734

Connections

GEESE seeking temporary pasture.
If you have a safe fenced yard,
they will mow and fertilize your
lawn. These three birds are fairly
quiet and quite gentle. Will deliver. Call 839-4256.

VALLEY CREEK COTTAGE: Southern
Oregon Bed & Breakfast with hot
tub (503) 476-8812. Weekend
Special for Two--2 nights, Saturday
dinner, Sunday brunch--only $110.
Expires 4-30-89.

LLEAD A LLAMA through the Lost
Coast! Woman-led pack trips.
For info., write: Nancy Peregrine,
Lost Coast Llama Caravans, 77321
Usal Rd., Whitethorn, CA 95489.

FREE to good home: Basenji cross
spayed female, all shots & license.
She's a good companion who needs
lots of love. 839-4664.

WOMEN'S BLUES BAND forming, no New
Wave. Rock, blues, old country.
Call 822-5232.

WANTED: Energetic young dog seeks
canine companion, your yard or mine,
while my owner is at work. Call
Hannah at 839-4798.

CLASSIFIEDS are $2.00 per 25 words.
Make checks payable to "The L Word,"
P.O. Box 272, Bayside, CA 95524.

Gorgeous heiress new to area,
child-loving, creative, warm,
totally together, great cook
and auto mechanic seeking lost
soul to nurture & cherish.
Would you like to meet this woman?
Write the "L" Word with your
personals--we get results!
$5.00 for each 30 words. We will
give your ad a box number and
forward inquiries to you on the
15th and 30th of the month.

Resources

The weekly LESBIAN RAP is on Tuesday evenings at the Women's Center (House 55) at HSU. It's from 7-9 pm, and drop-ins are welcome.

There is also a weekly BISEXUAL RAP, on Thursdays from 6-8 pm, also at the Women's Center.

Alchoholics Anonymous:
    24-hour answering service: 442-0711

    Womens' Meetings:
        Mondays, 12 noon
        Russ & I, Eureka

    Myrtletown Survivors (non-smoking):
        Tuesdays, 8 pm
        3100 Edgewood Dr., Eureka

    Gay Meetings:
        Wednesdays, 6 pm
        Russ & I, Eureka

 Both locations are wheelchair accessible.

Once a month, on the second Sunday, a sturdy band of outdoorswomen meets at the Women's Center on campus at 10:30 with daypacks and canteens. A destination is chosen, and several hours are spent hiking in good company. The hikes vary from easy to moderate. Join us.

The Women Artist's support group is open to all women and meets monthly. All media represented, location rotates. For information, call 822-2811.

The Women's Center, House 55 on the HSU campus (south of the library) is not just for students. A lending library, resource files, bulletin boards, and new friends are open to all women of the community. Tea, coffee, and bagels are available from 9-4. Phone 826-4216.

Unfortunately, the Women's Information Line at the HSU Women's Center will no longer be used, due to a new phone system. Call during office hours M-F, 9-4 for information.

The monthly WOMEN'S BRUNCH is a good way to meet lesbians, especially if you are new in the community. The location varies, and to find the current one, call the information line at the HSU Women's Center, 826-4216. The Brunch is the first Sunday of every month, and is a potluck.

The Disabled Women's Support Group meets Thursdays from 3:30-5 pm, at Humboldt Access Project, 2017 Third St., Eureka, 445-8404. The group started Sept. 15 and will run for at least 10 weeks and may continue. A lesbian Disabled support group may also be forming. Call for info.

Lesbian ACA-type group now underway, meets Mondays 7 pm, call 822 2811 for location.

"Through the Eyes of Women" is an excellent woman-identified public affairs show on KHSU, including news, interviews, music, and readings. It lasts ½ hour and is aired twice weekly, Tuesdays 4 pm and Saturdays 3:30.

Women's Rap Group, Mondays 7-9 in HSU Women Center, Rm. 106.

thanks to...

Lynda, Susan Nolan, Judith, "Hannah Senesch", Jonnie, Sandy, Sue H., Corinne, Roseann, Sally, Bev, Choi.

The "L" Word is distributed at Booklegger, 2nd & E, Eureka; Northtown Books, 957 H, Arcata; The Women's Center, HSU; Woodrose Cafe, Garberville.

23

PRINTMAKING/PAINTING

Betty LaDuke

"A successful artist," believes Betty LaDuke, "is able to pursue a vision and let that vision take that person places where they never would expect. It isn't the dollar bill at the end of having so many shows but having art be a part of your life—you want to do it, no matter what." LaDuke's definition is an apt description of her own life as an artist: "I think I'll be doing art always. I don't know anything else to do. It's a key part of my day-to-day being."

Betty's interest in art was encouraged by two African-American artists she knew while growing up in the Bronx. They had traveled and lived in Mexico and inspired her to go there following study at the Cleveland Institute of Art and the University of Denver. She spent three years in Mexico, first studying at the Instituto Allende in San Miguel and then working as an artist. Returning to the United States, she earned bachelor's and master's degrees from California State University at Los Angeles. Since 1964, she has been a member of the art faculty at Southern Oregon State College in Ashland.

LaDuke's efforts to develop a course on multicultural arts as part of the art curriculum led to her discovery of the "lack of information in our country about artists of other cultures and, in particular, about contemporary art from these cultures. We seem to appreciate the pre-historic—it's safe—but very little is known about non-Western art." Her preparation for a course on women and art revealed yet another gap. Available literature and slides "focused primarily on women's art from the United States and Europe. Because my students found relevance and excitement in that part of my course that dealt with our own country's artists of Native, Latina, African, and Asian descent, I was encouraged to search out and add examples of women's art from Latin

249

America, Asia and the Pacific."[1]

To gain the information she needed in these areas, Betty began to travel extensively, and she spends a good part of each summer exploring cultures outside of the United States. Her travels, which sometimes are partially funded by grants from sources such as foundations and humanities councils, have taken her to India, Sri Lanka, Indonesia, Thailand, Hong Kong, the People's Republic of China, Australia, Borneo, Chile, Peru, Nicaragua, Guatemala, Honduras, Ecuador, Bolivia, Brazil, Cuba, Haiti, Grenada, Puerto Rico, Yugoslavia, Nigeria, Egypt, Kenya, Morocco, Senegal, Mali, and the Ivory Coast. In each country she visits, LaDuke seeks out women artists, interviews them, studies and photographs their work, gathers information about the role of the arts and of women artists in their communities, and marvels "at their diversity and courage."

As she travels, Betty sketches, a habit she developed as a teenager as she traveled around New York City, fascinated by and wanting to capture the diversity of the cultures she observed. She returns from her journeys with her sketchbooks filled; these sketches then become the inspiration for her own work in printmaking and painting: "At the end of each journey my need was to convert the essence of these sketched events into universal and archetypal images that would reflect cross-cultural dreams and aspirations."[2] She elaborates: "I look back and realize that my travels were also a personal spirit journey. Like a serpent shedding skin, I had cast aside routine responsibilities to experience an extraordinarily different world view. Though it was only a brief period of sharing some of the intimacies of people's daily lives, customs and traditions, I was deeply touched in long-lasting ways. These feelings received visible expression in the paintings and prints later produced in my home studio."[3]

The dominant theme LaDuke explores in her work is women's roles. Her own experiences as a woman, which have included marriage and motherhood (she is the mother of two and the grandmother of one), always have been incorporated into Betty's work. But her work with women artists in other cultures led her to develop the role of women as a focal point. In particular, she explores women's lives as a duality — women as young bearers of new life, sustaining, and nurturing all life forms, and women as old, wise, healers and cultural guardians, offering strength and stability.

LaDuke's work also is characterized by a fusion of life forms; boundaries vanish between normally distinct entities, whether plant, animal, or human. Women's arms and heads turn into birds, bodies are trees, legs are roots, one person merges into another, and human forms contain multitudes of other humans, vegetation, and animals. Betty is interested not just in "being stimulated

---

[1] Betty LaDuke, *Compañeras: Women, Art, and Social Change in Latin America* (San Francisco: City Lights, 1985), p. xi.

[2] Betty LaDuke, "Images of African Woman," *KSOR Guide to the Arts* [Southern Oregon State College], March, 1990, p. 9.

[3] LaDuke, "Images of African Woman," p. 9.

by reality but wanting to reshape it in some way." The result is a rich, complex, dream-like universe of connectedness.

LaDuke's travels have resulted not only in vivid images in her own works of art but also in articles and books that explore the lives and artistic expressions of women. Her numerous articles have appeared in various art and feminist journals. Her books include *Mexico: A Sketchbook Journey of Easter* (1980), *Compañeras: Women, Art, and Social Change in Latin America* (1985), and *Africa Through the Eyes of Women Artists* (1990).

Betty acknowledges that her time is divided and fragmented, but, she asks, "what can I give up—teaching, traveling, writing or studio work? I continually struggle to master the juggling act . . . ." She sees a unity in her life and work that sustains and supports her: Bonding "with my family and friends on a multicultural, global level nurtures me. Therefore, I have the need to continue sharing, visually and verbally, examples of human dignity and hope." [4]

Four samples of LaDuke's works follow, one inspired by her travels in Latin America and three by her experiences in Africa. The first, *Tree of Life*, is part of a series of 21 prints and is 22 by 30 inches in size. It refers to the mothers of the disappeared in Argentina, Chile, El Salvador, and Guatemala. Betty depicts the tree as a woman's body, containing her despair; at the same time, she shows mothers transforming their anger and anguish into a common voice and visible action. She hopes such art serves as a vehicle for people to "reach out to help one another, to strive to grow out of the horror, to reach toward a situation that is more life producing, more life affirming."

The second print, 18 by 24 inches in size, is *Africa: Osun Calabash*, which depicts the celebration of Osun, A Yoruba fertility goddess. During the annual festival honoring her in August, a virgin is selected to carry a calabash or gourd filled with water on her head as she walks in a procession from the king's palace to the sacred Osun grove. Spilled water is considered a bad omen for the coming year.

In *Africa Bird Women, Carriers of the Dream*, a print 68 by 72 inches, LaDuke portrays the Yoruba market vendors who sit long hours with their children and baskets of fruits, vegetables, or kola nuts. Sometimes, their long, colorful head wrappers unwind and become mythical birds or guardian spirits, the carriers of their dreams.

Africa: Procession is a 68-by-72-inch acrylic painting, in which Betty honors the long processions of women bearing produce on their heads. Their produce burdens are transformed into spirit dreams that are guarded by black vultures, suggesting that the women are not free to realize their dreams. The flight of the white birds above, however, suggests that their aspirations continue to soar as they mobilize in unison to fulfill both their needs and their dreams.

⁴ J. F. Anderson, "Betty LaDuke: Acrylic Painting," in *Northwest Originals: Oregon Women and Their Art*, ed. Ellen Nichols (Portland: In Unison, 1989), p. 33.

Betty LaDuke, **Tree of Life**
Photograph: Douglas R. Smith

Betty LaDuke, **Africa: Osun Calabash**
Photograph: Douglas R. Smith

Betty LaDuke, **Africa Bird Women, Carriers of the Dream**
Photograph: Douglas R. Smith

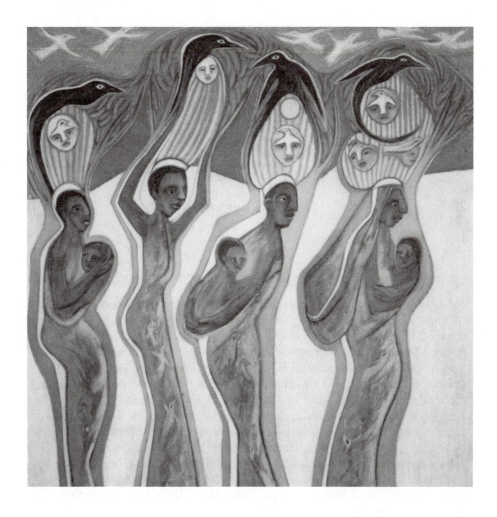

Betty LaDuke, **Africa: Procession**
Photograph: Douglas R. Smith

24

PHOTOGRAPHY

Diana Schoenfeld

Diana Schoenfeld is a photographer whose work already is known to readers of *Women Speak*; she is one of the photographers who took the pictures for the book. Her work has been exhibited at the San Francisco Museum of Modern Art; the Museum of Contemporary Photography in Chicago; universities across the United States; and galleries in Los Angeles, New York, and Amsterdam, among others. Schoenfeld has taught photography at the University of Hawaii, the University of Michigan, the University of Nebraska, and College of the Redwoods in Eureka, California. A resident of Loleta, California, Diana currently works independently as a photographer who exhibits and sells her own photographs. She recently curated an exhibition and catalog based on her research and writing about the picture-within-the-picture in photography. The exhibition, titled *Symbol and Surrogate: The Picture Within*, was sponsored by the University of Hawaii and later traveled to the Claremont colleges in Southern California.

Schoenfeld's interest in the visual arts began as a child: "I was an artsy kid—always painting and drawing." Theater was her first love during her high school years, however, precisely because it combined so many arts: "The theater not only involved literature . . . but also the visual two- and three-dimensional arts—the costumes, the staging, the sets, and that kind of three-dimensional reality of the theatrical production." At sixteen, she had to make a choice between continuing in theater or focusing her attention on the visual arts, a decision prompted by two equally interesting opportunities. She was offered the role of Antigone by the Actors' and Writers' Workshop in Atlanta; this would have been her first key role in a play. At the same time, she was chosen to attend a summer governor's honors program, where she would receive accelerated training in the visual arts. Schoenfeld chose the honors program and thus a focus on visual arts but feels her theater experience had a critical impact on her life: "I didn't realize until many years later that the theater program I abandoned, so to speak, has had tremendous influence on all of my professional activities—probably more so than the governor's honors program. But together, the two of them meshed to provide me with the grounding to be able to go on as an artist."

In college, Diana's interests switched from painting to photography as a result of a year spent abroad at the Université de Neuchâtel in Switzerland. Because she did not have studio space there to paint, she bought a camera and began using it as a form of artistic expression: "I was stranded high and dry with no place to do my art. It was then I realized how much that had been a part of my life and how much I missed it, and I went out with a camera and began looking at the world with a rectangular frame around my view, extracting bits and pieces of what was out there." When she returned to the United States to continue her undergraduate degree at Georgia State University, she began to study photography as an art form—although informally at first: "I still thought I was majoring in painting, but the first thing I did was to sneak down to the darkroom and find out what was happening down there." She began taking photography classes and soon became a major, although "everyone upstairs in the painting studio thought I was a painter because I was still painting. But the whole time my heart was down there in the darkroom."

As a painter, Schoenfeld had emphasized collage, combining paper, paint, and textured materials in the muted earth tones of nature. Her photographs continue to reflect many of these same qualities; they tend to be contemplative studies that emphasize placement, structure, stillness, and a connection with nature. Diana's theatrical interests also are evident in her desire to choreograph an illusion of three-dimensional space by combining a variety of raw materials for the camera in a still-life mode.

Schoenfeld's first series of still-life photographs, completed between 1973 and 1976, was called *Illusory Arrangements*. These photographs consist of fragments from her own photographs of posed nude figures, landscapes, and objects combined with portions of images from the works of Michelangelo and other classical painters. These pictorial scenes are embellished with specimens from nature such as dried plants, insects, and stones. She was interested in reorganizing familiar objects—from nature and from her own work—to create a new image that seems to be a photograph of a slice of reality but is, in fact, a carefully arranged illusion. The notion of putting her own photographs into these works would reappear later in her interest in the picture-within-the-picture.

Diana's photography evolved into even more carefully arranged still lifes of natural specimens, a series she called *Rhythmic Arrangements*. These photographs, completed between 1976 and 1981, consist of repetitive patterns of grasses, shells, insects, bones, and flower petals arranged on a light table so that an illusion of space is created by the shadows. In some, the male nude is incorporated, again using figures taken from her own photographic studies. Up to this point, Schoenfeld did only black-and-white photography: "I was not using any color at that point. I couldn't even imagine it. I actually had a huge non-imagination about it."

In 1981, while in this phase of her photography, Diana received a head injury as a result of an accident. After she had recovered enough to return to her photographic work, she struggled to deal with the changes in her brain: "It was strange that I could function as before, technically—that everything I knew, including my photographic skills, was available to me. I just couldn't relate them to my past or to how I had acquired them." She wanted to return, for example, to photographing the natural specimen still lifes she had been doing, but she discovered that those arrangements simply did not work for her anymore. At about the same time, the glass on her light table broke, and she was confronted literally, as well as metaphorically, with a shattering of her previous approach to photography. Consequently, she decided to try to symbolize, through photography, the invisible, emotional, and perceptual aftershocks of her injury.

The result was a series of 25 photographs, called *Fractures and Severances*, which reflects "a mind struggling to understand a world once taken for granted but now just beyond comprehension."[1] Some of these photographs relate to the sense of smell, which Schoenfeld lost permanently as a result of the injury. Others illustrate her temporary difficulty processing symbols, which she conveys by juxtaposing foreign languages, sheet music, and illogical phonetic writing. The photographs contain an occasional element found in her previous work— dried flowers and natural specimens—but in this series, their presence is dominated by fragments of shattered glass, illegible script, and bent nails, symbolizing the trauma of the accident. Disorderly maps, personal notes, old photographs, and diagrams of the brain represent the disconnected bits of her past and present, which she struggled to order through visual symbolization. These black-and-white photographs, chemically treated to have a bruised, blood-stained quality, suggest the physical evidence of injury.

The series of *Fractures and Severances* came to an end in 1983, when Diana wrote an essay about her experiences, published in *Family Survival Project Update*, a San Francisco publication about head injury. She realized that "once I could translate the visual images into words on a page, something happened.

---

[1] Bob Sheldon, "Artist's Work Describes Invisible Aftershocks of Head Injury," *Sunday Journal Star* [Lincoln, Nebraska], October 13, 1985, p. 8H.

I was liberated from this unconscious compulsion to make visible to myself what had happened inside of my brain. And oddly, once my visual language was translated again by me into the verbal, something was over. Experiencing the head injury was over. Now I could move on."

Schoenfeld traveled to Peru as a test to see whether she could manage the world again. On that trip, she began taking black-and-white landscape photographs of the high-mountain country. While landscapes were new for her in terms of the scale of the subject matter, they embodied many of the characteristic features of her earlier works. A rock pattern that occurred in an earlier still life, for example, is almost identical to a picture she took of a winding stone wall. Small specimens—this time of people and objects— are cast against enormous vistas.

Not until 1985 did Diana try landscapes in color, a change she attributes directly to the head injury: "Although I didn't start using color immediately after the injury, I definitely noticed a change in my sense of color or my receptiveness to color, my response to color. It's as if my world sprang into color." In addition, her sense of space had shifted as a result of the injury: "I have no sense of distance anymore. . . . What had been a previous sense of limits was gone." Similarly, she lost the need to touch physically the materials she composes.

What Schoenfeld calls "atmospheric, still-life landscapes," in color, continue to be her present focus. She has titled this series *The Serenity Studies* and sees them bringing together her sense of three-dimensional space, color, and structure into an integrated—though oddly ethereal—whole. She composes many of these square-format landscapes on the diagonal, experimenting with how to suggest, in a diamond composition, "a sense of the vastness of the sky and the depths of the earth, unfolding as they both do from the endless hinge of the horizon."

The photographs that follow reflect three stages in Diana's still-life period. The photograph with the female nude is from her *Illusory Arrangements* series; the female figure in it is from one of her earlier photographs. The male nude with natural specimens is from the *Rhythmic Arrangements* series, and the third photograph is from *Fractures and Severances*, the series done following her head injury.

Diana Schoenfeld, from Illusory Arrangements

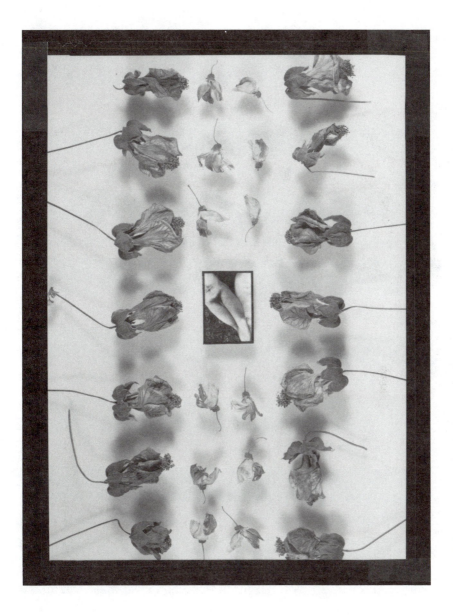

*Diana Schoenfeld, from **Rhythmic Arrangements***

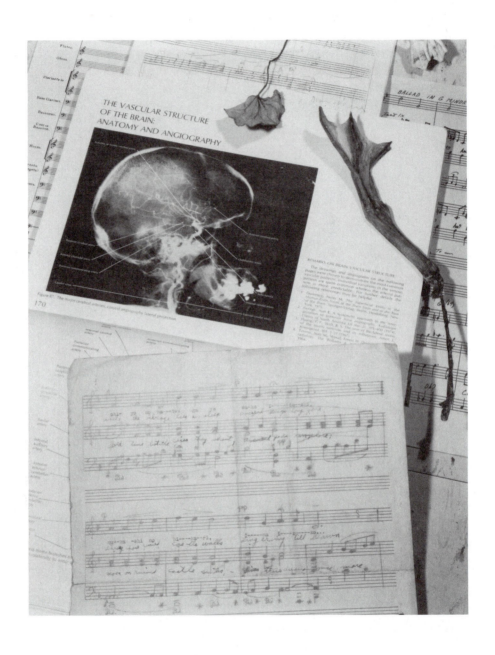

Diana Schoenfeld, from **Fractures and Severances**

25

POETRY

Michelle Boisseau

"Michelle Boisseau is a passionately feminine poet," says reviewer Robert Boyd, writing in the *St. Louis Post-Dispatch*. "She concentrates her work on facts as well as feelings, making compositions in which all can read plainly the exquisite tensions between society and sensuality by which, whether they like it or not, women in our place and time must define themselves."[1]

Born in Cincinnati, Boisseau holds bachelor's, master's, and doctorate degrees in English. She was director of creative writing at Virginia Intermont College in Bristol prior to assuming her current position as associate professor and director of creative writing in the English Department at Morehead State University in Morehead, Kentucky; she teaches creative writing, literature, and freshman composition. Her short stories and poetry have appeared in a variety of journals, and her poetry has been compiled into *No Private Life*, published by Vanderbilt University Press in 1990, and *East of the Sun and West of the Moon*, a chapbook published by the St. Louis Poetry Center in 1989. She is the winner of numerous awards and fellowships, including a National Endowment for the Arts Poetry Fellowship.

The impetus for Michelle's writing is a desire for surprise: "When I'm writing about a woman—either real or fictional/mythic—I'm not so much aware of the *fact* that I'm assuming a woman's perspective or that I am a woman, so much as I have a desire to surprise myself with what I come up with. . . . My

---

[1] Robert Boyd, "A Passionately Feminine Poet," rev. of *East of the Sun and West of the Moon*, by Michelle Boisseau, *St. Louis Post-Dispatch*, January 14, 1990, p. 5D.

motivation is a wish to surprise, to reveal a person, a woman, perhaps, who seems absolutely real—even if, ostensibly, she is a goddess—a woman who (like most of us) labors under and delights in all the human passions and the troubling and comforting notions that make life interesting."

After she finishes writing, between drafts of her work, and in her day-to-day life as a woman, however, Boisseau explains that she does have "more political motives." She wants "to redeem images of women from the simplistic treatments we're typically given: the cold bitch, the virgin, the whore, the mamma, the ditz, the superwoman, and their easy recombinations (the bitchy virgin, the virginal whore, the bitchy mother, the virgin mother), the creatures of popular culture, of soap opera, as well as creatures of fine art, of Tolstoy and Picasso." Her desire to redeem is not limited to women, however: "it's men, too, and children, even history itself." She acknowledges that this goal is a large one: "This redemption is not an ambition I foresee fulfilling, but it's one that poses interesting problems to work out, many surprises."

Michelle's writing process involves writing every morning and, if she has the time and energy, throughout the day. She warms up by reading the work of other writers and does not wait to write until she is inspired: "If I waited for inspiration, I'd never write anything." Boisseau tried "to do other, more responsible things" in her life prior to settling into a writing career, but she found that "only creative writing made me happy." She elaborates: "*Happy* is the wrong word. Writing often makes me miserable, but it gives me great satisfaction. I can't stop myself."

Three of Michelle's poems, all from her *No Private Life*, follow. "Counting" and "The Anniversary" were written before her marriage and are partly autobiographical, dealing with what Boisseau has learned about herself and other women in and out of relationships. "Gladiolus" was written when she and her fiancé were discussing having a baby, who since has arrived.

Counting

After a while, remembering the men you loved
is like counting stars.
From the arbitrary constellations
you pick out those the brightest. Then the others,
dimmer and dimmer until you can't tell
if they're real or only reflections
from your eyes watering with the strain.
 The body's memory is a poor thing. Ask the adopted child
who falls asleep against any steady heart,
to a lullaby in any language.
Between my first lover who was thin
and my second who was warm and nostalgic,
my arms remember little. Though, yes,
there was one who had that sweet smell in his skin
of a child who still drinks nothing
but milk. A milk ladled out
by the Big and Little Dippers. If you look up
long enough into the night sky,
it becomes surer of itself and you less sure
whether you're lying on the lawn, skirt tucked
against mosquitoes, a cigarette
about to burn your fingers,
or if you're falling, and the sky
is a net that can't catch you
since, like everyone else, you are water
nothing can stop. So you lie on your bed,
all night staring at the cracks
in the ceiling, terrified of falling through.

The Anniversary

Let's get this right.
First, that day was little different from others:
the argument between us like a torn bird
on a platter, the vague collapse of its parts
stuck to the cooled butter.

And second, all afternoon I'd watched you shedding the sea
off Naptree Point. The cormorants,
ticked by the invasion, unfolded from their aeries
like black newspapers. The book of my hands
lay open as I could not read it.

> But for you that afternoon
> was all irritations—
> the face mask leaked in strings of sea:
> you shot the spear gun into the rocks.
> When you swam in to straighten the shaft,
> I must have looked ridiculous, wedged
> into the water that pooled in your mask,
> and then my moodiness like a cloud of sand
> the tide rolled against you.

And last, on the way back—
didn't you drive?—
yes, you were glad to be intent on it—
the black mirror of Merritt Parkway,
the tunnel of traffic, no way you could turn to me
though you must have felt my eyes on you.
                                        But you're wrong.

I hoped for nothing from you. I'd become fascinated
with the browned skin of your arm, sea salt
crystalizing in the golden hairs:

                              though I was angry
I had to sit on my hands, I wanted to taste that salt,

take the blade of my tongue and travel
the length of you. For I could see the years
with me had left no mark on you.

Gladiolus

for a child who was never born

Where my life would have gone with you
is not as bad as I imagined:
stuck somewhere like Sulphur Springs, Ohio,
you thrashing in a grubby bassinet,
workweeks dropped like blank pie
from an office clock, weekends dragged
from an in-law's speed boat, lake water
like the green glass of a wine bottle
with me inside, a genie no incantation
could force out. Nor would it have gone

as easily as here in my 32nd year,
settling papery bulbs into silky pockets.
All day I need answer no one, so my thoughts
can spill quick as water from a rain spout
and fan out across last fall's leaves.
   Now that you're old enough to listen,
   now that you've come to that age
   you would have been,
   now that the soil has burned off the frost's glitter
   and rustles beneath my fingers,

I see how you have grown impatient for me.
It used to sicken me, earthworms uncoiling
from the roots of wild onion, the anarchy
of pill bugs beneath a fallen branch.
But smeared and shining to my elbows with mud,
the hand aching that held the claw,
I see now where you have gone to wait for me.
With canteen and rope I'm outfitting myself,
I'm coming down to get you, to bring you back
in crimson trumpets dense along the pliant spear.

26

PUBLIC SPEAKING

Ursula K. Le Guin

"I am an aging, angry woman laying mightily about me with my handbag, fighting hoodlums off. . . . It's just one of those damned things you have to do in order to be able to go on gathering wild oats and telling stories,"[1] says writer Ursula Le Guin about herself and her writing. Her "fighting" often involves subverting various "hoodlums" of tradition—traditional notions about literary genres, theories of literature, and appropriate roles for women. Her goal is "to subvert as much as possible without hurting anybody's feelings,"[2] a subversion she sees as inevitable simply because she speaks as a woman: "There is no more subversive act than the act of writing from a woman's experience of life using a woman's judgment."[3]

Le Guin earned degrees in French and Romance Languages from Radcliffe College and Columbia University, taught French briefly, and then moved to Portland, Oregon, where she has lived and worked as a writer for the last thirty years. Her works include fifteen novels, including *The Left Hand of Darkness* (1969), *The Dispossessed* (1974), and *Always Coming Home* (1986); about sixty short stories in periodicals such as *The New Yorker, Omni,* and *Kenyon Review*; seven books for children; poetry; criticism; reviews; screenplays; and two collections of essays. She has won a number of literary honors and awards, including the Hugo, Nebula, Gandalf, Kafka, and National Book awards.

[1] Ursula K. Le Guin, *Dancing at the Edge of the World: Thoughts on Words, Women, Places* (New York: Grove, 1989), p. 168.
[2] Le Guin, p. vii.
[3] Le Guin, p. 177.

Ursula currently is experimenting with the spoken word as performance and has been writing some pieces to be performed, in which the sound of the words is the primary focus: "It's playing with word as sound, as well as word as meaning. I get tired of word as meaning. People are always saying, 'What does that story mean?' and sometimes I think, does it matter? Listen to it! It's like music. Listen to the story. Hear it! And does it matter what it means if it satisfies you?"

Le Guin acknowledges that she has been able to write because of the support she has felt from her husband and three children, now grown: "Any artist must expect to work amid the total, rational indifference of everybody else to their work, for years, perhaps for life: but no artist can work well against daily, personal, vengeful resistance," suggests Ursula. "And that's exactly what many women artists get from the people they love and live with." Le Guin happily explains, "I was spared all that." "By the luck of race, class, money, and health, I could manage . . . and especially by the support of my partner. He is not my wife, but he brought to marriage an assumption of mutual aid as its daily basis, and on that basis you can get a lot of work done." [4]

Ursula sees the process of writing as "world-making": "An artist makes the world her world. For a little while. For as long as it takes to look at or listen to or watch or read the work of art." [5] Her process of creating a world through writing involves manipulation of five principal patterns: (1) Language— the sounds of words; (2) syntax and grammar—the ways the words and sentences connect to make the movement, tempo, or pace of a work; (3) images—what the words make or let us sense imaginatively; (4) ideas—what the words and the narration of events make us understand; and (5) feelings— what the words and the narration, through use of the other four elements, encourage us to experience emotionally or spiritually.[6]

Once she has written a story, poem, or novel, Le Guin rereads and revises it with a sense of collaborating with her readers, a process she begins by asking herself a number of questions: "Am I shoving them around, manipulating them, patronizing them, showing off to them? Am I punishing them? Am I using them as a dump site for my accumulated psychic toxins? Am I telling them what they better damn well believe or else? Am I running circles around them, and will they enjoy it? Am I scaring them, and did I intend to? Am I interesting them, and if not, hadn't I better see to it that I am? Am I amusing, teasing, alluring them? Flirting with them? Hypnotizing them? Am I giving to them, tempting them, inviting them, drawing them into the work *to work with me* — to be the one, the Reader, who completes my vision?" [7] She sees the role of the

[4] Le Guin, p. 233.
[5] Le Guin, p. 47.
[6] Le Guin, p. 194.
[7] Le Guin, p. 198.

audience in her work as critical: "Because the writer cannot do it alone. The unread story is not a story; it is little black marks on wood pulp. The reader, reading it, makes it live: a live thing, a story."[8]

A major theme in Ursula's work is an effort to challenge a culture that subordinates and mutes women's voices: "I don't want what men have. I'm glad to let them do their work and talk their talk. But I do not want and will not have them saying or thinking or telling us that theirs is the only fit work or speech for human beings."[9] She urges other women to speak in their own voices: "Now this is what I want: I want to hear your judgments. I am sick of the silence of women. I want to hear you speaking all the languages, offering your experience as your truth, as human truth . . . ."[10] She urges women to validate women's expressions and to resist men's efforts to subvert and resist them: "The English profs keep sweeping our work under the rug, but that rug is about three feet off the floor by now, and things are coming out from under it and eating the English profs. Housework is woman's work, right? Well, it's time to shake the rugs."[11]

Part of the process of speaking from women's experience, Le Guin believes, is for women to recognize their native language — women's language — to see it as valid and speak in it. Men's language, Ursula asserts, is "the language of thought that seeks objectivity," its essential gesture is "distancing — making a gap, a space, between the subject or self and the object or other."[12] This language "expresses the values of the split world, valuing the positive and devaluing the negative in each redivision: subject/object, self/other, mind/body, dominant/submissive, active/passive, Man/Nature, man/woman, and so on." It also is a language that "goes one way. No answer is expected, or heard."[13]

Women's language, according to Le Guin, is "the language spoken by all children and most women, and so I call it the mother tongue, for we learn it from our mothers and speak it to our kids."[14] She provides a sample of such language: "John have you got your umbrella I think it's going to rain. Can you come play with me? If I told you once I told you a hundred times. . . . Oh what am I going to do? So I said to her I said if he thinks she's going to stand for that but then there's his arthritis poor thing and no work. I love you. I hate you. I hate liver. . . . Is it grandma's own sweet pretty dear? What am I going to tell her? There there don't cry. Go to sleep now, go to sleep. . . . Don't go to sleep!"[15] Women's language, Ursula asserts, "expects

[8] Le Guin, p. 198.
[9] Le Guin, p. 159.
[10] Le Guin, p. 159.
[11] Le Guin, p. 177.
[12] Le Guin, p. 148.
[13] Le Guin, p. 149.
[14] Le Guin, p. 150.
[15] Le Guin, p. 150.

an answer. . . . It connects. It goes two ways, many ways, an exchange, a network. Its power is not in dividing but in binding, not in distancing but in uniting." [16] It is a language in which people offer their "experience to one another. Not claiming something: offering something." [17]

In the following speech by Le Guin, presented as a commencement address at Mills College in Oakland, California, in 1983, her concern with women's language is demonstrated. She urges the women to speak from their own experiences and to create and live in a world where they can grow and speak as women.

A Left-Handed Commencement Address

1983

I want to thank the Mills College Class of '83 for offering me a rare chance: to speak aloud in public in the language of women.

I know there are men graduating, and I don't mean to exclude them, far from it. There is a Greek tragedy where the Greek says to the foreigner, "If you don't understand Greek, please signify by nodding." Anyhow, commencements are usually operated under the unspoken agreement that everybody graduating is either male or ought to be. That's why we are all wearing these twelfth-century dresses that look so great on men and make women look either like a mushroom or a pregnant stork. Intellectual tradition is male. Public speaking is done in the public tongue, the national or tribal language; and the language of our tribe is the men's language. Of course women learn it. We're not dumb. If you can tell Margaret Thatcher from Ronald Reagan, or Indira Gandhi from General Somoza, by anything they say, tell me how. This is a man's world, so it talks a man's language. The words are all words of power. You've come a long way, baby, but no way is long enough. You can't even get there by selling yourself out: because there is theirs, not yours.

Maybe we've had enough words of power and talk about the battle of life. Maybe we need some words of weakness. Instead of saying now that I hope you will all go forth from this ivory tower of college into the Real World and forge a triumphant career or at least help your husband to and keep our country strong and be a success in everything—instead of talking power, what if I talked like a woman right here in public? It won't sound right. It's going to sound terrible. What if I said what I hope for you is first, if—only if—you

16 Le Guin, p. 149.
17 Le Guin, p. 150.

want kids, I hope you have them. Not hordes of them. A couple, enough. I hope they're beautiful. I hope you and they have enough to eat, and a place to be warm and clean in, and friends, and work you like doing. Well, is that what you went to college for? Is that all? What about success?

Success is somebody else's failure. Success is the American Dream we can keep dreaming because most people in most places, including thirty million of ourselves, live wide awake in the terrible reality of poverty. No, I do not wish you success. I don't even want to talk about it. I want to talk about failure.

Because you are human beings, you are going to meet failure. You are going to meet disappointment, injustice, betrayal, and irreparable loss. You will find you're weak where you thought yourself strong. You'll work for possessions and then find they possess you. You will find yourself—as I know you already have—in dark places, alone, and afraid.

What I hope for you, for all my sisters and daughters, brothers and sons, is that you will be able to live there, in the dark place. To live in the place that our rationalizing culture of success denies, calling it a place of exile, uninhabitable, foreign.

Well, we're already foreigners. Women as women are largely excluded from, alien to, the self-declared male norms of this society, where human beings are called Man, the only respectable god is male, and the only direction is up. So, that's their country; let's explore our own. I'm not talking about sex; that's a whole other universe, where every man and woman is on their own. I'm talking about society, the so-called man's world of institutionalized competition, aggression, violence, authority, and power. If we want to live as women, some separatism is forced upon us: Mills College is a wise embodiment of that separatism. The war-games world wasn't made by us or for us; we can't even breathe the air there without masks. And if you put the mask on you'll have a hard time getting it off. So how about going on doing things our own way, as to some extent you did here at Mills? Not for men and the male power hierarchy—that's their game. Not *against* men, either— that's still playing by their rules. But *with* any men who are with us: that's our game. Why should a free woman with a college education either fight Machoman or serve him? Why should she live her life on his terms?

Machoman is afraid of our terms, which are not all rational, positive, competitive, etc. And so he has taught us to despise and deny them. In our society, women have lived, and have been despised for living, the whole side of life that includes and takes responsibility for helplessness, weakness, and illness, for the irrational and the irreparable, for all that is obscure, passive, uncontrolled, animal, unclean—the valley of the shadow, the deep, the depths of life. All that the Warrior denies and refuses is left to us and the men who share it with us and therefore, like us, can't play doctor, only nurse, can't be warriors, only civilians, can't be chiefs, only indians. Well, so that is our country. The night side of our country. If there is a day side to it, high sierras, prairies of bright grass, we only know pioneers' tales about it, we haven't got there yet. We're never going to get there by imitating Machoman. We are only going to get there by going our own way, by living there, by living through the night in our own country.

So what I hope for you is that you live there not as prisoners, ashamed of being women, consenting captives of a psychopathic social system, but as natives. That you will be at home there, keep house there, be your own mistress, with a room of your own. That you will do your work there, whatever you're good at, art or science or tech or running a company or sweeping under the beds, and when they tell you that it's second-class work because a woman is doing it, I hope you tell them to go to hell and while they're going to give you equal pay for equal time. I hope you live without the need to dominate, and without the need to be dominated. I hope you are never victims, but I hope you have no power over other people. And when you fail, and are defeated, and in pain, and in the dark, then I hope you will remember that darkness is your country, where you live, where no wars are fought and no wars are won, but where the future is. Our roots are in the dark; the earth is our country. Why did we look up for blessing—instead of around, and down? What hope we have lies there. Not in the sky full of orbiting spy-eyes and weaponry, but in the earth we have looked down upon. Not from above, but from below. Not in the light that blinds, but in the dark that nourishes, where human beings grow human souls.

27

QUILTING

Ann Seemann

Ann Seemann began quilting in the late 1970s when, after wallpapering their bedroom, she and her husband needed a new bedcovering to match. She always had sewed but had not made quilts; she bought a yard of fabric that matched the wallpaper and incorporated it into a nine-patch quilt. She admits, "I didn't know what I was doing, and I selected all the wrong fabrics by weight and texture. I chose kettlecloth, polyester, and even a mock suede cloth for the lattice that separated the nine patches. You can't quilt through that, much less even tie! But I persevered, and I did tie!" This narrative is Seemann's first "quilt story"; quilt stories are about events that occurred as the quilt was in process or about the trials and errors of actually assembling it: "Telling a quilt's story, I've noticed, makes orators out of otherwise retiring people."

In creating her quilts, Ann uses traditional patterns and tends to prefer reds and blues for her quilts, although she doesn't limit herself to these colors. She took a week-long quilting seminar at Mills College one summer to "help me be more creative." While she appreciates contemporary quilts, she explains, "I'm not sure I want to create them." Seemann admits "it's fun to experiment, however, which has accounted for much of my growth as a quilter." She sees her individuality coming out in her choice and arrangement of fabrics in the traditional patterns. While quilts are becoming a "real art form" and she signs and dates her quilts as artists do, Ann's first love is with the utilitarian purpose of using a quilt as a bedcovering rather than as a wallhanging: "There's a very sensual feeling from the fabric sandwich that a regular blanket doesn't give."

Seemann identifies less with the quilt as a finished product that is a reflection

274

of her and more with the process of quilting. One of the most enjoyable parts for her is that "there's not just one thing to do. You've got fabric selection, the designs, you've got the actual piecing, and then you've got the actual quilting process." One of the aspects of the quilting process she particularly enjoys is "daydreaming and designing quilts mentally." She has even found herself dreaming of quilts and designs and patterns at night. Ann also appreciates the quilting process because it "allows you a lot of time alone where you can just let your mind wander. It provides me with quiet time where I can rethink interpersonal situations—figure out how I might have responded to something and so on. I find quilting just very therapeutic, very soothing." An unexpected outcome of her quilting is that "it rekindled for me an interest in history because there have been a lot of works out about the history of quilts, newly published diaries of the nineteenth-century trek west, and how quilts played a role. So a lot of things have come as sidelines of my interest in quilting."

Seemann's appreciation of quilts has developed both informally and formally. She recalls liking quilts as a child and remembers one in particular—a quilt made by her grandmother that was on her bed: "I remember I liked to study it whenever I was sick—it was a scrapbag quilt—and I remember my mother commenting, every now and then, that this was so-and-so's dress or whatever. It was a monkey-wrench design, and I just associated good feelings with it." She took a quilting class after she had made two quilts, "and that got me started. And I just kept on going since then, and my technique has developed over the years."

Ann joined the Redwood Empire Quilters' Guild in 1984, an organization formed in 1975 by a group of women in an adult-education quilting class interested in the revival of the art of quilting. Its purpose is to promote quilt appreciation and education and to provide a place where members can learn and talk about quilting. She has been active in various ways in the quilters' guild—working on group quilts; serving as president; and coordinating the first major quilt show, in which 200 quilts were exhibited.

While Seemann joined the group because of her interest in quilting, she came to realize that she also enjoys interacting in an all women's group—something she had not experienced since college: "It didn't hit me until after a couple years in the group how much I enjoyed the female companionship. In the beginning, it was just our quilting interests that were exchanged at the meetings, but then you become so much more personally involved." Ann, who is the mother of two sons, relied on the group for "information about runny noses or whatever."

Seemann works as a financial paraplanner and sees her primary commitments in life as her family and her faith. But quilting clearly dominates her free time as well as her house. Not only does she have many samples of her work in her home, but her bookshelves are filled with quilting books, and her cupboards are full of fabrics, designs, and quilts in process. Her car license-plate holder says, "I'd rather be quilting"; it was a gift from a special quilting friend and suggests the importance of quilting in Ann's life.

Two of Seemann's quilts are pictured below. The quilt shown hanging on the wall is a baby quilt done in yellows and aquas with accents of purple. Ann designed it deliberately with strong contrasts in order to catch a baby's eye. It was a gift to a quilting friend upon the birth of her first grandchild.

The quilt draped over the couch is done in white and a range of blues — from light to dark. A full-sized bed quilt, it is used in her home as a cover-up for naps. Most of the fabrics were from Seemann's collection, although she did "some additional shopping in order to find the 'right' fabrics to complete it."

Both of the quilts shown here are of the same pattern, which is called "Trip Around the World" (the Amish, using solid colors, refer to it as "Sunshine and Shadow.") It is a simple design because only one template is required throughout — a 1 1/2-inch square patch. The challenge comes in blending and contrasting the fabrics in concentric circles to create an overall pleasing effect. In both quilts, the quilting is also simple: it is done diagonally through the small squares in a concentric motion.

Ann Seemann, quilt, "Trip Around the World" pattern
Photograph: Diana Schoenfeld

Ann Seemann, quilt, "Trip Around the World" pattern
Photograph: Diana Schoenfeld

28

READING GROUP

Karen A. Foss, Lois A. Mellert, Jill K. Melton,
Jill L. Paydon, Peggy Peach-Fine,
and Kathy C. Thompson

Since the fall of 1982, a group of women in Humboldt County, California, has met monthly to read and discuss books by women. The group began after a failed effort to start a county-wide women's reading group at the local YWCA. Two members of the group — Jill Paydon and Karen Foss — were asked to lead a group the YWCA was hoping to get started; after disappointing turnouts at several meetings, the YWCA decided to abandon the effort. Foss and Paydon, who had met several years earlier at the Humboldt State University Women's Center, when Karen was faculty advisor to the Center and Jill was a work-study student there, decided to initiate a reading group comprised of their own friends. According to Paydon, "We realized we didn't have to wait for the YWCA for a reading group to work; we could just ask our own friends."

The motives for joining the group are varied. Several of the group's members were English majors in college who want to continue the opportunity to read regularly. Foss likes the idea of the reading group as a way of "allowing me to read something for pleasure at least once a month." All of the members share an interest in literature by women — something not given much attention when they were in college. Another reason for meeting is simply to make time for friends.

The first meeting of the group was held in the fall of 1982. The group meets in the homes of group members, with each member taking a turn in somewhat regular order. The hosting member is responsible for providing wine and snacks. The group generally meets Wednesday evenings at 7:30, although the group frequently adjusts the meeting day to accommodate members' other activities. While the plan is to read a new book each month, sometimes a book is discussed for two months—either because not many members were present for the discussion or not all members were able to finish the book in time. There are no guidelines governing what is discussed, although the portrayal of male-female relationships, the point of view embedded in the book, writing style, and feminist orientation are frequent starting points.

The book chosen to be read for the next month is selected in various ways. If someone has heard about a good book or a book by a well-known author is released in paperback, that book might be chosen. Availability plays a major role in the choice of a book. If someone has discovered several copies of a book the group has been wanting to read, she buys them and brings the copies to a meeting for distribution. At other times, a group member locates copies at the local libraries or has a local bookstore order several copies so the group is assured of easy access to the book. Fiction is read most frequently, although the group members have read several works of non-fiction, including Carol Gilligan's *In a Different Voice, Necessary Losses* by Judith Viorst, and *Co-Dependence* by Anne Wilson Schaef. Group members try to vary the kinds of reading from month to month; if a mystery by P. D. James is read one month, a more serious piece of fiction might be chosen for the next. The group tries to read authors with a national or international reputation—Marge Piercy and Margaret Atwood, for example—as well as local authors and women writers in other countries.

The original members of the group are Kathleen Baker, Karen Foss, Lois Mellert, Jill Paydon, Peggy Peach-Fine, and Kathy Thompson. Karen is a university professor of speech communication, Lois is a legal secretary, Jill is the director of programming and operations for a public radio station, Peggy teaches the early elementary grades at an alternative school, and Kathy is a staff service analyst in the county welfare office. Kathleen moved out of the area in 1986 but still stays in touch with group members. The reading group, in fact, made a quilt to celebrate the birth of her first child; each of the original members made a quilt square that depicts a shared interest with Kathleen. Other women come to the meetings from time to time but do not participate on a regular basis. In the transcript of the group meeting below, Jill Melton was attending her first meeting, having recently moved to the area; Peggy Peach-Fine was absent.

The following transcript is a segment of the discussion at the meeting of the reading group in November of 1989, which was held at the home of Kathy Thompson in McKinleyville, California. For this meeting, the group read

No Country for Young Men by Julia O'Faolain. While some portions of the conversation are not included because they were inaudible on the tape or everyone was talking at once and actual dialogue could not be distinguished, the transcript provides an accurate sample of the kind of talk that occurs at group meetings. As will become apparent, a wide variety of topics are discussed — not just the book the members have read that month.

Reading Group
November 29, 1989

[The conversation already has begun. Kathy has just told the group about her dog, Chip, who was accidentally left in the house one day that week, thus triggering the burglar alarm. She has just brought out food, and the group begins sampling.]

Lois: Dried tomatoes?

Jill P: Yeah.

Lois: And onions?

Jill P: And onions.

Lois: They're delicious.

Kathy: [Bringing in another plate of food] I think that's about it — and the cream cheese.

Lois: [Speaking for the dog] And my ears hurt so bad with that alarm! I think I need some cream cheese. (Laughter)

Jill P: [Addressing Karen] You sounded good today.

Karen: Did I? I was going to ask you.

Kathy: Were you on the radio or something?

Karen: Yes.

Kathy: What were you talking about?

Karen: Women's Studies. We're having a "coming-of-age" party on Friday. We've been around for eighteen years.

Lois: Eighteen! No kidding!

Kathy: What were you on?

Jill P: It was on *This, That, and the Other.*

Kathy: I just missed you. I was working late.

Jill M: The one thing I've read about that program [Women's Studies] is about the FBI investigation [for work-study fraud]. That's all I know about it is the FBI investigation.

Kathy: Oh, yeah?

Jill P: Unfortunately, in the past year, that's really the most anybody has seen about it.

Karen: The FBI investigation, you mean?

Jill P: Right.

Kathy: Is that still going on?

Karen: They've dropped the charges from two felonies to misdemeanors.

Jill P: Oh, they have?

Lois: Brother.

Karen: And it may not come to trial. It may be settled out of court.

Jill P: [Referring to the individual involved in the acts under investigation] Is she gone?

Karen: Yes.

Lois: What a stupid thing to do, though.

Jill P: She doesn't work there anymore?

Karen: No. She was there to help with the transition, but I'm trying to figure it all out. We kept coming up with all this stuff—like we owed $50.00 to some woman two years ago and hadn't paid her for two years. I don't know what else there is.
(All talk at once)

Kathy: This is not exactly the way you want the place to present itself to the world, right?

Karen: Yes! I don't know what's going on, but I'll work it out. Or at least I'll know (inaudible). I've been worried about Friday [the coming-of-age party] working out, but—

Jill P: But it will be whatever it is.

Karen: And I'll just run out and buy whatever we need if the donations don't come through, and it will work, you know. So anyway, if any of you are free then—

Jill P: Yeah, I'm planning on it.

Kathy: On Friday afternoon?

Karen: This Friday, 3:00 - 6:00.

Jill M: I have to take Jason [son] to see Santa Claus. (laughter)

Jill P: Well, maybe you can work this one in, Jill.

Kathy: After that [the visit to Santa Claus] you may need it! A drink! (laughter)

Kathy: So do we want to put off the discussion of this book until next month? [because not many members had finished it]

Jill M: Well, I'm interested in what impression it left you with of Ireland.

Kathy: Of what?

Jill M: Gary [husband] and I went about three years ago, and I had one impression when I went and I have a much different one when I left, and I was kind of curious of what kind of impression you had.

Karen: Did you go to Northern Ireland at all?

Jill M: No.

Kathy: I've never been there. I've never been to Ireland.

Jill M: Although we saw a faculty exchange and I was looking through that
         and I was reading something about Northern Ireland and it said
         something about areas safe for children or something. (laughter)

Jill P: Oh, wow.

Kathy: You mean there are any?

Jill M: Yeah. What kind of impressions do you have?

Lois: [Referring to the author] Is she Irish?
        (unintelligible)

Karen: I think you get a good outsider's view of Ireland from the American
        who goes over there with a certain set of impressions. And then usually
        they're kind of changing. Oh, I guess the image of Ireland in the book
        is my impression of Ireland when I was there, so I can't—

Kathy: You've been to Ireland before you read the book, right?

Karen: Right.

Kathy: Can you remember what your idea of Ireland was before you went?

Karen: No. [Chip, the dog, lies down next to the wood stove.]

Jill M: My dog has burned his stomach on the heater before.

Kathy: Really!

Jill M: He likes heat so much. Just lay on those old heaters, you know.

Kathy: It's actually cool down here where he is. That first ridge it starts to
        get a little bit warm, but the rest of it just stays kind of cool.

Jill M: Oh, there's a lot of recurring things about the history [of Ireland].
        Thinking about them living in their history and not really living now.
        Even though it wasn't so happy now, they weren't progressing.

Karen: That's a good point.

Kathy: Yeah, I think there was a lot of interesting contrast. And she kept sort
        of going back and forth on California consciousness and Irish
        consciousness.

Jill P: Right.

Kathy: It was a pretty strong contrast.

Lois: She's written a lot. I'm impressed with her biography.

Kathy: Oh, no kidding!

Lois: It was really very good.

Kathy: I thought as a novel that it was somewhat uneven. You know that there
        were bits and pieces, well—of course, that may have to do with how
        I read it, too, I mean I did not—

Karen: I read it in bits and pieces—it was jerky.

Kathy: I did, too, but I also, I found it to be kind of a jerky novel in some ways.

Jill P: Well, it was.

Kathy: I think maybe it was the way it was composed. I think maybe the way it was composed was kind of, I think—

Jill P: You went from now to 80 years ago, 70 years ago, without any kind of real transitions. And after you got used to it, you knew what was going on, but that was a real choppy area because we would be in the now and do one thing, and all of a sudden you would be in the other character 70 years ago, ummm, as if it was now, though, not really a memory but as—some of them were memories but some of them were as if it were now, so—

Karen: What an interesting way to do that.

Jill P: Yeah. But I think that is why we get the sense of depth. The history and what had been really still, I mean, if you think about why what happened in this book happened, it had a lot to do with that. Real concerns if what happened 70 or 80 years ago is still going to be a big deal now. Or if it would sort of change the whole history of the country if certain things came out or whatever.

Kathy: Even though we finally found out what it was wasn't at all what we thought it was! (laughter) I was, there are a couple of things here I don't want to say [referring to the fact that not all members have finished reading the book].

Karen: I mean I was not at all prepared for how it ended.

Jill P: Right.

Kathy: Yeah.

Karen: I wasn't prepared for the ending of the book.

Jill P: No, that's not what, that was, was not at all—

Kathy: In some ways, I found that almost a little sloppy—the way it was ended. Oh, let's just—

Jill P: Oh, yeah.

Lois: Right.

Kathy: I can't think of what else to do now so I'll just end.

Jill P: I was really aggravated because—

Jill M: When you said *No Country for Young Men*, I thought this was going to be about war, and no young man can belong to any country because he has to go to war.

Jill P: Well, in essence, they are at war, today, and they were and that sort of—

Karen: It's not a country for young men, but it's also that the young men had disappeared.

Jill M: Is this in Ireland or Northern Ireland? Is it distinguished or do you know?

Lois: That's a good question.

Kathy: Well, they talk about, he—what city they were in, they were in Dublin; well, they were outside of Dublin.

Lois: Probably in Northern Ireland. I bet it's Northern Ireland.

Jill P: Yeah, because he got, when his plane got turned around and he went back to Dublin, and he was there very quickly.

Karen: Yeah, right.

Jill P: I don't know, see I was; I don't have a real good—

Kathy: You know, I got a firmer grip on Irish history, and I realize that some way or another that I was totally awash as to where we were exactly. Oh, by the way, this is a Norwegian cheese, and it's got, it's got cumin, coriander, and caraway in it, and I think it's kind of interesting. Jack [husband] thought it was awful. He said it tastes like pencil shavings. (laughter) But I liked it.

Lois: That's a wonderful description for cheese.

Jill P: Does he like the cheese that Larrupin's [a local restaurant] has?

Kathy: Jack's not really that crazy about cheese.

Lois: I love cheese, but I can't stand that cheese. I hate it.
         (All talk at once)

Jill M: Do you like goat cheese?

Lois: Oh, I love it.

Kathy: I hate it.

Jill P: I like this. The cumin is very—

Kathy: I think it's very interesting. But Jack didn't like it at all. It does have cumin in it, I think, or some kind of—

Jill P: It's at the Co-op [the local natural-food store].

Kathy: Yeah, it does have a really strong pencil-shaving taste. Now I know what he means by the pencil shavings, but it was one of the more expensive pencil-shaving tastes! In fact, I bought it about three weeks ago. I thought, "Save that up for the book group." (laughter) Yeah, interesting sex scenes in this book, but—and I love, there was one that, you know the description of her—what was that guy's name?

Karen: Eric?

Kathy: No, umm, the Irish cousin. Owen?

Jill P: Owen.

Kathy: Owen. Did you notice the first description of Owen? In the book, it was just hysterical, I thought.

Jill P: I don't remember it.

Kathy: It was something or another about—it was, a a line about "dressed to the right," and I don't know if anybody else got that, but it's referring to what side his dong hung on.

Lois: Are you kidding?

Kathy: No, I'm not, I'm not kidding.

Lois: Dressed to the right?

Kathy: That was like military slang, sort of, you know, about where you hold your weapon and all that.

Lois: Oh.

Jill P: Dressed to the right?

Lois: How do you know that?

Kathy: I don't know—some boyfriend told me at some time.

Jill M: This is dreadful. You learn all kinds of things. Does that mean dressed
right versus dressed left?

Kathy: Yeah.

Lois: What if it's just like, right in the middle? (laughter)

Kathy: It was just, I was just, you know, beside myself with giggles when
I read that, "God, this is just a stitch." I hated the man intensely,
immediately, not because—because I mean he was just such a—

Lois: Oh, he's awful.

Kathy: Well, he is, but I mean the physical description of him was so vivid.

Jill M: What kind of book is this?

Lois: We read all kinds!

Jill M: What would this be?

Kathy: It's a novel.

Jill M: It's not, not a mystery?

Jill P: Well, mystery is in it, but the focus is not about mystery. It's sort of
a, how do you say, a social picture, you know, or a commentary, sort of.

Lois: Yeah, sometimes we pick books that sort of make a social comment
or so—

Jill P: Yeah, because it's really, sort of, kind of giving us a picture of Irish,
a certain segment of, a larger segment of Irish society.

Jill M: Can you tell me what some of her other books are?

Jill P: I don't know. I just remember seeing it in the library.

Lois: They're probably right in there. But I wouldn't be surprised if there
wasn't just one because I didn't know anything about her.

Jill M: I've never heard of her.

Kathy: I realize that there are at least two or three out, but I didn't realize
that she had put out quite as many as you had mentioned because,
you know, what you called the title. I know that I saw, I mean, I know
I've seen two or three in bookstores.

Jill M: Which library?

Jill P: In Eureka.

Jill M: Don't they have a card catalog where you can order books from the
main library and all the branches—isn't that how it works?

Lois: Well, they were there, but when I went to look at the shelf, they weren't
on the shelf.

Jill P: No, the branch library. The card catalog was—they're all part of the
county library system.

Jill M: Oh, OK.

Jill P: And if it's not there, you can just order it and they will send it up to that branch so you don't have to go into Eureka.

Jill M: Oh, OK. I didn't know that.

Jill P: I seem to recall doing that.

Kathy: You live here in McKinleyville?

Jill M: I live over, umm, off of, uh, off of—

Karen: Murray.

Jill M: Thank you.

Karen: Murray—over by the high school.

Kathy: Oh.

Jill M: On Fortune Street—that new subdivision.

Lois: And your husband works—

Kathy: Oh, wait a minute. OK, is it on this side of 101 or is it on—

Jill M: The west side. Toward the ocean.

Kathy: Oh, it's toward the ocean, so you're over by Knox's, Knox Cove.

Jill M: Oh, yeah. Over there by the castles [large homes with castle-like features].

Kathy: I know where you are, I know where you are. I've been to those; I've even met Harvey [Knox, a local developer].
         (Everyone talks at once)

Kathy: He's mad as a hatter. I think he lost it a few years back.

Jill M: [Referring to the castles] They're real different!

Lois: As close as they're built to the edge, and the way the rivers are moving north, aren't they a little worried or not worried?

Jill P: He doesn't worry about anything, Lois.

Jill M: Oh, he doesn't. In fact, he even told someone that some of those lots sold for ridiculous amounts—just outrageous. He was telling my sister and I that I think a duplex is the most that he can put on each, but he was going to build a triplex and what were they going to do after it was built?

Jill P: Ever since he's been here, since he came to town, he bought some land and he just cut the trees down without permits or anything. What can they do after that, after he's cut them down? Fire him, maybe. But they can't glue the trees back together and make them be back on land again, so once he does it, he's got it. They can't take the land away.

Jill M: He took the land and made it like shotgun lots, so everybody's got a little ocean that's long and narrow, and I asked him how he could do that with the Coastal Commission.

Kathy: Is he, do you think, I mean when I met him under circumstances which would, in which it would have been very fine for him to appear crazy. Do you think he's very crazy or do you think he's just real manipulative?

Jill M: He's real manipulative. I mean he's just very — I think, he goes with
         every situation.

Kathy: Uh, huh. But he appeared very weird and crazy when I met him, but
         as I said, whenever —

Jill M: He would do whatever was appropriate, when he was talking about
         this coastal thing, well, we didn't like the subdivision anyway, but
         when we were finished talking with him, my sister said she couldn't
         stand him. She was just seething.

Kathy: The Coastal Commission's there for the benefit of everybody; he didn't
         care, you know, and, you know, he even made a point that in twenty
         years he'll be gone.

Jill P: He's been here for ten years now.

Kathy: And he doesn't care what the result is when he's gone.

Jill M: Oh, I thought my sister was going to take him out right there! I mean,
         she was just fuming!

Karen: Here's the reference [to "dressed to the right"]. Are you ready? [reading]
         "The day after her visit to the R T E studios, Grainne's cousin came
         to call. Owen Roe was a redhead like herself, large, assured, youthful
         for his fifty or so years, a bit bloated about the gills, with jutting genitals
         which made a fold in his cavalry twill trousers — he dressed to the
         right — and a righteous blue eye which could, when useful, be made
         to glow like a gas glimmer (p. 145)."

Jill M: I wouldn't have got that.

Jill P: I know I didn't get it. I didn't know that. I've never heard that, but
         I'm never going to forget it now! (laughter)

Jill M: I would have thought that "dressed to the right" was being dressed
         to the tee.

Karen: Right.

Jill P: I think I interpreted it as something political.

Jill M: Oh, dressed to the right — conservative.

Kathy: I was afraid of that.

Karen: But coming after the phrase about his pants —

Jill P: Yes.

Karen: How were we to know? We found the reference, Lois. [Lois comes
         back into the room]

Lois: Oh, you did? Read it!

Jill P: Karen just did.

Lois: Read it again.

Jill P: [Reads the passage again]

Lois: Dressed to the right? I would think maybe dressed to the right would
         mean as in right wing versus left wing.

Jill P: Yeah, that's what I thought.

Kathy: But coming after the pants, that's kind of odd.

Jill P: Well, yeah, but you never know what made that, you know, I think I read that a second time to try to make sure that—

Kathy: Trying to figure out what that was.

Lois: Well, now we'll be able to say, "Look at that guy—he's dressed to the right!" (laughter) Oh, dear!

Kathy: [Addressing Lois] So anything new with this guy that you were going out with?

Lois: Oh, actually, no.

Kathy: Oh.

Lois: I mean, it just kind of happened and that was that, and then—

Kathy: So have you done anything to expand your options?

Lois: No, did I say what happened?

Kathy: No, did you run into John? [Lois' on-again, off-again boyfriend].

Lois: Well, worse. I happened to be in the movies with John and ran into Debra and Cort. Yes, well, anyway, they happened to have been at the banjo concert [which Lois had attended with the new friend], and I saw them there.

Kathy: Who was this banjo concert? (inaudible)

Lois: Anyway, the violin thing, anyway, it was really good, I really liked it. But anyway, I saw Cort and Debra in the lobby [at the concert], and so I'm at the movies with John, and we're sitting there and Cort comes up to us and says, "Wasn't that a wonderful concert?" And he starts going on and on, and he's looking at John—

Kathy: Oh, no!

Lois: And John is looking at me and looking at him and said, "I don't know what you're talking about." And I'm dying a thousand deaths—and I say I remember the concert and it was really good. And Cort keeps going on and on, you know, "Who was your favorite?" and so when he left, John said, "So what was that all about?" God, I mean you can't do anything in this county without some stupid thing happening like that. I saw Cort out in the lobby, and I said, "Gee, you know—" and he said, "I didn't realize until after." "Right! That's why you kept blithering on." He [her date at the concert] was a very nice man, but I probably wouldn't—

Karen: [Moving to the tape recorder] I'm just checking the volume. I just realized that I didn't check the volume. Did you check the volume, Jill?

Jill P: No, I just set it up.

Jill M: One time, my sister went out with a guy Friday night and a different guy Saturday night, and she saw the first guy about a week later and he said, "Oh, you sure did dress nicer for your Saturday date, didn't you?" (laughter)

Kathy: Oh, no!

Jill M: He saw this guy taking her home and walking around.

Kathy: Oh, God. Where was that, where, where was that?

Jill M: It was in Western Kentucky. In Kentucky. Yeah, a small town. (laughter)

Lois: Did you grow up in Kentucky?

Jill M: Yeah, Western Kentucky.

Jill P: Is that, is there a distinction? I mean, you said, "Western Kentucky."

Jill M: Well, I suppose; I mean, well, here you're talking history again. Western Kentucky went Southern and the rest of the state went Northern.

Karen: Oh, really?

Kathy: Oh, now, wait a minute, though!

Jill M: It's like in Tennessee — Western Tennessee went Southern, and Eastern Tennessee went Northern.

Lois: Really!

Jill M: So, you know, you think that when you come (laughter)
(All talk at once)

Jill M: We moved from Eastern and it was when I was five, and there were parents who wouldn't let their kids play with me because — so you know, it still kind of lingers. It's kind of strange.

Kathy: You teach?

Jill M: I teach one class; I teach a management class.

Kathy: At?

Jill M: At Humboldt [State University]. Out of desperation, they called me. It's Management 350 — it's really kind of interesting; it's human behavior and organizations.

Kathy: I'd like to find out what happened recently because, I just, you know, on Monday somebody told me that Joe, my boss, he apparently announced to my co-worker that he was, he was looking for jobs in other places because our agency was so sexist.

Lois: Oh.

Kathy: And I went, "Oh, Jesus," and I said, "Well, it must have been his wife that put him up to it." Something must have happened with her, and he said, "No, no, no." That wasn't what he was telling us, though — there is something else going on entirely. Give me a break, right! I mean, it must have been something so outrageous that even Joe was —

Karen: Noticed it.

Lois: You know, it's really funny how we put those labels on people because of where they're from. I work for the county in the public guardian's office. But anyway, we're getting a brand new boss, effective Monday, and he's been hired from Santa Cruz, and his name is Ramon.

Kathy: And you've never seen Ramon.

Lois: I've never laid my eyes on this guy.

Kathy: Oh, this is going to be weird! He's from Santa Cruz County, though, so there is some hope based on that.

Jill P: Because the Board of Supervisors, the county, is not very egalitarian at all.

Kathy: Not at all.
         (All talk at once)

Karen: You may have to stop making waffles in the office!

Lois: Geez! (laughter)

Jill M: You know, it's like — I can't remember what all this was about anyhow — two equally qualified people, and one was from L. A. and one was from Humboldt County, but the thing had to do with equality, and obviously we picked the one from Humboldt County and he's probably (inaudible).

Lois: Not very much, but I'm going to do what I want to do anyway.

Karen: Do you have any better plans of what to do here?

Jill M: No. I've been toying with the idea of finishing my doctorate. I've just been kind of working part time.

Kathy: Sounds like fun. (laughter)

Jill M: Yeah, it is kind of nice, although I've never worked part time. Yeah, it's kind of nice.

Lois: Do you have children?

Jill M: One. Sometimes, it seems like five. I have one of those.

Karen: Well, one of these days he'll start school.

Jill P: How old is he?

Jill M: Three and a half.

Lois: Oh, oh, oh.

Kathy: Oh, my gosh!

Jill M: He came downstairs Saturday while Gary and I were having coffee with nothing on, and I'm talking not even underwear, and I didn't have anything on except a pair of my stockings. (laughter) And for three days, every time he came by, he said, "You didn't have anything on." And for three days, he would come home from school everyday and take off his clothes except for his stockings.

Jill P: What are we drinking?

Kathy: This is a Sauvignon Blanc. I don't know whether you've discovered the Canned Foods [a discount store] lately.

Lois: I haven't been there for a while.

Jill M: They have wines?

Kathy: Oh, yeah.

Lois: I never know what to pick up.

Kathy: OK, well, OK, well, OK, my basic—I usually like Sauvignon Blanc.
Lois: So do I.
Kathy: Because it's dry. But I also usually try something new—Italian, Spanish—and they usually have a fair amount of French wines that aren't too bad, either. It just depends, but I usually go for the Italians first.
Jill M: What is, what is this?
Kathy: This is a California white. It's a Sauvignon Blanc.
Jill P: Their California reds are usually pretty marginal.
Kathy: Yeah, reds, usually your California reds are not as good as Spanish.
Jill P: Right, right.
Jill M: You can't go too wrong, price wise.
Lois: Isn't there a discount liquor place, too, over by the mall? I saw the thing in the paper.
Jill P: It looked like it's by the Bayshore Mall.
Jill M: It's before it, on the right.
Jill P: What about that place—by the Victorian Mall?
Jill M: No, no, it's before that. It's kind of by a gas-station place.
Kathy: What kind of place is that?
Lois: I read about it in the paper, and it's supposed to be some sort of discount liquor place.
Kathy: I've never tried it.
Lois: It said specifically in the paper that it doesn't have everything—but wines and alcohol.
Kathy: Well, that's interesting. Maybe we should go check it out.
Jill P: Some lunch hour. (laughter)
Kathy: But I've had good luck with Canned Foods. My greatest bargain at Canned Foods was that one time I remember we were buying this Italian white, and it came in a box, and it was 59¢ a liter. (laughter)
Lois: Oh, you're kidding!
Kathy: It was real good!
Karen: Really!
Kathy: I mean, it was probably better than this white.
Lois: Really? 59¢?
Kathy: It was originally 99¢, but they marked it down.
Jill M: They had 99¢ on it?
Lois: Really? I'm going to have to go down there. I can walk down from work.
Jill M: Symphony—have you ever had Symphony wine? Someone said, "Have you ever had Symphony wine?" and it was like $1.29 and it was really good.
Kathy: Hmmm.
Lois: Really. I just didn't check out the wine the first couple times, you

know, but it's just kind of neat to try new beer. They had some apple cider, you know, hard cider.

Kathy: It's somewhat hard cider, hard apple cider. It tastes like apple beer almost.

Lois: Well, you can certainly tell from this tape what we enjoy doing! (laughter)

Jill M: We'll discuss cheeses and food after this. But it's probably Velveeta.

Kathy: [To Chip] Oh, you don't want to step in that, right, OK. And actually, I've gotten some pretty good deals in the frozen-foods department like Lean Cuisine and things like that. But I found that, they have some weird luxury products there. I mean, like I've gotten things like, I've spent $1.49 for like half a quart of Dijon mustard.

Lois: I don't know what those things are at Mark and Save.

Kathy: Well, some things are probably, you know, geared, I mean, like this would probably be a restaurant-sized jar, you know.

Lois: Was it a straight-sided thing? The one I get is even larger than that — at Mark and Save.

Kathy: But this is the Poupon, Grey Poupon. I mean, it's like, it's a fairly expensive label, but it was cheap there and —

Lois: Hmmm, I'll have to check it out.

Kathy: They have things there sometimes like anchovies packed in olive oil, you know, like from Spain, so they're, you know, they're not —

Jill P: They don't always have things like that so you have to keep going there several times and look through things. (all talk at once)

Jill M: They had some great butter cookies there, butter crackers, but then they were never there again, so now we know if you like something, stock up because you can't just buy one of something. Oh, this is something you really like and here it is and then —

Kathy: The sample of people I know who actually, you know, see, I work where I can go there anytime, but we also make a point to try any wines that we get that are new to us as soon as possible so if we like them, we can go back and stock up.

Lois: Really? Do you stock up on things?

Kathy: Oh, yeah.

Lois: I mean, how cheap are the wines over there?

Jill P: You can get a $2.00 bottle.

Kathy: You can get 99¢ bottles.

Karen: Or 59¢ bottles!

Kathy: It's just one of those things, you know, if they're there, you want to go back and get a case. Usually, after work, you know, I'll cruise through for about fifteen minutes — I do that, every so often. It's that

time again, I'm running low. We had to search for a bottle of red that
was, you know—

Jill M: It's kinda fun. They have 99¢ cereals.

Kathy: I saw something really silly the other day—cereals—it must be
amusing, but there was something about Barbie Doll cereal.

Jill M: I've seen Ghost Busters cereal. I just saw Batman cereal. (all talk at
once)

Lois: Barbie Cereal? Is it shaped like high heels or something? (laughter)

Jill M: I bought it one time for Jason, but he didn't like it, but Gary did.
Gary did! Too much sugar, I guess.

Kathy: So, have you folks been moving around a lot?

Jill M: We were in Arkansas for eleven years.

Kathy: Oh, so you haven't been moving around a lot, then. Well, that's good.

Jill P: I was there when Gary came here for an interview one time, and all
he wanted to do was to get out so bad.

Jill M: We were kind of wanting to get out of Arkansas before Jason, but after
Jason, the narrow mindedness and things like that in Arkansas. You
know, for us, we could ignore it.

Jill P: Right.

Lois: Yeah.

Jill M: But he was absorbing it. It made us more anxious to get out. And
then we traveled a lot, too, before hand.

Kathy: McKinleyville isn't the finest place in the world.

Jill P: Well, you know, it's a real mix.

Jill M: It was a lot more like Arkansas than I expected.

Kathy: I'm sure it is. (all talk at once)

Jill P: But there's still that real—well, the nickname is "Oklahoma by the sea."

Kathy: I mean, it's sort of gotten, you know, sort of, you know, ah,
fundamentalist churches of all sorts, in McKinleyville, it's all sort of—

Jill M: It reminds us a lot of Arkansas.

Jill P: A lot of people from Arkansas are from Oklahoma, aren't they?

Jill M: Yeah, oh, sure.

Kathy: Have you ever been down around A Avenue in McKinleyville? OK,
well you go up Sutter Road, you go up Sutter Road and head out one
way, you know, you go if you go one way toward Azalea. It's kind
of posh, but if you go the other way, it's A Avenue, and basically a
lot of those houses were housing for some logging mill.

Jill M: That's out where the guy makes redwood planters and redwood wishing
wells and some strange stuff.

Jill P: A barrel factory basically owned McKinleyville; what is McKinleyville
was basically owned by this company. They were one of the largest

employers at one time. When they cut down the redwood trees, they
were kind of, things were changing and barrels weren't really —

Kathy: They started making metal barrels.

Jill P: The company was dissolving, so what they did is they gave many of
their employees little plots of land, and there were many people from
Oklahoma and such and so what many of them did — suddenly they
were property owners — and what they did was call all of their relatives,
and they all moved out there onto these tiny plots of land and built
shacks there, and so that's why it's like that in some areas. Really
tiny shacks really close together.

Lois: And what was the name of the company?

Jill P: California Barrel Company. I knew, sort of, the history, when I worked
in the recorder's office; I learned more about history. Anybody that
died in Humboldt County during a certain period worked for California
Barrel.

Jill M: You know, I read the obituaries here because I find them so fascinating!
(laughter) They talk about who the people's friends are and all kinds
of real folksy — and the pictures!

Kathy: Actually, I read somewhere in the *Chronicle* [*San Francisco Chronicle*]
that one time or another — I don't know if they are still doing this —
every once in a while there would be these obituaries that were really,
we were wondering why they weren't being sued for libel, routinely.
There were some really weird ones in there.

Jill M: It's like they're using it as some sort of an outlet.

Karen: The family and friends write them.

Lois: Particularly now because a lot of people aren't married, so they say
that they are survived by —

Karen: A lot of gay couples.

Lois: Yeah, and gay couples.

Jill M: They were mentioning their friends, and I thought that was really nice.
I'd just never seen that before. And old pictures from about 30 or 40
years ago. All kinds of — and I just thought it was kind of neat.

Jill P: Is it traditional? I'll bet it's small town.

Lois: It is in Washington.

Kathy: What are you used to? Like that?

Jill M: It must not be written by the family. It's a small town, but it was
basically your traditional, here's the family of whoever dies.

Jill P: Yeah.

Jill M: Just survived by and when the funeral is. And if you want to leave
something, send flowers, and that's it. And some of the papers I noticed
when they did the wedding anniversaries they would put pictures of
the wedding in, too, and I've never seen that before.

Karen: Really.

Kathy: Well, Jack and I never even had a wedding photograph. We got married in Reno, so—

Lois: How long have you been married?

Kathy: Twenty years.

Jill M: Did you get married in one of those chapels with the birds flying?

Kathy: No, we got married by the justice of the peace office in Reno, Nevada. Jack hates needles. He has a blood test, and he's really—he's just really one of those people that has veins, that you know, dive for cover when somebody goes looking for them so, you know, we decided that this was by far the simplest.

Lois: How many years have you been married? Twenty years? That's a very long time for most people that I know.

Kathy: Wait a minute, I'm sorry, it will be twenty years in December.

Lois: Well, that's next month.

Kathy: Yeah, come to think of it.

Lois: I don't know anybody, except for my relatives, who've been married that long.

Karen: Well, you're almost there, aren't you, Jill?

Jill M: Hmmm, yeah, let's see, I'll be married around sixteen in August.

Lois: I would have been married twenty-one, but— (laughter). That's like a lot of people—it would have been, it would have been.

Kathy: Well, maybe it's nineteen. It was so memorable, I think it must have been in 1970 that we got married when I think about it.

Lois: Wow, twenty years.

Jill: Twenty-five is silver.

Lois: It must mean something.

Jill M: Pewter.

Kathy: I put a great deal of store by this, you can tell! It must be something like rubies or something important. But, well, you see the whole point is that—I've probably told you this story before—but Jack's best friend is married to a black woman. And my father's a total bigot and, so, you know, any kind of traditional family wedding would have been a total pain in the ass for both of us because, you know, they wouldn't have been able to invite her friends, you know, and—

Jill M: Right, you know, this whole family has lived in the United States forever and my grandparents, too, you know, so it's like, you know, we can't spell their last name.

Kathy: I think my father is, you know, a total bigot, you know, so I mean, it would have been awful.

Lois: It would have been awful, yeah, exactly.

Jill M: Where is your family from?

Kathy: My father's from Oklahoma.

Jill M: Oklahoma?

Kathy: Yeah. Oklahoma. (inaudible) Yeah, well, you know I didn't have to go through any of that wedding hassle, you know. [Addressing Karen] Did you go through trauma?

Karen: I think weddings are always traumatic unless you keep in mind that it's your wedding and not your mother's. (laughter)

Jill M: That's a major thing to keep in mind.

Jill P: If I ever get married! (laughter)

Kathy: Well, my father, true to form—we went to my cousin's wedding in Berkeley, oh, about six or eight years ago—something like that. She is getting—she's a costumer for the Berkeley Shakespeare Theatre—so they were married in Shakespearean costumes.

Jill M: Oh, neat!

Kathy: In the park, you know, and my father, true to form, absolutely true to form, you know, he was out there and they did, you know, a wedding where it was, you know, they didn't have a presiding cleric, they basically made speeches to each other. My father stands up after the wedding and says, "If that's a real wedding, I'll be damned!" (laughter) Everybody in the whole amphitheater heard it; it wasn't just us. (all talk at once)

Lois: Were you standing next to him?

Kathy: We were standing in front of him and pretending that I'd never seen him.

Jill M: Nobody invited him!

Lois: Oh, that's good. (all talk at once)

Jill M: You know, my sister had a simple one outside at Mamma's. Well, we just had, you know, we had just a little reception and a tent. And then it was, oh, you're never going to get married and then it was, and then when she set the date when she was going to get married, it was, are you sure you want to get married? (laughter)

Kathy: [To Chip, who wanders back into the room] He just couldn't stay away from all those nice ladies. (laughter)

Jill M: [Referring to the dog] He's going to make the rounds now.

Kathy: But Jill's his favorite. Well, Jill has taken him for many walks and, you know, pampered him.

Jill M: Do you have another dog besides this one?

Kathy: Nope, this is, this is the only dog. Actually, we used to have three labradors and that was, hmmm, quite a herd.

Jill M: Dogs really seem to be in around here. I'm amazed how people seem to take their dogs everywhere! Everywhere! It's amazing, you know, they said no dogs in the classroom, no dogs in the building, you know, it's obvious.

Jill P: They didn't used to have that rule.

Lois: That's not true in the South?

Jill M: I haven't seen dogs everywhere.

Kathy: Really. Well, that's interesting.

Jill P: This is definitely a Northern California phenomenon.

Karen: The other is not to keep them tied up most of the time. A dog's not happy unless it runs free.

Jill P: Well, that's a, right, that's the McKinleyville, Fields Landing, Fieldbrook—

Jill M: I thought there was a leash law in McKinleyville until we built this fence—but everybody else's dogs are running free.

Lois: Do you keep Chip tied, Kathy?

Kathy: No, but he won't leave the property, either. He's not really close to people here.

Jack: [Coming into the room] He's not supposed to be on the rug, either.

Kathy: He gets spoiled, special treatment at the reading group.

Jill P: Speaking of reading group, I have to bring this up—I got a new Daedalus catalog today.

Kathy: I was hoping you'd made a list [of books to order].

Jill: Anyway, I know I've heard of this one—maybe in one of these before— but especially the title, *The Book Class*.

Kathy: OK, where?

Jill: Well, hmmm, well, here's a quote from him: "'If I have a bias, it is my suspicion that women are intellectually and intuitively superior to men, writes Christopher Davey,' narrator of this book."

Jill M: Where was he raised?

Jill P: That's a quote. "'And so he begins to describe the twelve women who, as debutantes, instituted his mother's book class in 1908 and met every month to discuss selected titles.'"

Kathy: Oh, my God! (all talk, laugh at once)

Jill P: It's only $2.98. We can afford that.

Karen: That's wonderful!

[The evening ends with the group deciding to read *Wayward Girls and Wicked Women* by Angela Carter and to meet at Jill Paydon's house in December.]

29

RITUALS

Starhawk

The word *Witchcraft* tends to conjure up images of "Witches flying around on brooms or brewing up noxious potions,"[1] suggests Starhawk, an activist, feminist, and Witch. But *Witchcraft* means something quite different for her: "To be a Witch is to make a commitment to the Goddess, to the protection, preservation, nurturing, and fostering of the great powers of life as they emerge in every being."[2] Witches see the cosmos as the living body of the Goddess, who encompasses and who is immanent within all beings. This life force is called "Goddess, not to narrowly define her gender, but as a continual reminder that what we value is life brought into the world."[3]

Participants in Witchcraft seek to develop an awareness of and to activate power-from-within, which Starhawk distinguishes from power-over and power-with. Power-over is linked to domination and control; power-with is social power, the influence wielded among equals. Power-from-within, in contrast, stems from a view of the world itself as a living being, where all things have inherent value. By drawing on power-from-within, Witches "bend energy and shape consciousness"[4] to achieve liberation — to "challenge hierarchies that keep us unfree and create structures that embody values of immanent spirit, interconnection, community, empowerment, and balance."[5]

[1] Starhawk, *Truth or Dare: Encounters with Power, Authority, and Mystery* (San Francisco: Harper & Row, 1987), p. 7.
[2] Starhawk, *Truth or Dare*, p. 8.
[3] Starhawk, *Truth or Dare*, p. 7.
[4] Starhawk, *Truth or Dare*, p. 7.
[5] Starhawk, *Truth or Dare*, p. 24.

These goals are met in Witchcraft by means such as poetry, metaphor, symbol, and myth; among the most powerful means used are rituals—consciously structured collective experiences or patterned actions. Rituals function as "seed crystals of new patterns that can eventually reshape culture around them."[6] Rituals foster such growth and create change by restoring to their participants a sense of immanent, inherent value. They also provide a symbolic space of protection and safety, in which participants are free from judgment and punishment—both from themselves and others.

Starhawk's interest in Witchcraft and ritual began when she was a student at the University of California at Los Angeles during the late 1960s. Her questioning of the forms of power she witnessed as part of the turbulence of this decade led her to explore Witchcraft as a means of creating empowering, life-oriented cultures. She joined a coven; became a licensed minister of the Covenant of the Goddess; and helped to found the "Reclaiming" collective, a center for feminist spirituality and counseling.

Starhawk adopted a new name to represent her commitment to Goddess spirituality, dropping the name she had been given at birth, Miriam Simos. She explains the origin of the name she selected: "My own name came from a dream about a hawk who turned into a wise old woman and took me under her protection. The star came from the card in the Tarot that symbolizes hope and the deep self. Taking on the name Starhawk for me meant making a commitment to the Goddess and to new levels of my own power-from-within. The name itself became a challenge."[7]

Starhawk pursues this challenge in a variety of ways—as a filmwriter, writer, teacher (she has taught at several colleges in the San Francisco area), non-violence trainer, lecturer, and political activist. She participated in the nonviolent blockade at the Diablo Canyon Nuclear Power Plant in California in 1981 and is active in "Prevention Point," an ongoing nonviolent action dedicated to halting the spread of AIDS through a needle-exchange program with drug addicts.

Starhawk is the author of three books designed to introduce readers to Witchcraft. *The Spiral Dance*, published in 1979, is an overview of the growth, suppression, practices, and philosophy of Witchcraft. Her master's thesis in feminist therapy, earned from Antioch University West in 1982, became her second book, *Dreaming the Dark*. In this work, she fuses feminism, Witchcraft, and politics by applying ritual techniques to anti-nuclear activism and non-authoritarian group structures.

The rituals that follow are from *Truth or Dare*, Starhawk's third book. They are meant to be only suggestions—"a framework meant to spark imagination; they will go dead," she explains, "if you take them as unchangeable, universal,

---

[6] Starhawk, *Truth or Dare*, p. 98.
[7] Starhawk, *Truth or Dare*, p. 121.

or definitive."[8] Rituals should be designed, created, evaluated, and revised to fulfill the needs of a particular community at a particular time.

Starhawk does suggest that a ritual follow a certain general pattern. It begins with an entrance transition that focuses on cleansing—incorporating elements such as water, fire, movement, or sound—and grounding, connecting in some way with the earth, participants' own centers, and the others involved. The next step is the creation of sacred space, perhaps by marking off a circle, opening windows, or hanging banners or scarves. In the next step, the participants evoke the powers and qualities of the four directions—North, South, East, and West—acknowledging the basic life-support systems of earth, fire, air, and water to which the directions correspond. Invoking constitutes the next step and is the body of the ritual; stories, dances, meditation, drumming, and visualization are used to invoke the power of the Goddess within to create the changes desired by the participants. A transition of return concludes the ritual, which involves opening the circle and returning to ordinary time and space through poetry, songs, chants, or improvised speeches. The ritual usually ends with the sharing of food and drink among participants as tangible expressions of mutual nurturing.

The seven rituals below are designed to empower their participants in a variety of ways. "Giving Names in Threes" is a ritual participants can use to restore their sense of immanent value through coming to feel seen and valued. "Gifts of Power" can be used to empower someone who is undergoing a transition or lacks confidence for a task or effort ahead. In "Gifts for the Newborn," a welcoming ceremony is held to mark the birth of a newborn child. "The Servants' Masked Ball" is a ritual in which participants work to free themselves from self-hatred and the judgment of self and others, and "Dream Challenge" focuses on dreams as a gateway to creativity and self-knowledge. "Cleansing Ritual for Groups" is designed to help a group let go of a conflict. The final ritual, "Ritual to Prepare for Struggle," as its name suggests, is designed to prepare participants for political action or for a major battle in work, relationships, or any area of life.

[8] Starhawk, *Truth or Dare*, p. 100.

Giving Names in Threes

When a new group comes together, break into groups of three. Tell stories about yourselves: what brought you to the group, what your journey has been, what race or class or religious background you come from, what transition you are undergoing. Each person in the triad should have a protected time to talk without being challenged, questioned, or interrupted. Five minutes each is a surprisingly long time. Then take a few minutes to discuss what common threads and differences you hear in your stories.

Now, two of you focus on the third member of your group. Choose a name for her or him, or choose an epithet, something to add to her or his name, as in "Catherine the Great." When you finish with the first person, recombine and do the same for each member of your group.

Bring the whole group back together. Go around the circle. Each person sings her or his name, stepping forward into the circle and expressing its power with movement or dance. The group sings the name back.

Gifts of Power

When someone you care about is undergoing a transition, taking on new responsibilities or power, and perhaps doubting her or his abilities or value, give that person a power gift. In sacred space, put her or him in the center of the circle. Each person in the group can give a gift, which may be simply a symbolic statement, an active wish: "I gift you with the ability to stay grounded under pressure in your new job."

Something tangible may or may not accompany the wish. "I give you this special button to carry in your pocket for your first day at school. It came off Grandma's coat, and I want you to remember how much she loves you."

Chant the person's name, hug, and feast.

Gifts for the Newborn

A similar ritual [to Gifts of Power] forms part of a welcoming ceremony for a newborn baby. The child is held in the center of the circle, and each person expresses gifts of qualities she or he hopes for the child. These are most powerful when they reflect some quality the giver has. So before beginning, allow some time for reflection. One person might say, "I give you the quality of perseverance against difficulties." Or, "I would like to give you the benefit of all my experience in rotten relationships—but I know I can't, so I give you the hope that you can always remember to love yourself."

A candle is passed around to be held as each gift is expressed. Later, snuff it (don't blow it out—that dissipates the energy) and save it to burn during future celebrations in the child's life, or when she or he is in danger.

The Servants' Masked Ball

In the group, make a mask that represents the face you wear to please others. Talk about it as you make it. For each mask, find a one-line phrase or sentence that represents the essence of what the mask says: "Stay covered up," "I'm sweet, don't hit me," "I won't ask anything of you," and so on.

Put on the masks, and play some music. Dance, saying your phrases to each other. Periodically stop the music. Interact with the person you face. Then exchange masks and phrases. Try on someone else's persona: speak in someone else's voice as the music resumes and the dance continues.

To end, hold up the masks. Dancers ransom their own back by saying or doing something that reveals their personal power.

Talk about how it felt to wear the different masks. Then decide what to do with them, perhaps creating a ritual for their destruction, perhaps keeping them as reminders of the game.

Dream Challenge

Ask everyone to bring to the ritual a disturbing dream. In sacred space, form into small groups.

Take hands; breathe together. Then someone begins drumming or clapping a rhythm. Everyone joins in clapping until the rhythm becomes well established.

One by one, each person tells her or his dream to the rhythm. Members of the group then give each person a challenge that comes from the dream.

A challenge is *not* an analysis or an interpretation. We do not attempt to explain the symbols or apply some preconceived idea of what they mean. The challenge emerges when we allow the characters and the events in the dream to tell us what the person needs to do. For example, if you dreamed of your dog being hit by a car, I might say your challenge is to learn to protect your animal self. If you dreamed of a monster chasing you, your challenge might be to turn and face it.

When all have received challenges, form a large circle again. One person enters the center of the circle, tells her or his challenge, and the group cheers, shouts, drums, and chants her or his name for empowerment. Then the first person chooses another, and so on until all have been empowered.

Meditate on your challenge; see in what guises it appears in your daily life, and use it as the basis for a dream story.

Cleansing Ritual for Groups

Establish a ritual space. In the center, place a large bowl of salt water.

One by one, come to the water. Breathe deep: imagine your breath coming up from the fiery center of the earth, through your feet and legs, through the base of your spine, belly, heart, down your arms and out your hands, past your throat, through your eyes, and out the top of your head, carrying with it the hurt, the anger, the mistrust that you have collected. Let it all come out through your breath: imagine it as a stream, muddy or flaming, or in whatever form works for you. Let it flow into the salt water.

Name aloud what you are letting go: the conflict, the hurt, the unmet needs. Don't be diplomatic. If you feel moved to do so, yell, scream, moan, gag. Pour it all into the salt water.

As you listen to others, you may find their words arouse further hurt, anger, resentment, pain. Imagine breathing all of that into the water, letting it pass through you.

When all have been to the water, take a lit candle and pass it clockwise around the circle. As you take the candle, name something positive you feel about the group or the people in it, something the group has done that has benefited others or realized your desires.

When the candle has been around the circle, whoever has been the most involved in the conflict takes the candle and douses it in the water.

Sit there in the dark and feel miserable for a while.

Then softly begin to chant:

> Free the heart, let it go
> What you reap is what you sow

Let the chant build power and energy. Raise power: imagine it lighting a new candle, rekindling the group trust and spirit. When the power falls, ground it. Light a new candle and pass it around the circle clockwise. When you take the candle, say what it is you rededicate yourself to doing in the group, what changes you commit to making, what new hopes you now hold.

Pour the water out on the ground. Set the candle in the center of the circle. As it burns down, feast and feed each other.

Open the circle.

Ritual to Prepare for Struggle

Before gathering, each person who is to take part spends time in individual meditation and cleansing. You might plunge in the ocean, a lake, stream, or river, or take a long ritual bath in salt water. Burn sage, for purification, or steep sage leaves in the bath. Rub yourself with cedar boughs—used by Native

Americans to draw helpful power, or with rosemary—a traditional herb of protection. Or use whatever herbs or incense seem right to you. Take time to feel your fears, doubts, any emotions that might cloud your judgment. Let them go into the salt water, not to be lost, but so that the energy locked up in negative images can be released and become available to you as clear power.

Those who are about to embark on an action, a struggle, a conflict gather with their community of support. Ground, create sacred space, and invoke the sacred powers.

Pass a crystal (or other sacred object such as a rattle, a stone, a shell, or something the group chooses) around the circle. As each person holds the crystal, (or whatever), clearly state your intention for the coming struggle. Why are you embarking on it? What do you hope to accomplish or gain? How do you intend to conduct the struggle? For example:

"I intend to go to Cape Canaveral and with my own body interfere with the testing of the new Trident 2 missile. I intend to act in loving nonviolence and maintain my sense of humor." Or: "I'm about to take the bar exam and I intend to pass it so that I can have the credentials I need to be a better fighter for justice. I want to stay calm, remain in touch with my sharpest intelligence and clearest memory, and retain my sanity."

Those who will offer support to the struggle tell what they intend to do.

When the circle is complete, those who will be at risk go into the center. Together, they hold the crystal. The group begins to chant, and raises power around them, while they focus on taking in that power and filling themselves with the love and protection of their friends. Each person may also create a personal image of power—a scene or an object to think of or remember in times of danger or stress. Visualizing the image of power during this time will help fix it in mind. Remembering it in tense moments, while breathing and grounding, will bring needed strength, calm, and power. A physical object can be used instead of a mental image and may be easier for beginners to work with.

Ground the energy. Affirm each person in the center—sing their names, hug them, bless them with power and protection.

Place the crystal in a pouch and bind the power as you close it up. Decide what you will do with it. Will you bury it on the Air Force Base? Place it on your desk during the test? Share food and drink. Entertain each other. Open the circle.

If you don't have a group to do this ritual with, adapt it to do alone.

30

SHOPPING

Marla R. Kanengieter

"Shopping isn't considered acceptable behavior if you're a serious student because it suggests you're frivolous, materialistic, and only care about your looks," observes Marla Kanengieter, and she remembers clearly the first time she admitted to someone in her professional life that she likes to shop. Although the fact that she likes shopping still is not something Kanengieter advertises to her colleagues and students at Seattle Pacific University, where she teaches communication, shopping serves important functions for her and for many women she knows.

Marla has warm memories of shopping experiences while she was growing up. She recalls "the distinct pleasure of walking downtown by myself to buy penny candy" when she visited her grandparents in a small town in Iowa when she was very young. She also remembers going shopping with her mother for new dresses before school started every fall and at Easter. When she was in high school, she and her mother would go to the nearest large city, Ann Arbor, which was about 50 miles away from where they lived, and spend the day shopping: "shopping was an event, an outing." Kanengieter recalls, "I could always count on having a real good time with my mom while shopping, and that's still true. We go shopping whenever we visit each other, and we make a big deal of it. It has become an important part of our relationship."

Marla also recalls with fondness the time the man who became her husband came to visit her when she had gone home from college for the summer. Kanengieter went shopping to buy her mother a birthday present, and he went along. Although they didn't know each other well, she remembers thinking,

"This is a man I could probably spend a great deal of time with" since he didn't mind going shopping. He did bring along a copy of Aristotle's *Rhetoric*, and now and again, he sat down on a bench to read or "would lean over the racks and have this book open. I don't know if he was trying to impress me or what." He continues the tradition today, Marla notes, "accompanying me shopping. He doesn't like shopping and brings something to read, but it's a way we spend time together."

Kanengieter has a typical routine she follows when she goes to downtown Seattle, her favorite place to shop. She has something to drink at a coffee bar and watches people for a while. Then she goes to the Bon, a department store, where she visits the linen department, the women's department, and the shoe department; she concludes by "checking out the earrings." She also goes to Nordstrom's, another department store, and The Rack, the sale outlet for Nordstrom's. She usually spends a great deal of time at The Rack because "I'm a deals person; part of the fun or the challenge of shopping for me is finding great buys." Then she heads to Sur le Table, a kitchen store, and finishes up at Pike Place Market, an indoor/outdoor city market, where she buys fruits, vegetables, and flowers.

The joy of shopping for Marla isn't confined to shopping for clothing or gifts. She also enjoys grocery shopping and, in fact, this was a form of entertainment for Kanengieter and her husband when they were in graduate school and didn't have much money. Sometimes, she knows what she wants to buy for the coming week and goes to the grocery store with a list. Her preference, though, is to come up with her ideas and plan the week's menus during the process of shopping. She does a lot of comparison of different food items and proceeds at a leisurely pace. She prefers not to go grocery shopping with her husband because, as she explains, "I feel like I have to hurry up."

Another shopping context that Marla finds enjoyable is thrift stores and garage or estate sales. Her mother-in-law took her shopping at thrift stores for the first time: "When I first met her, I thought it was the oddest thing. She asked if I wanted to go to the thrift stores. Being polite, I went." Kanengieter's reaction at first was, "This is so stupid. This is the last place I'd want to go. I had to grow to like it; it wasn't immediate for me." Her mother-in-law taught her how to find good fabrics and how to tell size, and Marla has found "wonderful things" at thrift stores, including wool blankets, a lamp, and a rocking chair. Part of the appeal is the unknown history of the items: "You wonder whose it was before and think about the stories around the item."

Making the rounds of garage and estate sales is something Kanengieter does with her in-laws and husband. They aren't the kind who get to the sale early and sign the admission list; their commitment is much more casual. They go to the sales close by and try to avoid ones in nice neighborhoods; garage sales in these areas generally offer "junk—usually children's junk—and it's way overpriced." One of the fun things for Marla about exploring at garage and estate sales is trying to figure out what things are: "A question we frequently ask each other is, 'What is this thing and can you describe it in ten words or less?'"

Shopping can be an unpleasant experience for Kanengieter. She doesn't like to go to hardware stores, nor does she like to shop for running shoes: "I just think they're boring," she explains. She also doesn't enjoy shopping when she feels pressured. "I get an idea in my mind, and I have to find exactly that," she says. She gets frustrated when she doesn't have the time to find precisely the items she has conceptualized. Sometimes, the shopping styles of others make the experience less than enjoyable. Marla has a difficult time shopping with one of her sisters, for example, who "floats too much — goes from one department to the other too quickly — it feels too disorganized to me." She also finds shopping with her sister-in-law difficult because "we don't talk very well when we're shopping; we usually have interesting, enjoyable conversations, but not when we're shopping."

"In contrast to my husband," says Kanengieter, "I don't just go shopping when I need to buy something. I go for very different reasons and, in fact, I almost prefer shopping when I'm not looking for something in particular." In the following essay, Marla explores the functions shopping serves for her.

Shopping

Only women absorbed by the self, consumed by the material, and elevated by the superficial enjoyed shopping. Not me. This little elitist attended to matters more important than the musings of dressing-room banter. I feigned complete and total repulsion toward the act of shopping and sneered at any woman who willingly spent her time pacing miles of aisles at the mall of her choice.

The first time I admitted to someone that I liked to shop, I felt an odd sense of relief — the sort that usually accompanies some easily accomplished, yet horribly dreaded task — like confession, for example. I remember the occasion well. As I walked out of my classroom, a student who usually remained guarded, while laden with questions, lingered. We met with usual salutations appropriate within the fortress of knowledge — our student-teacher relationship was in that liminal state somewhere between revelation and redundancy. We had had one previous conversation, I remembered.

As we traveled from the formal to the more mundane, our dialectic turned toward a more casual and carefree tone. Soon I found myself leaning toward her and asking, "So what do you do in your free time?" She rattled off several noble artistic pursuits and then mumbled into her turtleneck sweater. "Excuse me," I said. "What did you say?" She replied, "Well, sometimes I like to, you know, shop. I find it cathartic." She had a good reason for this pasttime, one that I understood instinctively but was unable to articulate.

I like to shop. I still hesitate to admit it openly (I thought about changing my name for this essay). I also feel a strained ambivalence about the act itself. In a culture where mass markets crawl with images of women that feed gnawing desires of the "male gaze," why do I participate in such an innocuous, even somewhat degrading, activity?

I think I discovered the answer when I was in graduate school. I would announce periodically to my husband that I needed to go shopping. My proclamation usually was prefaced by a fierce declaration that I was depressed — the causes being inaction of the mind and paralysis of the soul that accompany graduate school. My husband found my inclination to shop rather confounding. Why would I deliberately place myself in a situation that reinforced the obvious fact that I possessed neither money nor time to purchase such fetishes (and luxuries) as clean, white linen napkins, drafting pens, flowers, copper pots, wool gaberdine, and red suede shoes? I was not bothered by my inability to satiate my material appetite; I was satisfied to return home empty handed. For me, shopping was not the act of *buying* or even the love of buying; shopping was a way of coping.

Shopping is one way I establish and maintain friendships. I remember a pair of giggling girls tripping down mainstreet with a dollar in their pockets ready to take charge of their lives at the local Woolworth's. We sipped cherry cokes, hammed it up in the 25-cent photo booth, and stared with wide-eyed curiosity at the clerk as she flashed her firey-red fingernails while ringing up our penny candy. We owned ourselves. We traded secrets. We exchanged plots. We purchased Nancy Drew.

At sixteen, I tightly clenched the family car keys. My mother clenched her teeth. We sped to the store, breezed down the grocery aisles, searched for the ever-elusive bargain, and attempted to influence one another's taste. We learned to talk (not always effectively and not without conflict). Now, at thirty, I clench her hand; we both move slower, but we both still breeze. Bargains remain the challenge. Issues of taste are resolved — we agree ours are different. We talk of regrets. We whisper visions. We laugh. Long. Hard. Together.

I sail to garage sales with mother-in-law as navigator. Coasting, lilting, reeling, we finally whirl out histories of forgotten items. Vacant lineages now become my own. I seize with unexpected pleasure bowls of brass, pitchers of glass, and books of leather, appreciating the clean artistry of years unknown to me.

We shop for therapeutic reasons, I think. Hooks of expectations placed by career and education bend and become malleable as I lose myself in the Lenox.

Avoidance. Release. No one's judgment but my own.

My friend, grieving for her father who lies sleeping in the next room, his body consumed by cancer, turns to her sister, looking for a glimpse of the familiar, and cynically states, "Let's go get our memorial service dresses." We lose a job. We go shopping. We lose a father. We go shopping.

Elegance. Kitsch. Artistry unraveled by the necessity of utility. Matching textures, weaving colors, we meander seamlessly through the mirrored fields. What we hope for rarely matches what we see. Often, we are as infatuated with our own ugliness as we are with our beauty. Spying, trying, and lying to ourselves, we place our potential even in the midst of the most banal. I am rescued while picking out yellow peppers and smelling for a glimpse of the sun from ripe tomatoes.

We exchange. We linger. We return. Communion with one another and necessary anonymity, not possessions, are what we seek.